Was It Yesterday?

THE SUNY SERIES

HORIZONS OF CINEMA

MURRAY POMERANCE | EDITOR

Was It Yesterday?

Nostalgia in Contemporary Film and Television

Edited by

Matthew Leggatt

Cover image: *Stranger Things*, courtesy of Photofest.

Published by State University of New York Press, Albany

© 2021 State University of New York

All rights reserved

Printed in the United States of America

No part of this book may be used or reproduced in any manner whatsoever without written permission. No part of this book may be stored in a retrieval system or transmitted in any form or by any means including electronic, electrostatic, magnetic tape, mechanical, photocopying, recording, or otherwise without the prior permission in writing of the publisher.

For information, contact State University of New York Press, Albany, NY
www.sunypress.edu

Library of Congress Cataloging-in-Publication Data

Name: Leggatt, Matthew, 1986– editor.
Title: Was it yesterday? : nostalgia in contemporary film and television / edited by Matthew Leggatt.
Description: Albany : State University of New York Press, 2021. | Series: SUNY series, horizons of cinema | Includes bibliographical references and index.
Identifiers: LCCN 2020058279 (print) | LCCN 2020058280 (ebook) | ISBN 9781438483498 (hardcover : alk. paper) | ISBN 9781438483481 (pbk. : alk. paper) | ISBN 9781438483504 (ebook)
Subjects: LCSH: Motion pictures—United States. | Nostalgia in motion pictures. | Television programs—United States. | Nostalgia on television.
Classification: LCC PN1993.5.U6 W35 2021 (print) | LCC PN1993.5.U6 (ebook) | DDC 791.43/0973—dc23
LC record available at https://lccn.loc.gov/2020058279
LC ebook record available at https://lccn.loc.gov/2020058280

10 9 8 7 6 5 4 3 2 1

Contents

Illustrations ix

Acknowledgments xi

Introduction: History in Reverse 1
   Matthew Leggatt

Part 1
What Is Nostalgia?

1 Clearing Up the Haze: Toward a Definition of the "Nostalgia Film" Genre 15
   Jason Sperb

2 Midcentury Metamodern: Returning Home in the Twenty-First-Century Nostalgia Film 35
   Christine Sprengler

3 Touched by Time: Memories of the Faded Star 51
   Daniel Varndell

4 Mimetic Tangible Nostalgia and Spatial Cosplay: Replica Merchandise and Place in Fandom's Material Cultures 71
   Ross P. Garner

Part 2
When Is Nostalgia?

5 A Nostalgic Exception: Warren Beatty's Star Performance in *Rules Don't Apply* 91
   Steven Rybin

6 The Past as a Temporal Free-Zone: The Nostalgic 1970s in Contemporary Crime Film and Television 105
   Fran Mason

7 On the Limits of Nostalgia: Understanding the Marketplace for Remaking and Rebooting the Hollywood Musical 121
   Justin Wyatt

8 "I'm Going to My Friends . . . I'm Going Home": Contingent Nostalgia in Netflix's *Stranger Things* 137
   Tracey Mollet

Part 3
The Politics of the Past

9 A Confrontation with History: Re-Viewing the Horror Film Sources of *Get Out* 155
   Vera Dika

10 "Why Can't We Go Backwards, for Once?" Nostalgia, Utopia, and Science Fiction in Steven Spielberg's *Ready Player One* 179
   Matthew Leggatt

11 Replaying Cowboys and Indians: Controlled and Commercial Nostalgia in *Westworld* 197
   Christina Wilkins

12 Contradictory Reminiscences: Post-9/11 Cold War Nostalgia, *The Americans*, and *Deutschland 83/86* 211
   Ian Peters

Part 4
Not My Nostalgia

13 Remembering It Well: Nostalgia, Cinema, Fracture   231
    Murray Pomerance

14 Nostalgia Ain't What It Used to Be   247
    William Rothman

Contributors   265

Index   269

Illustrations

1.1	Cub Photographer (Noah Matteo). *Nebraska* (Alexander Payne, 2013). Digital frame enlargement.	16
2.1	George (William H. Macy) and Betty Parker (Joan Allen). *Pleasantville* (Gary Ross, 1998). Digital frame enlargement.	40
2.2	Dorothy Vaughan (Octavia Spencer), Mary Jackson (Janelle Monáe), and Katherine Johnson (Taraji P. Henson). *Hidden Figures* (Theodore Melfi, 2016). Digital frame enlargement.	45
3.1 and 3.2	Gloria Swanson on-screen in *Queen Kelly* (Stroheim 1929) and "in the flesh" in *Sunset Blvd.* (Wilder 1950).	53
3.3 and 3.4	A haunted study: Negri in *A Woman of the World* (St. Clair 1925) and *The Moon-Spinners* (Neilson 1964).	57
3.5 and 3.6	Reversing the rot: Gloria Stuart in *The Old Dark House* (Whale 1932) and *Titanic* (Cameron 1997).	59
3.7 and 3.8	Enduring love: Maria (Julie Andrews) dancing with the Captain (Christopher Plummer) in *Sound of Music* (Wise 1965), and Clarisse dances with Joe (Héctor Elizondo) in *Princess Diaries* (Marshall 2001).	64
3.9 and 3.10	Enchanting: Julie Andrews in *The Sound of Music* (Wise 1965) and *Princess Diaries 2* (Marshall 2004).	66
4.1	Hot Toys' life-size replica of the Infinity Gauntlet from *Avengers: Infinity War*.	72

5.1	Marla Mabrey (Lily Collins) sings a song as *Hell's Angels* (1930) flickers behind her in *Rules Don't Apply* (Warren Beatty, 2016). Digital frame enlargement.	100
7.1	Danny (Aaron Tveit) and Sandy (Julianne Hough) at the beach, the opening of *Grease Live!*	131
9.1	Chris (Daniel Kaluuya) falls into the Sunken Place: *Get Out* (Jordan Peele, 2017). Digital frame enlargement.	159
10.1	Tomb Raider, Mortal Kombat, Overwatch, Street Fighter, Army of Darkness references, and more in *Ready Player One* (Steven Spielberg, 2018). Digital frame enlargement.	183
10.2	Parzival (Tye Sheridan) watches an entry in the Halliday Journals in *Ready Player One* (Steven Spielberg, 2018). Digital frame enlargement.	184
10.3	The Overlook Hotel, the setting for Stanley Kubrick's *The Shining* (1980), as recreated in Steven Spielberg's *Ready Player One* (2018). Digital frame enlargement.	188
11.1	Dolores (Evan Rachel Wood) waking up in *Westworld* episode 1 (Jonathan Nolan, 2016). Digital frame enlargement.	201
11.2	Maeve (Thandie Newton) encountering the Westworld reception in *Westworld* episode 10 (Jonathan Nolan, 2016). Digital frame englargement.	208
13.1	Benjamin (Dustin Hoffman) racing across San Francisco's Bay Bridge to find the love of his life in *The Graduate* (Mike Nichols, Lawrence Turman/Embassy, 1967). Digital frame enlargement.	245

Acknowledgments

As I've learned since beginning this journey, a collection of this sort relies on the patience and hard work of a huge number of people. It would be difficult to thank them all here. No doubt, behind every chapter in this collection is a story and a list of people without whom the work may never have been completed. All I can do is offer a big thank you to all of these unnamed and kindly people. I owe a huge debt to the following people: my partner, Laura, for her love and good humor; Murray Pomerance, without whom there would be no collection at all; and Daniel Varndell, who has given up so much of his time during this journey to offer advice and feedback. I also want to personally thank all the contributors in the collection for making this a thoroughly enjoyable experience. Thank you for your professionalism and for putting your trust in me.

Introduction

History in Reverse

Matthew Leggatt

> The entirety of our history is now being written at the speed of light, which is to say in nanoseconds, picoseconds and femtoseconds whereas the organization of time was previously based on hours and minutes. We no longer live even in a world of seconds; we live in a world of infinitely tiny units of time.
>
> —Paul Virilio (113–14)

In spring 2018, as I sat down and began to pen ideas for how to open this book, I was suddenly struck by the uncanny symmetry between the worlds of culture and politics that I was inhabiting at that moment. My partner and I had decided to catch up on *The Americans*, a Joe Weisberg creation then in its sixth (and final) season. We were on the fourth season. For those who aren't familiar with it, *The Americans*, an FX television show that first aired back in 2013, follows the exploits of two deep-cover KGB spies, Elizabeth and Philip Jennings (played by Keri Russell and Matthew Rhys) and their family, as they attempt to navigate the perils of a job that involves numerous undercover operations all while trying to maintain the appearance of normality in 1980s America.

Much of the plot for season 4 revolves around the couple's attempts to smuggle biological weapons being developed by their US adversaries out of the country and to the Soviet Union. Strange, I thought, given that at that very moment Sergei Skripal, a former Russian counterintelligence operative for the UK government, and his daughter, Yulia, lay recovering in a hospital some weeks after they had been the target of an attempted murder by shadowy figures in the Kremlin (or so the UK government insisted). That this attack had happened in Salisbury, England, using a military-grade nerve agent in broad daylight some fifty miles away from my quiet hometown on the south coast of England was like something out of a fictional realm. The event, which dominated the UK media for about a week before disappearing, will no doubt be little more than a footnote by the time you read this. Like so many similar political instances, these events demonstrate the increasing ephemerality of the public memory. As Virilio suggests, history is being written at the speed of light. How could one possibly remember?

There were more uncanny similarities to be observed. As Ronald Reagan's rosy cheeks appeared on the television screen in season 4, episode 5, giving his March 1983 Strategic Defense Initiative speech—the family in *The Americans* are often shown gathered round watching the fortieth president of the United States address the nation—I was reminded that a Reagan-like impostor currently occupied the White House. In the run-up to the 2016 presidential election, I was struck by Donald Trump's boast in the debates that his corporate tax cuts would be the biggest since Reagan's. Reagan's economic policies may have boosted the economy, but that never translated into increased wages. Figures from the Economic Policy Institute show that the 1980s marked a period in which productivity grew rapidly, but wage growth was stagnant (Bernstein). Indeed, the structural changes to the US economy in the 1980s under Reagan are often cited as the beginning of the neoliberal stripping of wealth from hard-working citizens. Yet Donald Trump's Ronald Reagan was reconfigured—at least in his rhetoric—as a hero of the working class. History was not just being written but, rather, rewritten.

This is a book about history. Or rather, this is a book about time; more specifically, time travel. One might even go as far as to call this a science fiction text. It is no coincidence that cinema has often been called a time machine (see Friedberg 100; Penley; Lee 2); while on the international political stage nostalgia has been wreaking havoc, movies with their action set in other time periods have been booming at the box office. Of the nine Best Picture Oscar winners between 2011 and 2019

(*The King's Speech*, *The Artist*, *Argo*, *12 Years a Slave*, *Birdman*, *Spotlight*, *Moonlight*, *The Shape of Water*, and *Green Book*), only one was set in the present. Even that movie, *Birdman*, was a story about memory—protagonist Riggan's (Michael Keaton) career is defined by his early role as Birdman (mimicking Keaton's own role as Batman in the late 1980s and early 1990s) and the movie centers on his struggle to escape his past and reinvent himself as a serious actor. Not to say that all of these movies are explicitly about nostalgia, but they do seem to speak of our obsession with the past. If we take *Green Book*, for example, it is difficult to argue that the movie encourages a longing for the 1960s, given its depiction of the racism and homophobia encountered by Dr. Donald Shirley (Mahershala Ali), but the use of the iconic 1962 Cadillac driven by Tony Lip (Viggo Mortensen) does lend an air of romance to the road trip that is the subject of the movie. Such films often seem to appeal through what one might call the texture of the past. Rather than operate on the narrative level, nostalgia is evoked via the aestheticization of the period setting to which the viewer is transported. Often these aesthetics alone are enough to distort our understanding of history. As Robert Burgoyne has argued, even as we have become increasingly accustomed to and comfortable with the manipulation of film through digital methods, "film appears to have acquired, more than ever, the mantle of meaningfulness and authenticity with relation to the past—not necessarily of accuracy or fidelity to the record, but of meaningfulness, understood in terms of emotional and affective truth" (223). Indeed, wrapped up in this is an argument about fidelity to history and authenticity, but as the essays in this collection attest, there's considerably more at stake than just this.

Where the movies mentioned above might evoke nostalgia for their periods in a formal sense, a recent flurry of Disney films seems to show the industrial process at its most ruthlessly efficient. When you think about it, it's a great marketing strategy: if you were ten when *Beauty and the Beast* (1991), *Aladdin* (1992), or the *Lion King* (1994) came out in the early 1990s, there's a good chance that your children (if you had them) might be about ten when the remakes hit the screens in 2017 and 2019. Your nostalgia becomes the perfect excuse to take your ten-year-old child to the cinema. I have often wondered what the point of the live-action remakes are, given that Disney's 1990s animation techniques don't really age—in fact, the remakes will probably age more rapidly—but given their box office success, it would appear that Disney has found a formula that works. Of course, we can still enjoy this nostalgia. *Toy Story 4* (2019), for example, showed that Disney can still create original narratives that mobilize nostalgia to get patrons through the doors but that ultimately have a heartbeat of their own. But there is a sense that these new old movies are in some way haunted by the ghosts of their originals. Is it possible to watch the new *Aladdin* movie without comparing Will Smith's performance as the Genie (unfavorably) to Robin Williams's show-stealing work in the original? Likewise, why is it that James Earl Jones reprises his role as Mufasa in the live-action *Lion King*, whereas other stars, like Jeremy Irons, who voiced Scar, are missing? Mufasa's ghostly presence quite literally haunts the movie, perhaps. All of these decisions are talking points for fans who crowd internet fora, and while it's true that Disney's takeover of Lucasfilm in 2012 had many *Star Wars* fans up in arms, the pull of new old material was just too strong for the franchise's continuation not to be a commercial success.

In the introduction to his 2017 work *Retrotopia*, published only a week after his death, sociologist Zygmunt Bauman reworks an image of the Angel of History that he draws from Walter Benjamin's "Theses on the Philosophy of History" (1940). Interpreting a 1920 print by Paul Klee titled *Angelus Novus* (New Angel), which he bought in 1921, Benjamin envisions an angel forced backward by the onslaught of history, a "storm" that "irresistibly propels him into the future to which his back is turned, while the pile of debris before him grows skyward. This storm," pronounces Benjamin, "is what we call progress" (201). Bauman notes that nearly a century after Klee's painting was made, "one would catch the Angel of History once more in full flight" (1). Now, however, Bauman imagines the Angel in full reverse, "the storm blowing this time from the imagined, anticipated and feared in advance Hell of the future towards the Paradise of the past" (2). For Bauman, one senses, there was little to recommend the debris of history. Yet it would seem that the past, at least in the public consciousness, has become a haven into which one can escape an increasingly uncertain future. In such circumstances, it might appear easier to go backward than forward. Progress becomes synonymous with reversal; nostalgia becomes the symptom of a complete loss of faith in what's to come.

Similarly, Mark Fisher writing in 2014 saw the twenty-first century as a time uniquely predisposed toward nostalgia: a product of the inadequacies of our present and the failed promises of neoliberal capitalism. For Fisher, ours was a moment devoid of the intellectual and cultural creativity of earlier periods like the 1970s and 1980s, and he argued that even the "recombinatorial delirium" of postmodernism now seemed exhausted (8). Fisher asked, "could it be that neoliberal capitalism's destruction of solidarity and security brought about a compensatory hungering for the well-established and the familiar?" (14). Or is it that "neoliberal capitalism has gradually but systematically deprived artists of the resources necessary to produce the new," creating "an increased tendency to turn out cultural productions that resembled what was already successful" (15)? Whereas Bauman saw our nostalgia as something to be wary of because it seemed to mark an end to our belief in progress, Fisher seemed to see in it the ultimate indictment of our present political and cultural moment.

So, are we more susceptible to nostalgia today? That's certainly what some scholars have argued. Ryan Lizardi writes that "in today's hypermediated world, technological affordances make it easy to create our own "playlist past" of downloaded vintage video games and DVD boxsets of long-forgotten television shows" (3). Fisher also ties our nostalgia to technological shifts: "In conditions of digital recall," he laments, "loss is itself lost" (2). Just as Michael Dwyer highlights the new technologies of the 1970s and 1980s that were inspiring a younger audience to revisit and nostalgize the America of the 1950s, it would be worth pausing here to note the similarities in how such technology is now shaping a new nostalgia (especially for the 1980s and 1990s) for the Netflix generation. An increase in scholarly interest in this area, as demonstrated in the recently published *Netflix Nostalgia: Streaming the Past on Demand*, edited by Kathryn Pallister, suggests that there is something specific to today's media platforms that have encouraged this move toward a nostalgic culture and with it a nostalgic politics. But what to make of this shift is more challenging. For Lizardi—who coins the phrase "narcissistic nostalgia" to help describe an environment where "new technologies [have enabled] the inclusion, exclusion, and ordering of individual media texts to be played back at any time," often at the cost of the "dismiss[al] of collective cultural experiences" (3)—we are being "exploited by contemporary media to develop individualized pasts that are defined by idealized versions of beloved lost media texts pumped up with psychic investment to a level of unreality" (2). Thus nostalgia, particularly when considered as an industry tool, becomes a highly conservative force. Rather than bring us closer to our past, it has a tendency to erase certain histories (often the marginal) replacing these with a cathartic, whitewashed, and sanitized simulacrum that can be used to escape from a collective guilt and responsibility for today's political confrontations.

Christine Sprengler, on the other hand, sees a debate between good and bad nostalgia as ultimately somewhat fruitless because "the tendency to assess nostalgia on the basis of its object . . . informs nearly all attempts to evaluate [it]" (32). Sprengler highlights the changing fortunes of nostalgia in academic criticism over recent decades: in the 1980s and 1990s, she argues, Reagan's use of nostalgia "made it difficult for anyone but staunch Republicans to find value in it" (32). One might note Fredric Jameson as the cultural theorist most associated with this more pessimistic understanding of the role of nostalgia in the cultural and political sphere. At the beginning of the twenty-first century, however, Sprengler notes a shift toward a new, more optimistic engagement with nostalgia in scholarship. She cites Grainge, Moran, McDermott, Cook, and Cashman as figures who reevaluated nostalgia during this period (33). Another more recent example might be Gilad Padva, whose 2014 book, *Queer Nostalgia*, offers an important contribution to the field. While this volume's focus is firmly on mainstream US film and TV culture, Padva's positive evaluation of the way nostalgia has helped shore up more marginal identity constructions offers a useful counterpoint to the sometimes cynical take on nostalgia found across a number of chapters in this collection, my own included.

Whether you believe that the wave of nostalgia we're currently experiencing offers positive hopes for reengaging with history, or whether you see a warning that our culture is in full retreat from the present, there is evidently much more to nostalgia than just the formation of catchy political slogans or the recycling, remaking, and rebooting of a few old movies and TV series. Nostalgia is an industry, but it is also, as scholars have noted, an amalgam of a complex web of different affects, practices, aesthetics, emotions, and fetishes. This volume is an attempt to work through some of these and to explore how nostalgia has come to dominate today's media, culture, and politics in an effort to assess what this all means for us. Beyond this, on a conceptual level, a collection on nostalgia must touch on issues relating to time, history, and memory—three hugely important touchstones for identity. Many of the questions raised in this volume highlight these touchstones as areas of contestation. As Paul Grainge has written, "the desire for memory as stable, reassuring, and constant has always been plagued by the fear of its instability and unreliability, and its disposition towards fantasy and forgetting" (5). A number of the papers in *Was It Yesterday?* treat memory as a battleground on which individuals compete with multinational corporations and the movie and TV industries to help shape certain conceptions of history.

In this introduction, rather than attempt to set out a clear definition of nostalgia, I opted instead to set the scene and give a little background about what inspired this collection. There are just too many different nostalgias to theorize in such a short introductory note. Instead, the first four chapters in part 1 of this book are all in some way dedicated to finding a mode of discourse by which we might better explore, define, and frame nostalgia. Thus, in the opening chapter, Jason Sperb brings together a host of competing definitions and ideas of the nostalgia film. He identifies the characteristics of affective, peripheral, representational, and narrative nostalgias before considering the role of identity in the nostalgia film. In chapter 2, Christine Sprengler begins by considering the theoretical landscape spawned by studies of nostalgia. She argues that the "metamodern" offers perhaps the clearest understanding of how nostalgia has tended to operate in recent movies, using the examples of *La La Land* (2016), *Hidden Figures* (2016), and *Carol* (2015) as a means to demonstrate the metamodern style. In the third chapter, Daniel Varndell explores an array of filmic moments, focusing particularly on the role the star image plays in evoking various types of nostalgia. For Varndell, these intertextual moments sometimes reveal the aging star as fading and at other times act as triumphal returns demonstrating that true star power can overcome the passage of time and the ravages of aging. He also examines the gender dynamic that often seems to energize such moments and our reactions to them. Ross P. Garner's chapter on fan cultures closes this part and moves the debate around nostalgia to material cultures by focusing on merchandise. Garner seeks to redeem nostalgic merchandise, which he argues is often dismissed as an offshoot of consumer exploitation by giant conglomerations, arguing through his concept of mimetic tangible nostalgia that nostalgic commodities offer a bridge between the consumer and the spatial and temporal worlds of their franchises.

In part 2 each chapter effectively draws on the history of their respective periods to unpack the various films and TV series they explore and identify what it means for a movie or show to transport us back to a particular decade. In chapter 5, Steven Rybin focuses on the re-creation and sentimentalization of 1950s Hollywood in his work on Warren Beatty's evocation of Howard Hughes in *Rules Don't Apply* (2016). In chapter 6, Fran Mason raises questions about why crime texts, particularly *American Hustle* (2013), *The Nice Guys* (2016), *Free Fire* (2016), and season 2 of *Fargo* (2015), return to the 1970s for their action set pieces. For Mason, the 1970s offers a blank canvas, or a temporal free-zone as he calls it, which locates the action beyond the politics of the period. Next, in chapter 7 Justin Wyatt considers nostalgia from an industry perspective, exploring the different formulas by which nostalgia can be successfully and unsuccessfully marketed to today's audience through the musical reboots of *Fame* (2009), *Footloose* (2011), and *Grease Live!* (2016), which have their roots in the late 1970s and early to mid-1980s. In chapter 8, Tracey Mollet "goes home" to the 1980s in her exploration of *Stranger Things*. She explores how the show applies the values of today to the America of the 1980s to "correct" the politics of the period, thus testing the meaning of the idea of going home, both in terms of the show's focus on a missing child wanting to return home, and for the viewers whose nostalgia means that the 1980s feels like going home.

Part 3, which contains chapters centered more explicitly on the political implications of nostalgia, opens with Vera Dika's examination of the dialogue between Jordan Peele's 2017 Oscar-winning hit *Get Out* and its horror sources. Like those works identified in her earlier and crucial book on nostalgia (*Recycled Culture in Contemporary Art and Film*), Dika's chapter locates a spirited resistance to the nostalgia of our times in Peele's glances backward in *Get Out*. Dika argues that for Peele, the use of intertextual references, which might evoke nostalgia on their own, together expose the codes of the horror movie and reconfigure history itself as horrific rather than nostalgic. In chapter 10, I tackle a different genre by exploring science fiction and nostalgia in Steven Spielberg's *Ready Player One* (2018). I use the film as a basis to explore how nostalgia often depoliticizes the past and thus produces conservative rather than radical texts, even those that might otherwise use progressive ideas and technology in their explorations of the future. In opposition to this, Christina Wilkins explores HBO's *Westworld* (2016) series in chapter 11, offering a more upbeat conclusion by arguing that nostalgia in the show operates as a progressive rather than conservative force because it brings about self-actualization. Chapter 12, by Ian Peters, follows some of the lines of inquiry put out by this introduction in its analysis of the role that the Cold War has played in television series after September 11, 2001, focusing on *The Americans*, *Deutschland 83* (2015), and *Deutschland 86* (2018). Peters shows how different nations, depending on their cultural history, respond differently to Cold War nostalgia deployed in the face of uncertain times and uncertain threats in the twenty-first century.

The final part of the collection contains two essays that stand apart from the others in seeing the contemporary period as no more or less nostalgic than earlier times in film history. Murray Pomerance offers a personal account of his own nostalgia for a number of films, particularly *The Graduate* (1967), to consider the generational nature of nostalgia. He argues that nostalgia films of today often get the past wrong, and he considers how memory operates. In a final flourish, William Rothman argues that "nostalgia ain't what it used to be," questioning the premise of the collection as a whole and arguing that today Americans spend less time living in the past than they have historically, highlighting the movies of the 1940s and 1950s as offering overwhelmingly nostalgic experiences. In doing so, he questions whether the films of today could ever be nostalgic objects for future generations in the same way.

Let me finish this introduction by thinking again about nostalgia in a personal sense. In Italo Calvino's wonderful little novella, *Invisible Cities*, Marco Polo tells the inquisitive Kublai Khan of a city he encountered on his travels around the Khan's empire:

> In Maurilia, the traveler is invited to visit the city and, at the same time, to examine some old postcards that show it as it used to be: the same identical square with a hen in the place of the bus station, a bandstand in the place of the overpass, two young ladies with white parasols in the place of the munitions factory. If the traveler does not wish to disappoint the inhabitants, he must praise the postcard city and prefer it to the present one, though he must be careful to contain his regret at the changes within definite limits: admitting that the magnificence and prosperity of the metropolis Maurilia, when compared to the old, provincial Maurilia, cannot compensate for a certain lost grace, which, however, can be appreciated only now in the old postcards, whereas before, when the provincial Maurilia was before one's eyes, one saw absolutely nothing graceful and would see it even less today, if Maurilia had remained unchanged; and in any case the metropolis has the added attraction that, through what it has become, one can look back with nostalgia at what it was. (Calvino 26)

In this passage, Polo neatly illustrates the value of nostalgia—its power to allow us to reevaluate the present—and its dangers. Indeed, as Polo intimates, one "must be careful" with nostalgia. While looking backward can help us appreciate a certain beauty and simplicity in the past, there must be a recognition that returning to that past would only reveal the fraudulence of nostalgia. In most cases, nostalgia is the site of harmless whimsy. Our passing regrets at the changes we have witnessed are a way of coping with the turbulent times in which we live. But when we take the time to consider how far we have come, I personally believe that very few would honestly wish to go back in time. When we look back on the past, we do so not just with an affection but with an understanding that it would be folly to turn back the clock. The expression "to look back through rose-colored glasses" neatly reveals nostalgia's artifice. Hence, nostalgia should never provoke in us a genuine desire to return to the past because such a romantic vision is always understood as just that—a romance.

Today, there is a space, just as there has always been, for the nostalgia film—and with it a little romance in one's life. Indeed, many of the contributions in this volume demonstrate their author's passion, reverence, and even adoration for the nostalgic texts that have held our collective interest over the past decade and more. It might seem there can be little harm in indulging wistful fantasies of postcard by-gone days now buried beneath the sediment of the ever-shifting present. Today, however, there is not just a space but a genuine need for cultural artifacts that can mobilize our imagination and inspire us to look forward. Perhaps for this reason, it is vital to understand how nostalgia circulates in our culture. In uncertain times, we must look ahead toward the possible rather than behind toward the "catastrophe" of history, as Benjamin's Angel sees it (201). Our new catastrophes cannot simply be covered over with the old ones.

Works Cited

Bauman, Zygmunt. *Retrotopia*. Cambridge: Polity Press, 2017.

Benjamin, Walter. *Illuminations: Essays and Reflections*. Ed. Hannah Arendt. Trans. Harry Zohn. New York: Mariner Books, 2019.

Bernstein, Jared. "Productivity and Wages: What's the Connection?" *Washington Post*, August 14, 2018. https://www.washingtonpost.com/news/posteverything/wp/2018/08/14/productivity-and-wages-whats-the-connection/?noredirect=on.

Burgoyne, Robert. "Memory, History and Digital Imagery in Contemporary Film." *Memory and Popular Film*. Ed. Paul Grainge. Manchester: Manchester University Press, 2003. 220–36.

Calvino, Italo. *Invisible Cities*. London: Vintage, 1997.

Dika, Vera. *Recycled Culture in Contemporary Art and Film: The Uses of Nostalgia*. New York: Cambridge University Press, 2003.

Dwyer, Michael D. *Back to the Fifties: Nostalgia, Hollywood Film, and Popular Music of the Seventies and Eighties*. Oxford: Oxford University Press, 2015.

Fisher, Mark. *Ghosts of My Life: Writing on Depression, Hauntology and Lost Futures*. Winchester: Zero Books, 2014.

Friedberg, Anne. *Window Shopping: Cinema and the Postmodern*. Berkeley: University of California Press, 1994.
Grainge, Paul. "Introduction: Memory and Popular Film." *Memory and Popular Film*. Ed. Paul Grainge. Manchester: Manchester University Press, 2003. 1–20.
Lee, Christina. "Introduction." *Violating Time: History, Memory, and Nostalgia in Cinema*. Ed. Christina Lee. New York: Continuum, 2008. 1–11.
Lizardi, Ryan. *Mediated Nostalgia: Individual Memory and Contemporary Mass Media*. London: Lexington Books, 2015.
Padva, Gilad. *Queer Nostalgia in Cinema and Pop Culture*. New York: Palgrave Macmillan, 2014.
Pallister, Katherine, ed. *Netflix Nostalgia: Streaming the Past on Demand*. London: Lexington Books, 2019.
Penley, Constance. "Time Travel, Primal Scene, and the Critical Dystopia." *Camera Obscura* 5.3 (1986): 66–85.
Sprengler, Christine. *Screening Nostalgia: Populuxe Props and Technicolor Aesthetics in Contemporary American Film*. New York: Berghahn Books, 2009.
Virilio, Paul. "Paul Virilio: Interview with Jérôme Sans." Trans. Henry Martin. *Virilio Live: Selected Interviews*. Ed. John Armitage. London: Sage, 2001. 113–20.

Part 1

What Is Nostalgia?

Clearing Up the Haze

Toward a Definition of the "Nostalgia Film" Genre

JASON SPERB

ONE MOMENT IN THE POST–WORLD WAR II drama *The Master* (2012) features US soldier Freddie Quell (Joaquin Phoenix) discussing a letter he received from a girl back home, one that caused him to have an intense emotional reaction. Asked by a psychologist to describe his feelings, "I believe I suffered what, in your profession, you call 'nostalgia,'" Freddie says, laughing it off. This nods to the term's (almost mythical) origin as a clinical term—a doctor's diagnosis for Swiss soldiers experiencing a profound sense of homesickness way back in the seventeenth century (given its Swiss roots, Svetlana Boym notes that the word *nostalgia* "is only pseudo-Greek, or nostalgically Greek" ("Nostalgia," 7; see also Boym, *Future*). This sequence was an homage to a similar moment in John Huston's documentary *Let There Be Light* (1946)—also about the trauma of US soldiers struggling to adjust to civilian life after experiencing the horrors of war—but there were important differences. The soldier in the documentary (an African American man) was provoked into a state of melancholic despair not by a letter but a photograph. Upon recalling this episode, the real-life soldier breaks down again in shameful tears.

Figure 1.1. Cub Photographer (Noah Matteo). *Nebraska* (Alexander Payne, 2013). Digital frame enlargement.

There was always something uniquely nostalgic about the photographic image. Like nostalgia itself, the frame isolates; it blocks off as much about the past as it reveals. The image suggests a moment frozen in time, both powerful and deceptive in what it shows. As Roland Barthes, Hollis Frampton, and others have tried to capture, those images of years gone by permanently wall off from us the past as much as they may also allow us to glimpse its fragments—creating a decisive visualization of the gap between "then" and "now." Writing or speaking, in contrast, creates a greater sense of immediacy, as the reader/listener is able to visualize in the present what is being described. This was part of the effect of Frampton's *Nostalgia* (1971)—narration is present, image is past. Sarah Polley's autobiographical film *Stories We Tell* (2012) operates similarly—the voice of her putative father (Michael Polley), as he reads his account of family events, creates an intimate sense of presence, while the Super 8 footage of those same past moments (both actual home movies and Polley's uncanny re-creations) immediately and overwhelmingly conveys a sense of pastness.

It's unsurprising that a collective preoccupation with nostalgia increased across the span of the twentieth century in direct proportion to the rapidly expanding presence of visual media, such as cinema and television. As Fred Davis noted long ago, popular culture only intensified nostalgia—the ubiquity of older media in recirculation and repackaging meant being in the audible and visible presence of the past. It is one thing to try to recall such times as a hazy abstraction and quite another to have it (in a way) physically present. As culture became increasingly confronted with its mediated past (fueled in part by the cheap conveniences of endlessly repackaging the same content through various aesthetic forms and technological platforms), it stands to reason that the centrality of nostalgia's power would soon follow. In a thoroughly mediated, globalized, mobilized culture, the image becomes a substitute for home—as in a repository for (increasingly collective) memories of the past (Davis has noted how the general lack of geographic stability in our modern mobile society suggests that perhaps "media products may now serve memory where once houses, streets and persons did"; 129). And yet while few would question the centrality of nostalgia in media culture today, there remains little in the way of a working genre definition for that most often-used term: the "nostalgia film." This chapter is an attempt at such a project—to quantify textually what we mean by "nostalgic" media texts and what's at stake in highlighting it beyond either just reliving reassuring fantasies of days past or (coexisting with that) blocking out the ugly realities of history.

The "Nostalgia Film"?

Specific textual attempts to define what nostalgia might look and sound like have been—like nostalgia itself—powerful and persuasive, but also fragmentary and incomplete. For instance, Alexander Payne's *Nebraska* (2013) is obviously a deeply nostalgic film. In some ways, the movie evokes Fredric Jameson's notion of the "nostalgia film," a highly stylized vision of a father (played by Bruce Dern) and son (Will Forte) road trip that knowingly equates some notion of the past with its cinematic mediation (the vintage Paramount logo, black and white cinematography). But it is also, importantly, a story *about* nostalgia. Woody (Dern) returns to his hometown, encounters old friends and family, and even visits his eerily abandoned childhood home in an elusive quest to recapture some semblance of a lost past—most directly symbolized by his desire to be allowed to drive again, that great "frontier" myth of the open road and all its possibilities that defined his post–World War II generation. In this regard, *Nebraska* attempts to capture a nostalgic journey (narrative), as well as a nostalgic look (black and white 35mm film stock). There remains, too, the question of what possible nostalgic relationships the film itself will evoke in another thirty years—when someone looks back as longingly at 2013 as some now do at the hazily defined era of classical cinema the film's pastiche visually simulates. Finally, the fact that the movie was shot on what will continue to be the increasingly quaint anachronism that is celluloid film suggests another layer of (technological) nostalgia. In sum, saying *Nebraska* is a "nostalgia film" presents as many questions as it does answers.

There are, as Rick Altman argued, different ways to conceptualize genre—through an exhaustive list that includes every possible film in the category, or as a more exclusive group of the best cinematic examples whose textual commonalities collectively define the genre in question. Or we can define it as a relatively stable category with fixed narrative and thematic and iconic elements (semantic), or as a more historically contingent one whose basic genre features are defined more by core ideological meanings that tend to be in dialogue with larger cultural contexts (syntactic). The task of analyzing the nostalgia text from a syntactic perspective has been more thoroughly explored than its textual mechanisms, as demonstrated by Davis's *Yearning for Yesterday*, Jameson's *Postmodernism, or the Cultural Logic of Late Capitalism*, or Boym's *The Future of Nostalgia*. Jameson's use of the phrase "nostalgia film" is an important and usefully contested point of reference that has permeated countless discussions since. On its own, though, the phrase is vague—particularly as Jameson admits that the word *nostalgia* is unsatisfactory for his purposes. For a touchstone, the title of my chapter deliberately uses the phrase "nostalgia film" in a nod to this well-known term—at the risk of unintentionally implying that these ideas do not also apply to possibilities in TV and other mass media (advertising, video games, and so forth). For Jameson, the nostalgia film is a simplified, superficial pastiche of stylistic clichés, "conveying 'pastness' by the glossy qualities of the image" (19), which for him evokes a collective, largely conservative, vision of an idealized past that is ultimately more approachable in opposition to its double: the messy, at times unknowable contradictions of history (for more on nostalgia, postmodernism, and late capitalism, see also Stewart).

Thus, a working demarcation for what might actually define nostalgia as a genre of media remains more abstract, despite there being a working assumption that such a concept already exists. As Christine Sprengler notes, "genre labels continue to suggest a degree of coherence and singularity markedly absent from the various ways in which nostalgia's relationship with the cinema can be theorized" (67). From a strictly semantic standpoint, Marc Le Sueur's often overlooked essay, "Theory Number Five: Anatomy of Nostalgia Films," followed Davis's work by attempting to give shape to the emerging centrality of nostalgia in popular culture by the 1970s. Le Sueur's work focused primarily on nostalgia's thematic consequences and visual elements, such as mise-en-scène. Pam Cook has explored how the language of cinema can evoke nostalgia through the stylistic use of freeze frames, slow/step motion, ellipses, repetition, and other visual means of stopping, preserving, and reversing the flow of time. Richard Dyer has shown how we might use nostalgic pastiche to engage with the history of genre. The concept is perhaps underdefined in part because we tend to think of nostalgia as an affect—a by-product of media consumption as often as an inherent textual feature.

Affective, Peripheral, Representational, and Narrative Nostalgias

Generally we can distinguish at least four broad types of mediated nostalgia, and the more elusive question of affect may be the best place to start. An "affective" nostalgia is a form that does not extend directly from any element planned in the text itself and can only be acquired over time. It is not a text necessarily set in the past or targeted toward a melancholic audience, but triggers in the present a yearning for yesterday by virtue of its relationship to some distant audience memory. Davis has written about "future nostalgia" or "planned *revivification*" (133)—how media products will be increasingly conceived with an eye toward their potential nostalgic value in subsequent cycles of consumption after their initial shelf life expires. In a sense, most products' inevitable, often preplanned state of anachronism is a necessary first component to their lasting value. As an affective experience, for instance, reruns of *Saved by the Bell* (1989–1993) today can offer an intensely nostalgic journey for certain generations, despite the fact that there was (we can reasonably presume) no sense of appealing to nostalgia at the time of its production. This contrasts sharply with, say, *Freaks and Geeks* (1999)—a loosely similar concept about the ups and downs of high school–aged students, but one deliberately set two decades earlier to at least partially capture a nostalgic desire for that time. For my present purposes, I set aside such affective forms of nostalgia—endlessly fascinating and equally infinite to map (as audience reception studies has already shown)—and stay confined to more quantifiably textual components.

There are those types of nostalgia that straddle the fine line between purely affective and more explicitly textual forms. For lack of a better term, we can call this "peripheral nostalgia." These texts are where nostalgia is clearly one possible source of appeal—two prominent forms are star vehicles (which can refer to well-known writers or high-profile directors, as well as established actors) and franchise properties (which would include sequels, prequels, and reboots, alongside broader nostalgic media brands such as Disney and Pixar). The latest Julia Roberts movie, James Bond epic, or TV show featuring Cedric the Entertainer undoubtedly appeals to those who—either passionately (fans) or more casually—look forward to the reassurances of medias past which those texts can potentially offer on top of other visceral and narrative pleasures. Here, the nostalgic value of a proven star or durable franchise is clearly evident, thereby negotiating the boundaries between knowingly incorporating that appeal into the text and yet still depending mostly on the affective engagement of the audience to more explicitly articulate that nostalgic value. I am tempted, moreover, to place Dyer's work on genre imitation somewhere in this category of the peripheral. His definition of pastiche, wherein new movies call forth the longer history of preexisting genre conventions before them, offers up an engagement with (but not necessarily a dependence on) earlier media periods and forms—meaning, the knowledge of genre history is not essential to the text's resonance (or lack thereof) with contemporary audiences. Of course, the actual degree to which such nostalgia is truly peripheral or possibly intended to the text's appeal is a subjective point open to debate. My point is merely structural—some stories are not directly about nostalgia in any technological, visual, narrative, or thematic way. Peripheral nostalgia is an unspoken, if generally agreed on, element of the text's appeal, which otherwise offers no direct engagement with such melancholic desires.

On that note, we can begin to more directly examine nostalgic modes by distinguishing "representational" forms from "narrative" ones. *Representational* refers to the ways in which—somewhat like *Stories We Tell*'s kitschy 1970s flashbacks—a text might seek to emulate a nostalgic time and place. We can break this down further to highlight "period nostalgia"—that is, movies, TV shows, and so on, set in the recent or historic past with the conscious intention of appealing to some kind of nostalgia associated with that time. Meanwhile, period pieces are not necessarily the same as those representationally nostalgic media that try to simulate earlier media forms. We can refer to this as "simulacric nostalgia"—as in, not just (or even necessarily) set in the past but meant to literally emulate a mediated look from the past. For instance, *Nebraska* is presumably set in the present day, despite its visual evocation of an earlier film aesthetic. *Grand Budapest Hotel*'s (2014) frame narrative, meanwhile, establishes multiple past time periods—and the film's shifting aspect ratios (1.37:1, 1.85:1, and 2.35:1) match the common aspect ratios of the corresponding period. Le Sueur's work is an important precedent in this regard, as he made the distinction between "surface realism" (mise-en-scène) and "deliberate archaism" (textual simulation of obsolete media) (192) as separate forms of what I am choosing instead to call representational nostalgia (I prefer the word *simulacric* not only because of its play on *simulation* but also its Baudrillardian evocation of an absence of history).

Such diverse cases of representational nostalgia must be distinguished from the more common form of narrative nostalgia. Such storylines can be set in either the past or the present (or perhaps most intriguingly, in the future—Pixar's *WALL-E* [2007] offers a paradoxical nostalgia for our own immediate present seven hundred years into the future). Narrative nostalgias do not necessarily depend on any particular fan base, franchise connection, historic time period, or simulacric look—rather, they are simply stories explicitly about nostalgic impulses (just as, oppositely, movies that depend on representational nostalgia do not necessarily concern themselves with overtly nostalgic plots—such as *Argo* [2012], *The Wolf of Wall Street* [2013], and so on).

Some common nostalgic plots might involve one or more of the following.

1. Major life events, such as reunions, weddings, milestones, graduations, or deaths—wherein reflecting on the past and the inevitability of change becomes a central narrative and thematic point.

2. Road trips, vacations, or other forms of "home-coming"— where there is the assumption or hope that at the end of the journey, one will enter into a physical space that is either literally or symbolically associated with an earlier period in one's life (a place often, but not always, associated with childhood).

3. Time travel—where the journey into the past becomes literal.

4. "Return" to nature—here, nature is defined by its opposition to competing notions of "society," "modernity," "civilization," and other concepts that work in some way as a code for the complexities, temporalities, and challenges of everyday, modern life from which nostalgic impulses offer

an escape. A return to nature would entail not just overtly "naturalistic" locations such as sandy beaches, wooded forests, deserts, and whatnot but also more populated settings, such as small towns or other vaguely frontier-type environments. The nihilistic violence of actual frontiers is more or less nostalgically erased, either by being safely situated in the past (i.e., the western) or omitted entirely. In this context, nature is marked symbolically by its imagined connection to a simpler, more innocent, time in the world. The key is that such locations offer the protagonists a reassurance or escape from the realities of the modern world (i.e., the present).

Nostalgic plots, moreover, often involve some element of a repressed memory that coexists, spoken or otherwise, with those same representations of the past. The repressed memory can be relatively insignificant, such as a personally embarrassing anecdote, a secret crush that finally comes to the surface in any number of reunion movies, or the fact that in the *Vacation* (1983–1997) films, the character of Clark Griswold admits he never actually had any fun during his childhood summer road trips and Christmas gatherings past. Or they can be far more significant, such as collective negotiations of war's memory or cultural transition. The reasons for this difficult memory are at the very least dual—for one, the threat that the repressed memory poses for the protagonist provides the narrative with some manner of dramatic conflict to help drive the story beyond the otherwise potentially flabby indulgences of simply reliving the past. The other reason, however, is less narratological and more inherent to the nature of nostalgia itself.

Nostalgia's appeal coexists with that "since then . . ."—the upsetting event that causes one's desire to return to a past moment before that trauma. Thus, these narratives involve a dissatisfaction with the present (and, often implied, a fear of the future). The nostalgia text is often about a resolute resistance to these concerns—either through their narrative overcoming (think of a more conventional time travel story, where the present becomes modified by changing the past, a reunion narrative where the two would-be lovers finally achieve happiness together, or some other kind of wish-fulfilling closure), or through its complete disavowal (the period piece that never addresses the present at all, let alone what might have happened in the intervening years to create a desire for such a longing look back). Most genres deal with ideological issues that largely go directly unspoken, of course, but perhaps most of all the nostalgic text evokes the urgency of that (historical) question that is its structural absence—what is that repressed memory, the "since then . . ." that causes one to be nostalgic to begin with? Although this reactionary nostalgia was not necessarily intended, such historical questions are nonetheless raised by their popular appeal.

Today's nostalgic convergence, however, feels like a very different matter. The era of sequels, prequels, and reboots certainly suggests a much more conscious industrial effort to exploit nostalgia's economic potential. More important, that traumatic historical event today is not only less defined but perhaps absent entirely. While such structuring absences still exist (the terrorist attacks of September 11, 2001; conflict in the Middle East), nostalgia films are more ubiquitous today and less tied to any particular time period now that we are overwhelmed with media archives of all kinds that increasingly accumulate artifacts from overlapping historical periods. If nostalgia for audiences once felt akin to something like Swiss homesickness or US melancholia in a time of war, today's mediated version feels more like nostalgia for nostalgia's sake—the completion of nostalgia's ahistorical journey from traumatic antidote to sanitized memory.

We can add that figurative and actual reenactments are also a reoccurring element in nostalgic plots. Sometimes, as with *Stories We Tell*, this can simply come in the form of the standard use of flashbacks (perhaps simulacric), where the narrative represents an interpretation of what happened in an earlier moment. Or, as with Woody's final drive down main street at the end of *Nebraska*, reenactments can also appear in the form of characters in the present diegetically re-creating moments from the past (either consciously or unconsciously) with the hope of achieving some kind of celebratory or therapeutic end. Such moments are implied in many variations of the aforementioned life event, time travel, and road trip narratives, since all take as their narrative starting point the need to reinhabit physical or social spaces that embody the past.

Finally, many nostalgic period pieces and reunion narratives are marked by the extensive use of popular music from the time. Like the use of mise-en-scène, some of this may simply be an effective form of narrative shorthand—immediately indicating the historical setting for the story without the need for more elaborate explanations. Yet more than simply helping establish the mood of the era, nostalgic music also offers a greater sense of intimacy between past and present, allowing the viewer to feel a more direct engagement with the period in question. If images of the past construct a hermetically sealed time capsule that audiences can observe but never enter, the more abstract presence of sounds from that same time—as mediators of a powerfully collective cultural memory—operate on a different affective level. As with Zero Moustafa's (F. Murray Abraham) narration in *Grand Budapest Hotel*, they generate a more immediate feeling of the past—allowing audiences to relive and inhabit the nostalgia in a way (here) that the distancing effect of images (there) do not. At the same time, we should be mindful of how such retro music carries with it the specter of endlessly lucrative soundtracks. (For more on the nostalgic recycling of music as commodity see Baade and Aitken.) Old songs (like old movies) thrive on their ability to be infinitely repackaged for new generations, new markets, and new technologies. New cinematic and televisual narratives offer, if nothing else, the chance to reintroduce outdated tunes back into the cycle of consumption—first as a means to help sell the film or show, and then the soundtrack itself (here again, after numerous creative detours, the discussion of the nostalgic text finds itself trapped in another dead-end of commodity consumption).

All of these factors finally move us toward a better understanding of why a certain kind of nostalgia text has been so prominent—the period, coming-of-age narrative, complete with a soundtrack of classic hits. These stories achieve a dual form of nostalgic address to audiences—older generations can look back fondly to what they imagine as the simplicity of the good old days (representational nostalgia), while younger generations can relate to the so-called timeless appeal of the poignant challenges in transitioning from childhood innocence to adult responsibility (narrative nostalgia). Older audiences can perhaps forget their own present reality of choices made and not made, and younger ones can find reassurance in the limitless universality of dreaming for the future. Seen through this light, it becomes easier to see why one of the original "nostalgia films" par excellence, *American Graffiti* (1973), became the genre trailblazer it did (or why more recent fare like *Freaks and Geeks* developed an eventual cult following). *American Graffiti*'s success is not simply the result of a kind of early Reagan-era political fantasy of traveling back to a life of loving 1950sness (even though it's technically set in 1962), before the various movements of the 1960s counterculture (the "since then . . .") disrupted the beloved normality of Eisenhower's white, heterosexual suburbia, as others have argued (though it was also undoubtedly that). Like many generational touchstones, *American Graffiti* benefited from conflicting appeals to ideologically contradictory audiences.

Better still, this may account for why *Back to the Future* (1985) has maintained its popularity as well as (if not better than) any other iconic

1980s Hollywood film. Not only do we have the dual address of the period piece and a coming-of-age narrative, but the film also has that other staple of the nostalgia genre: time travel. The appeal is self-evident, as this device allows character and audience to go back into the fond spaces of yesteryear. But the use of time travel highlights an important paradox (and not just the usual space-time problems associated with that device): the nostalgic desire to return to that idealized past is also ironically about trying to improve that past, just as Marty not only tries to preserve his parents' courtship to save his own existence but also plays a part in toughening up his father for the eventual betterment of his entire family. This at first suggests a contradiction—if the nostalgic past was imagined to be so perfect, presumably there would be no need to change it. But if we take the appeal of nostalgia to be based at least partly on (as I've been arguing here) the assumption that somewhere "things got worse" in the intervening years and decades—the "since then . . ."—it's perfectly logical to assume there would be a nostalgic desire to return to that better time while also changing things just enough to ensure that the subsequent future will no longer be deemed deficient.

This paradoxical logic fits a modern advertising-driven consumer culture that rests on the core belief that no matter what condition it may be in, present life can always be much better with the right antidotes. "Perhaps the first and most obvious thing to note about contemporary nostalgia," Davis highlighted decades ago, "is that it is very big business" (118). The experience of nostalgia is arguably the commodity being sold—consumers are often less invested in purchasing the actual product and more in somehow reobtaining that elusive yearning for yesterday which the commodity conceivably mediates for them. "Nostalgia is delicate, but potent," advertising executive Don Draper (Jon Hamm) noted in a well-known episode from the first season of *Mad Men* (2007)—meaning that if the wrong memories of the past are activated (the "since then . . ."), the product will be worthless (for more on nostalgia and *Mad Men*, see Spigel). But if they hit just the right note, its value is potentially limitless—hence the need to increasingly sanitize nostalgia, so that its "delicate" power can be made more resilient. It is worth noting that Draper's presentation in the sequence explicitly involves using photographs in a sales pitch for the new "Carousel" Kodak projector, Carousels, meanwhile, are a common nostalgic motif from *Grand Budapest Hotel* to at least as far back as *Twilight Zone*'s "Walking Distance" (season 1, episode 5, 1959), a circular machine that evokes both childhood and symbolically returning home. Thus, the reference to *Mad Men*, a show ostensibly about the successes of the modern advertising industry, highlights the other significant aspect of nostalgia's emergent centrality in the postwar period—it is too dependably lucrative to be anything but a dominant force (perhaps as dominant as sex itself) in contemporary consumer culture, as a means to sell new products and as an incentive for repackaging older ones (for more on nostalgia and advertising, see Stern).

Nostalgia and Identity

Like *American Graffiti*, *Back to the Future*'s appeal was, for some, in returning to the Reaganesque conservative fantasy of 1950s small-town suburbia. Such texts that looked back to a childhood innocence of the 1950s have been read, as Michael Dwyer notes, as a reaction against the subsequent social upheavals of the civil rights, anti–Vietnam War, and feminist movements. Of course, this also prompts the larger question of nostalgia's assumed interdependence with whiteness. Part of nostalgia's modern connotation as an excessive indulgence in only the most reassuring aspects of the past (real or imagined), along with the emergence of modern advertising industries, coincided in the postwar period of economic growth and suburban expansion with issues of white flight from urban spaces and reactions against progressive social upheavals. Although it's too simplistic to say that mainstream nostalgia's appeal is purely reactionary, many of its most popular nostalgic periods (late nineteenth-century Americana in the postwar period, 1950s small-town life in the age of Reagan, the ubiquity of 1980s-era franchises today) seem to fit some of the eras most associated with conservatism, while messier periods of progressive change, such as the civil rights movement, seem to serve as a structuring absence in those historical timelines. Perhaps no less troubling, they may be relegated to nostalgic narratives (i.e., *The Help* [2011]) whose primary role is not to advocate for continued progressive change today but to insist on the reassuring fantasy that any deep-seated cultural problems—such as institutional racism—were already addressed long ago. Or at best, perhaps the most successful period pieces of this latter kind appeal to ideologically opposed audiences—progressive audiences see a historical lesson regarding the value of continuing the fight, while conservative audiences see the comfort that any such problems, if they ever really existed, have long since been dealt with safely and decisively.

At the same time, can we really call mainstream Hollywood movies about the civil rights movement "nostalgic" since some may not think of that violent and bloody history as particularly romanticized or sanitized?

I would be inclined to say "yes," primarily because their appeal for most commercialized representations today is invariably a certain kind of idealization of historical moments to be celebrated, not repressed. The possible distinction beyond that may be to what future end that romance with the past is put—not unlike the distinctions between Boym's theories of "reflective" and "restorative" forms of nostalgia. If the goal is only to embrace accomplishments of the past and avoid the pressing urgencies of the present (restorative), then images of the civil rights movement serve only regressive ends. But if the ideal is to see in history a path forward, as part of a continuum of unfinished causes stretching into the future (reflective), then such nostalgia is necessarily reactionary.

Continuing the idea of more "reflective" forms, nostalgia's long relationship with whiteness should not preclude the possibility of a nostalgia text that foregrounds and negotiates the ambivalent memories of traditionally marginalized racial identities (Cook's work on nostalgia, for instance, focused on Wong Kar-Wai's *In the Mood for Love* [2000]). What if we were to say that Julie Dash's seminal *Daughters of the Dust* (1991) should also be regarded as a "nostalgia film" par excellence? Not that it is only or primarily concerned with nostalgia, but it touches on many of the issues and plot points highlighted in this chapter in uniquely illuminating ways. Set in 1902, Dash's film is about a major family reunion, and with that, the difficulties in dealing with profound life transitions that are more or less permanent. A group of daughters return to their family, descendants of West African slaves living on islands off the coast of Georgia. Isolated from most whites and other slaves living closer to the plantations and urban centers, they had come to develop a culture of their own, which now is coming under threat from the modernity of a new century. Importantly, *Daughters of the Dust* is situated on the border between the traditions of the nineteenth century and the so-called progress of the twentieth, between the embodied time of one era and the mediated time of another.

If *Daughters of the Dust* does not strike one as a nostalgia film, it is more a reflection on just how narrow the term and its attendant assumptions about race, ethnicity, gender, sexuality, and temporality have become in the limitations of modern consumer culture. Thus, its contrast is extremely useful. In essence, it is the introduction of a Western (colonialized) notion of linear temporality by the "modernized" couple, Viola Peazant (Cheryl Lynn Bruce) and Mr. Snead (Tommy Hicks), into the Gullah culture, which raises the question of nostalgia. The couple lived in the "civilized" society of Philadelphia and return with a fundamentally different sense of time, along with a desire to romanticize the family's history in a way that does not align with the community's memories (such as Tommy's need to have the one elderly man wax nostalgic about his childhood, a conversation that quickly focuses instead on the brutality of a life in slavery). We may resist the idea of seeing nostalgia in *Daughters of the Dust* because of melancholia's relationship to traces of a longer history of colonialization. But what the film brings nicely to the fore is the arbitrariness of that European perception of time, while positing a different sense of nostalgia on its own. When we are introduced to Viola as she returns to the islands, she waxes nostalgic about the land as she remembers it from childhood. In addition to subtly suggesting the Western understanding of time she internalized while living in the city, it also foregrounds the extent to which nostalgia, since the days of the homesick soldiers, depends on the displacement of not just time but also of space—only in leaving this place can she find herself nostalgic for some imagined loss when returning to it. This contrasts sharply with the rest of her family, who have never left that land, and thus do not have the same sense of linear time or desire to romanticize the geography. The "past" for them is embodied presently in the land itself and in the elders who have retained the history of their culture.

Meanwhile, Mr. Snead offers a more explicit visualization of nostalgia's presence, as he is a cameraman who becomes obsessed with documenting this world through the photographic image—often while ironically asking people to pose in ways that are inconsistent with or counterintuitive to their day-to-day physical behavior (photography captures lies as much as it does truth). By walling off the past from the present, the photo creates the conditions for nostalgia. Snead focuses on "preserving" this culture, but by doing so he ensures its continuing disappearance by insisting on separating through mediation the "then" from the "now." In *Daughters of the Dust*, the process of photography arguably creates a sense of linear temporality within that diegetic world—visually separating the (framed) past from the contingent present in a way that is fundamentally different from the culture's own sense of time.

But finally, I would caution against one possible reading of *Daughters of the Dust* as only criticizing a kind of (white) nostalgia associated with the imperialist imperatives of modernity. Rather, the film's callback at the time of its production in the 1990s to an earlier moment in African American history should be regarded at least partly as an act of reflective nostalgia by the filmmakers for the cultures and traditions therein lost—a way to preserve something now gone with the hope that it might inspire contemporary audiences going forward. This impulse is not entirely unlike that of Mr. Snead—though one magnified further by the profound passage of time as the film production approached yet another century. As an independent film production, *Daughters of the Dust* is very much technically also a product of the twentieth century—one struggling to hold onto that lost period. Just because we usually situate nostalgia as coexisting with hegemonic discourses of whiteness, masculinity, and modernity does not preclude the possibility that some other films might offer challenges that rethink some of those same assumptions. Looking at films like *Daughters of the Dust* widens and clarifies our understanding of nostalgic representations in contemporary media culture, while the frustration some mainstream audiences feel regarding the movie's counterintuitive (non-Western) approach to historical memory and time should also compel us to see just how limited, and limiting, the scope of popular culture's mediated nostalgic representation of history has become. A final point to take away from *Daughters of the Dust* in this immediate context may not simply be that there are fascinating cinematic meditations on nostalgia that elude its usual connotations of masculinity and whiteness, but that the more interesting forms of nostalgia in media must by necessity exist as much as possible outside the commercial imperatives of Hollywood's modern entertainment industry.

The Return of History

Two broader concerns arise regarding nostalgia's thoroughly commodified role in popular culture today—the more collective sense of our relationship to and understanding of history, and the more intimate feeling that our personal nostalgias are neither unique to our individual selves nor immune to manipulation. As for the former, sanitized nostalgia carries the risk of further erasing any sustained commitment to historical consciousness. Does it matter that Wes Anderson's highly stylized pastiche, *The Grand Budapest Hotel*, is not simply a wistful look back but also a nostalgic erasure of World War II—its structuring absence? The real fears and horrors of fascism in twentieth-century Europe become safely transported into a fantastical make-believe world (a question all the more powerful given its literary origins' tragic authorial context). Or what of Disney's neoliberal corporatist fantasy *Tomorrowland* (2015)? Brad Bird's film longs for the Baby Boomer days of early Space Age optimism—as well as the ambitions and innovations of successful industrialists like Thomas Edison—without seeming to recognize that its massive parent media conglomerate, the Walt Disney Company, is a perfect modern-day exemplar of Thomas Edison's disturbing ambitions for total market control. Its corporate nostalgia for the lost innovative potential of NASA or Jules Verne works to disavow how effectively the mechanisms of modern capitalism have made impossible the kind of radical political and cultural change to which the movie's messages pay superficial lip service.

In contemporary media culture, as in some of the films discussed here, nostalgia is often a starting point for populist engagements with larger historical questions, and thus nostalgia's value certainly extends beyond aesthetics. In this regard, Dyer's work in *Pastiche* on the critical worth of imitation remains essential—seeing nostalgic media as a potential entry point back into genre and cultural histories—as long as we remain mindful that most audiences won't bother doing that kind of research on their own. More than anything, this may be the larger ideological value in defining the nostalgia genre—to highlight not only the "since then...," and its basic generic features, but to reiterate the frightening extent in contemporary culture to which nostalgia is so often masked superficially as history (the complexities of the latter seem to be increasingly fading in light of its little commercial value). In our hypermediated society, the distinctions between nostalgia and history (particularly in documentaries like *Stories We Tell*, and other oral narrative forms) have become effectively blurred—a commodified culture where it's common to conflate the consumer's personal reaction to older media artifacts with a thoroughly researched and contextualized one. Pam Cook has previously noted that history and nostalgia are not opposed but parts of the continuum of past time (along with memory). "History," she writes, "suppresses the element of disavowal or fantasy in its representation of the past, [while] nostalgia foregrounds those elements" (3). It might be useful to review some possible distinctions between the two, laid out in the following table.

Table 1. Distinctions between Nostalgia and History

Nostalgia	History
Simplification	Contradiction
Seduction	Negotiation
Imagination	Documentation
Wholes	Fragments
Reassuring	Unsettling
Monologue	Dialogue
Innocence	Knowledge

The fact that we can see overlaps (indeed, history requires a certain kind of "imagination," just as nostalgia is a certain kind of "documentation") only reinforces the extent to which the two have come dangerously close to collapsing together in late capitalist media culture. This makes the constant acknowledgment of nostalgia as nostalgia in accounts of history all the more valuable. Any discussion of the nostalgic media text must begin with a recognition that we do not think enough about the differences between nostalgia and history in a culture that—with either a constructively aware lens, or a regressive and oblivious one—increasingly gravitates to their commonalities.

In the end, three trends have emerged in Hollywood's increasing fascination with nostalgia. The first is its troubling (and unresolvable) tensions with historical consciousness in a consumer culture that largely defines the past according to its financial worth. The second, following that point, is that nostalgia is itself often the commodity that people desire when consuming popular media, not the film or TV show that facilitates it. The third, which binds the previous two, is that nostalgia is defined textually through assumptions about style—the aesthetic looks of the past (pastiche) become synonymous with the past itself. None of these trends offer much optimism if we are focused on thinking about the nostalgia film as (1) a substantive engagement with history, (2) offering a personal relationship with the past that is actually personalized, or (3) activating a special feeling that resists or eludes heavy industry manipulation. Perhaps the last two are the most distressing, as nostalgia's "delicate" power comes from its ability to evoke the feeling of a unique or spontaneous personal engagement with the past. This echoes Altman's other point about a genre contradiction between the opposing pulls of desire and manipulation. Can we still feel genuinely connected to certain tropes, formulas, and so forth once we become wholly aware of a genre's inherent commonalities and even clichés? As nostalgia's ubiquity becomes more concentrated and coordinated in popular culture today, this is perhaps the most important question to ask.

It would be ideal to end by noting that the critic's holy grail of nostalgia texts might be those that shrewdly and reflexively integrate several of the above textual and thematic genre elements into the same story. However, such textual shrewdness in the age of late capitalism should not be accepted at face value. For instance, *Tomorrowland* is intensely reflexive regarding its representational and narrative nostalgic impulses, using its fondness for innovations past to valorize new possibilities in our digital future. But it's also a multimillion-dollar corporate fantasy fully conscious of nostalgia's potential to sell both movie tickets and an illusion of historical and cultural change that paradoxically leaves room for neither. Such nostalgic narratives obscure questions in their attendant economic histories far more than they illuminate. Given Hollywood's self-evident obsession with the market dependability of nostalgic appeals and its generally transparent self-awareness about its own products, it's difficult to envision how any of its nostalgic texts—affective, peripheral, representational, narrative, or otherwise—really offer much in the way of a critical space for using the past as a reflective guide for the future.

In short, this is one key limitation for more progressive definitions of pastiche that see nostalgia as offering a critical intervention into our understanding of history. Unfortunately, the various incarnations of nostalgia for medias past are already too central to Hollywood's business model to easily offer up such spaces for hypothetical readings that are truly deviant, resistant, or in any other way unexpected in the context of the movie's intended address (not that those spaces are impossible, just extremely and undependably rare). If we haven't already, we may find ourselves yearning for that kind of media nostalgia that we imagine to have once seemed untainted (not to mention wholly undetermined) by capitalist imperatives. Has Hollywood's rabid obsession with nostalgia already reached a breaking point, causing audiences to pine for that idealized, simpler moment of the "good old days" of media consumption that weren't only about fulfilling dependable market niches for easily predictable and manipulated audience demographics? A next trend in nostalgic pop culture might be a yearning for that past mass-mediated experience that felt somehow genuinely "our own" once, and not something that was always already programmed for us—a postnostalgia nostalgia for a prenostalgic past.

Works Cited

Altman, Rick. *The American Film Musical*. Bloomington: Indiana University Press, 2003.
Baade, Christina, and Paul Aitken. "Still 'in the Mood': The Nostalgia Aesthetic in a Digital World." *Journal of Popular Music Studies* 20.4 (2008): 353–77.
Boym, Svetlana. *The Future of Nostalgia*. New York: Basic Books, 2001.
Boym, Svetlana. "Nostalgia and Its Discontents." *Hedgehog Review* 9.2 (2007): 7–18.
Cook, Pam. *Screening the Past: Memory and Nostalgia in Cinema*. London: Routledge, 2004.

Davis, Fred. *Yearning for Yesterday: A Sociology of Nostalgia*. New York: Free Press, 1979.
Dwyer, Michael. *Back to the Fifties: Nostalgia, Hollywood Film, and Popular Music of the Seventies and Eighties*. New York: Oxford University Press, 2015.
Dyer, Richard. *Pastiche*. London: Routledge, 2006.
Jameson, Fredric. *Postmodernism: or, the Cultural Logic of Late Capitalism*. Durham, NC: Duke University Press, 1991.
Le Sueur, Marc. "Theory Number Five: Anatomy of Nostalgia Films: Heritage and Methods." *Journal of Popular Film* 6.2 (1977): 187–97.
Spigel, Lynn. "Postfeminist Nostalgia for a Prefeminist Future." *Screen* 54.2 (2013): 270–78.
Sprengler, Christine. *Screening Nostalgia: Populuxe Props and Technicolor Aesthetics in Contemporary American Film*. New York: Berghahn Books, 2009.
Stern, Barbara. "Historical and Personal Nostalgia in Advertising Text: The Fin de Siècle Effect." *Journal of Advertising* 21.4 (1992): 11–22.
Stewart, Kathleen. "Nostalgia—A Polemic." *Cultural Anthropology* 3.3 (1988): 227–41.

2

Midcentury Metamodern

Returning Home in the Twenty-First-Century Nostalgia Film

CHRISTINE SPRENGLER

THE LABEL "NOSTALGIA FILM" CASTS a wide net around representations of pasts documented and fictionalized, eras ancient and recent, stretches of time brief and extended. It inspires taxonomies that account for varying claims to taste and authenticity in specific national contexts as well as classificatory schemes that foreground different ways of aesthetically engaging the past. The nostalgia film encompasses a range of genres that have evolved their own visual, aural, and narrative grammars, transforming how we understand the epic or romance, for instance. The concept of evolution is key here, for as much as genres develop over time, so too does the concept of nostalgia. From its origins as the medical condition of homesickness afflicting Swiss mercenaries through various manifestations aligned with loss and longing at the hands of industrialization, psychology, and commodification, nostalgia has accrued and shed the resonances of its travels through time, space, theory, and media.

For decades, definitions of filmic nostalgia have been tied to postmodernism's aesthetic modes (e.g., parody, pastiche, and irony), famously derided by Fredric Jameson for impeding meaningful engagements with history, trading in depthlessness and supplanting the 1950s, for example, with "fiftiesness." Linda Hutcheon challenged Jameson's thinking on this by salvaging postmodern historiographic metafiction, recuperating the critical possibilities of parody and irony and arguing that the past has only ever been accessible through its textualized remains (96). Later, Svetlana Boym, Pam Cook, Vera Dika, Michael Dwyer, Richard Dyer, Paul Grainge, Elizabeth Guffey, myself, and others extended these critical-analytical powers to pastiche and nostalgia itself. They (and I) remained deeply indebted to Jameson's persuasive arguments about postmodern nostalgia but also sought to acknowledge its capacity, in certain cases, to initiate critical reconsiderations of the past, to tap into previously overlooked experiences, and to reveal the processes by which histories are constructed, engaged, and challenged. Since then, the literature on nostalgia has splintered along several trajectories. One includes Jason Sperb's compelling and nuanced reconsideration of the analytical potential of postmodern aesthetic modes. He introduces a healthy dose of skepticism and a much-needed account of the film industry's continued economic stakes in nostalgia. Jilly Boyce Kay, Cat Mahoney, and Caitlin Shaw's edited collection also accounts for such complexities as well as its many permutations in relation to memory. Another trajectory foregrounds a concern with nostalgia's value, though in a way that bypasses the Jameson/Hutcheon debate (Cross, Niemeyer).

However, explorations of the potential criticality of (postmodern) nostalgia in the early years of the twenty-first century coincided with proclamations of postmodernism's death and its replacement by something else: digimodernism, hypermodernism, altermodernism, metamodernism, and so on. These periodizing labels were initially introduced with a fair amount of hyperbole and required the homogenization of an often contradictory set of discourses. After more studied reflection, however, the proponents of some of these new -isms have tempered their claims, acknowledging how older tendencies—be they modern or postmodern—persist across our cultural forms. In other words, they started to account for the complexities of periodization, an issue Michel Serres describes through his "theory of percolation." For Serres, time itself is understood not as linear or chronological, as "geometrically rigid," but as a turbulent and chaotic force that percolates (58). He accounts for flow and filtering, and thus a process whereby some things pass and others are held at bay. In historical terms, percolations rupture the boundaries that circumscribe temporally defined eras, puncturing and then infecting periods with the residues—material, representational, and/or ideological—of even earlier times. His insistence that time percolates and that all eras are multitemporal and polychronic are apt reminders of the continuing entanglements of seemingly discrete moments in history. The premodern, modern, postmodern, and post-postmodern coexist. They do so in broad cultural terms but also within a single object, like a film. This is an important point to keep in abeyance here, and one partially accounted for in the postmodern replacement most adept at explaining certain tendencies in recent nostalgia films: metamodernism.

In what follows, I suggest that metamodernism provides a useful—although imperfect—lens through which to consider a recent batch of nostalgia films invested in midcentury America, that period most derided by Jameson for instantiating our sense of postmodern nostalgia. Following a few brief observations on postmodern nostalgia films and, by way of introduction to metamodernism, *La La Land* (2016), I consider how certain strategies related to nostalgia in *Hidden Figures* (2016) and *Carol* (2015) might benefit from the analytical framework introduced by this post-postmodern discourse. Timotheus Vermeulen and Robin van den Akker argue that metamodernism describes a new cultural logic characterized by an oscillation between modern enthusiasm and commitment and postmodern irony and detachment but, in the end seeks to replace the latter's penchant for deconstruction with an investment in reconstruction, hope, and meaning (5–6). Metamodernism may be marked by a desire for sincerity and authenticity, but such earnestness is—and ought to be—mitigated by a degree of skepticism. To me, this overstates a little the degree to which postmodern strategies supposedly effaced meaning and feeling, for sincerity and irreverence coexist in nostalgic representations of regressive and progressive visions of the past. That is, irony and parody may have indeed reigned, but their prominence did not occlude an investment in a kind of historical reality or deeper affect even in the most quintessentially postmodern films. Nevertheless, Vermeulen, van den Akker, and others take metamodernism beyond the recuperative projects aimed at nostalgia to identify a newer sensibility.

This sensibility, explained with recourse to Raymond Williams's "structure of feeling," describes the nature of metamodernism, including its capacity to link a diverse range of creative expressions borne from the political and economic realities of the 2000s (van den Akker and Vermeulen 6). For instance, in the realm of literature, metamodern fiction like

Toni Morrison's *Beloved* is "historioplastic" rather than historiographic in its "infinite yet bound pliability of the past" (Toth 43). For James McDowell, the "quirky" cinema of Wes Anderson or Miranda July makes up a category of films that share "an overarching tone of defiant affirmation, commitment and sincere engagement in the face of an implicitly acknowledged potential for despair, disillusionment or ironic detachment" (39). McDowell offers a convincing argument for a particular strain of metamodernism in contemporary cinema, one that replicates Vermeulen and van den Akker's exclusion of nostalgia, a curious omission given the prominence otherwise given to questions of historicity and affect. If we introduce nostalgia into metamodernism, a range of other films open themselves up to consideration through this scaffolding. For instance, *La La Land* may fail to register as quirky in the way McDowell describes, but it can certainly be understood through an investment in sincerity as one of the privileged poles to which metamodernism's pendulum swings (Vermeulen and van den Akker 6). The film charts Mia (Emma Stone) and Sebastian's (Ryan Gosling) unapologetic devotion to the art forms that structure their lives, acting and jazz, respectively. More accurately, they are deeply passionate about nostalgic visions of these creative pursuits, grounded in their views of classical Hollywood cinema and the work of Charlie Parker and Thelonius Monk. The authenticity of their investment is never questioned, even though it should be, given how the racial dynamics of Sebastian's particular commitments play out in the film, including the erasure of jazz's many alignments with civil rights struggles. In other words, the characters' (and film's) nostalgia for the cinema and music of the past is genuine, meaningful, unaffected, and offered up as problematically unproblematic.

But nostalgia in *La La Land* is also signaled aesthetically. As such, the other privileged pole of metamodernism's pendulum is not irony (as it is for McDowell) but pastiche of a postmodern variety that surfaces in a number of varied ways. The film is shot in CinemaScope and introduced and concluded with retro-style titles. It references its classical Hollywood musical source material at every turn. It plays with visual artifice through location shots that look like painted backdrops and matte paintings that move through the real space of a Hollywood backlot. It recalls the cinematography, color palettes, and framing of midcentury American cinema. As such, although *La La Land* is readily identifiable as a nostalgia film because of its aesthetic trappings, its structure of feeling—one where feeling itself is emphasized and guided along distinctly unironic emotional vectors—results in a rather different type of engagement with the past.

To explore the metamodern thrust of twenty-first-century nostalgia films would be an irresponsibly large undertaking. Even narrowing my purview to midcentury representations, as a point of connection to Jameson's nostalgia critique, would be unwieldly given the continued prominence of this era in the cinematic imagination. Therefore, I focus on how home is represented in nostalgia films invested in postwar America, specifically those inhabited by marginalized constituencies. Doing so returns us somewhat poetically to nostalgia's origins but in a way that echoes metamodernism's implicit concerns with sincerity and ultimately even truth. As a concept, home has been subject to much cultural criticism and in ways that extend into questions of patriarchy, migration, exile, childhood, trauma, memory, subjectivity, and geography. While some of this informs what follows, at issue here is how home is cinematographically figured through otherwise postmodern aesthetic modes and what this alignment produces if we track shifts in its representation from the 1990s to the 2010s.

Pleasantville (1998), *Blast from the Past* (1999), *Far from Heaven* (2002), and *Down with Love* (2003) are all quite typical examples of postmodern nostalgia films for both their cinematographic aesthetic and ways of representing home. In each case, the look of the film trades in "deliberate archaism," the practice of creating new images to resemble older ones by mimicking black and white, sepia, Technicolor, rear projection, and so on (Le Sueur 193). *Pleasantville* looks like a black-and-white 1950s television sitcom until a Technicolor palette slowly supplants the monochrome. *Blast from the Past* draws much of its postwar energy from "period casting" Brendan Fraser as Adam, whose previous alignment with 1950s-set films permeates this one. *Down with Love* makes use of CinemaScope, long takes, highly choreographed movements, period casting, wide expansive sets, matte paintings, and original rear projections from the 1950s and 1960s. These deliberately archaic gestures imbue the film with an artifice that hearkens back to the sex comedies that served as its aesthetic template. *Far from Heaven*'s deliberate archaism is even more precisely calibrated. Here, director Todd Haynes re-creates the look of Douglas Sirk's melodramas like *All That Heaven Allows* (1955) in painstaking detail. Haynes does so to celebrate the ways Sirk transformed the screen into a visual spectacle of garish and complementary color to unsettle the audience, initiate a kind of critical distance, and launch (through visual means) a stinging critique of postwar America's racism, sexism, and homophobia. Deliberate archaism remains a staple of recent nostalgia films. *The Aviator* (2004), *Good Night, and Good Luck* (2005), *The Good German* (2006), *The*

Artist (2011), *Hugo* (2011), and many others re-create the look of past media forms. Some, following the footsteps of *Far from Heaven*, do so to engage critically with history, historicity, mediation, and nostalgia itself, whereas others are the progeny of *Blast from the Past*, uncritically reveling in past popular forms or perpetrating troubling historical constructions.

In *Pleasantville*, home is a 1950s domestic sitcom construct and not, for the most part, an object of longing. Home as a site of comfort and plenty is parodied through an overabundance of chintz, knickknacks, decor, and breakfasts that could feed a crowd (figure 2.1). It is a space whose (mock) sanctity requires protection: a conversation between father and son about dating cannot take place inside its walls. Consciousness—of sex and of gender inequality—bring all this crashing down. This is signaled most forcefully by the distinctly cinematic clap of thunder that follows the father's cheery refrain, "Hi honey, I'm home!" and the tree that erupts into flames with the mother's first orgasm, a conflagration that threatens to engulf the entire house. *Far from Heaven* similarly deconstructs a mythologized construct of home. Initially a picture-perfect suburban dwelling and site of familiar routine, its underbelly is revealed through Sirkian stylistic maneuvers that foretell its unraveling. Increasingly violent clashes of complimentary color signal growing unease while its design perfection signifies its unhomeliness. It is a stage set, a function made

Figure 2.1. George (William H. Macy) and Betty Parker (Joan Allen). *Pleasantville* (Gary Ross, 1998). Digital frame enlargement.

clear by the photo session that captures Cathy's (Julianne Moore) artificial poses in what we are prompted to read as an artificial environment. She and her home are little more than images for the consumption of others in a desire economy. In this way, *Pleasantville* and *Far from Heaven* perform that quintessential postmodern function of deconstructing representations of home, showcasing the suffocating effects of oppressive patriarchal structures.

Postmodern nostalgia films can hardly be considered homogeneous, and neither can their representations of home. In *Down with Love*, home is not a middle-class suburban dwelling but a city apartment. Here, too, it announces itself as a carefully styled fabrication and not a meaningful object with the capacity to evoke melancholic longing. The protagonists' apartments are tasked with little more than exemplifying the personalities of those who inhabit them and the 1960s sex comedies that served as inspiration. Barbara Novak's (Renée Zellweger) apartment is wholly unrealistic in its size and scale. Such artifice is further reinforced by the (obvious) matte painting of the Manhattan skyline that betrays an impossible geography. Here, the Chrysler Building, Empire State Building, and Statue of Liberty are in close proximity. How can home be real in a city that is not? Likewise, Catcher Block's (Ewan McGregor) apartment trades equally in artifice. His bachelor pad, complete with mechanized contraptions like a hidden bed and bar, is missing a kitchen. It too announces itself as a cinematic set piece but also does some work at intimating how Catcher is falling behind the times. Its design scheme is more angular (i.e., late 1950s), and its technologies parodied as outdated for the period. Barbara's home, by contrast, makes full use of the vocabulary of early 1960s interior design and beyond. After all, she represents the future of gender relations and Catcher, the past.

Blast from the Past is centered on home's meaning, destruction, and replication. Although parody and irony abound in the film, it is not an exercise in critical postmodern deconstruction. It opens with a cocktail party hosted at the height of the Cuban missile crisis by Calvin (Christopher Walken) and Helen (Sissy Spacek), who is nine months pregnant. News reports of escalating nuclear tensions spark fear in Calvin, who drags Helen into their fallout shelter. As they enter, a wayward jet crashes into their house, wrongly convincing them that an attack has occurred. They set the locks for thirty-five years. Their shelter is not only fully stocked but a precise replica of their home on the surface, and thus it provides (in outward appearance anyway) a bastion of domestic comforts and a protected oasis in which to raise their son. For Andrea Vesentini, the film's representation of the fallout shelter accords with how cinema showcased such shelters as spaces of "retreat from upsetting historical processes in which the present could be brought to a standstill and preserved from complete annihilation." They were "mirror spaces" of suburban homes, "domestic utopias" immune from "dangerous" social forces or, in other words, progressive movements that were feared as challenges to white heterosexual male privilege (42).

Calvin's first foray into the 1990s confirms this. Upon leaving his "domestic utopia," one where he and Helen reproduce in their son all the virtues of patience, respect, education, good manners, and graces, he encounters a character who embodies several 1960s social movements at once: a Black sex worker who offers, "If you want a boy, I can be a boy. If you want a girl, I can be a girl." Calvin describes this person as a "mutant" and part of a landscape of degeneracy, crime, and countless other moral failings. This is just the beginning of the film's deeply problematic representations of race, gender, and sexuality. By the end, when Calvin and Helen finally return to the surface, they are whisked out to the country where their son has re-created their original home. Like their fallout shelter, it is a perfect simulation of their early 1960s dwelling, one that permits them to remain in the past. As such, they enact not only a geographical kind of "white flight" but a temporal one as well.

In each case, these late postmodern nostalgia films offer highly mediated, heavily parodic constructs of home that play reflexively with the signifying elements that constitute them, the ideological discourses in which they have been activated, and the mythic images of postwar America at whose service they have been mobilized. For deconstructive purposes, this reflexive play often (but not always) ends with the critique of its subject and of nostalgia for home, too. So, what shifts might we detect in nostalgia films produced since the purported "death of postmodernism"? Specifically, what new roles does home play now in films representing the postwar period, ones that still announce their nostalgic status aesthetically? I argue that although constructs of home continue to be mobilized to myriad ends, we find several cases in which home has been reconfigured in a metamodern vein. That is, we find in a series of nostalgia films—ones that continue to trade in deliberate archaism—representations of home that eschew parody and artifice in favor of sincerity. In these examples, home is treated as a site with a connection to a purportedly real, lived past, one capable of evoking a genuine nostalgic mood in a way that hearkens back to nostalgia's origins in the feeling of homesickness. However, this order of nostalgia is not akin to that found in *Blast from the Past*, where the object of longing is a mythic vision of white middle-class patriarchy. Instead, we find nostalgia for a vision of home that centers and, to a certain degree, guards marginalized subjectivities against a series of truly "upsetting historical processes," namely, racism, sexism, and homophobia.

In these films, home has been tasked with an anchoring function, the locus of stability and comfort and an object worthy of longing. It has been reinscribed with the power to access histories—personal and public—especially ones too often neglected. *Hidden Figures* tells the story of the integral role played by Black women in the NASA space program in the early 1960s, focusing specifically on Katherine Johnson (Taraji P. Henson), Dorothy Vaughan (Octavia Spencer), and Mary Jackson (Janelle Monáe). It makes use of the aesthetic trappings of postmodern nostalgia cinema, opening in 1926 on a world described through sepia tint and two-strip Technicolor. As we shift to the film's present in 1961, the desaturated bluish greens transform into the vibrant greens made possible by three-strip technology. This moment of self-reflexive mediation in turn ushers in a scene that establishes the present as a lens through which to consider what follows. The newly verdant rural landscape becomes the setting for a stressful encounter between the women—whose car has broken down—and a white police officer who, with billy club in hand, interrogates them. The resulting tension pierces through the conventionally nostalgic image of the rural postwar past by bringing to mind the many recent instances of police brutality. Past and present collide to remind us of the long history of this kind of violence. This engagement with the visual language of postmodern nostalgia plays an important function, for set against these well-worn aesthetic strategies is a critique of racism and sexism that runs deeper than what *Pleasantville*, for instance, offers us—although one that remains problematic in several respects. Segregation and its effects may be foregrounded throughout the film, but many of the collective efforts of the civil rights movement—as well as its relationship with the Cold War context—are obscured. Also troubling are the inaccurate dating of events and especially the undue dramatic energy that swirls around several invented white savior moments, including Al Harrison's (Kevin Costner) desegregation of NASA's washrooms (Morris 417–18).

Whereas public spaces, including workplaces, are beset with an unending stream of humiliations and injustices, the space of home is a source of nostalgia in terms of mood and not just aesthetic modes. Home is not offered up as a mediated construct but as a space of comfort, community, safety, and belonging. It is a space where both family and community congregate, a space of nurturing and sociality. Houses, despite their (class) differences, are sources of pride and their interiors bathed in warm light. For instance, Katherine's home is working-class, something communicated through its size, furniture, and mismatched and abundant patterns. Mary's is distinctly middle-class, with modern tulip chairs, sleek wooden dining set and paneling, and use of modernist patterns. However, both perform the very same function by providing a space for the types of experiences that feed an authentic nostalgia. For example, our first view inside Katherine's home takes place on her return from work and reveals her loving relationship with her mother and three children. But in foregrounding this, the film doesn't privilege some regressive notion of feminine domesticity. Whether she should work is not a vexed question or even an option, as it is in other postwar set dramas; she is challenged by and receives fulfilment from both her roles, as a mathematician and a mother.

For Katherine, home is not simply a space of family, at least not in any narrow sense that excludes the political realities in which familial relationships are necessarily imbricated. It plays out through Jim Webb's visits, whereby his actions counter any patriarchal practices ideologically ingrained in domestic space; he makes soup for Katherine to nurse her back to health and serves dinner to her family. The civil rights movement and the space race are also part of the experience of home life for both Katherine and Mary. Archival footage of key events is mediated by the TV sets and radios around which family and friends congregate. They consume, process, and discuss the significance of everything from Sputnik to the words of Dr. Martin Luther King Jr. A card game at Mary's house between Katherine, Mary, and Dorothy provides the backdrop to a conversation about the continued segregation of Virginia's schools (figure 2.2). The radio program that scores the dancing at Dorothy's son's birthday party is interrupted by a news bulletin detailing the successful completion of Yuri Gagarin's first orbit in space. The scene then cuts to archival footage of this event. A family dinner at Katherine's house is followed by actual footage of Alan Shepard's launch into space, while scenes of Katherine and Jim's engagement cut abruptly to footage of the Mercury Atlas rocket preparations. A news report of the bomb attack on the Freedom Riders functions as a bridge between scenes set in Katherine's and Mary's homes. Despite Mary's pleas to turn off the television, her husband insists that everyone needs to see this. These moments and images flow in and through family dinners, parties, and other decidedly domestic events. The nostalgia-worthy moments of home life (birthdays, engagements, familial love, friendship) are entwined with both actual and staged footage of broader social and political forces at work.

Figure 2.2. Dorothy Vaughan (Octavia Spencer), Mary Jackson (Janelle Monáe), and Katherine Johnson (Taraji P. Henson). *Hidden Figures* (Theodore Melfi, 2016). Digital frame enlargement.

Home may be a refuge, but it isn't a retreat from the many historical events that make up the world of the film. Katherine, Mary, and Dorothy are shaped by them and, in turn, shape history. But the space race is also a part of Black history in many ways beyond their specific contributions, something mainstream cinema has long overlooked. As such, history matters here, publicly and personally, in ways that introduce several important complications. Although certain postmodern aesthetic modes keep our consciousness in the film's present, they are not mobilized to deconstruct, demystify or challenge history. The authenticity of the past represented matters as a contextualizing framework for the events that unfold therein. This is not to suggest that the framework itself—one that privileges a white, patriarchal, individualist, and nationalist American history—isn't ingrained with racist and sexist tendencies. To my mind, one of the film's greatest problems is how it elides the complexities of the civil rights movement and the many facets that constitute the protagonists' subjectivities. However, *Hidden Figures* does allow us to contend with what is excluded by a postmodern treatment of the past that reduces all history to textualized remains. For instance, how do we celebrate the very real contributions Katherine made to the space program if historical events are offered up as little more than ironic constructs? How do we represent the postwar histories of marginalized communities when the cinematic language typically used to describe that era has been colonized by regressive nostalgic agendas but also critical ones that originate from a white perspective on the world that can afford the various consequences of playing parodically with history? This is as important for validating—and feeling nostalgia for—the protagonists' intersections with History as it is their own personal ones. For excluding Black women from the experience of nostalgia, as Janelle Wilson's studies have shown, denies the powerful, identity-forming, and affirming value of nostalgia for home as a salve in the racist context of postwar America. Indeed, we may be unlikely to ever truly know history, or even agree on what constitutes such knowledge, but a metamodern approach suggests that sometimes the stakes are high enough that we are obligated to try.

The historical world of *Hidden Figures* derives some of its authenticity from the archival footage that links—and necessarily inflects with verity—its dramatized representations of home life, enabling us to see, among other things, the affective truths that can emerge from even fictionalized family dynamics. Something similar is at work in the lesbian romance drama *Carol*. The titular character's house is in some ways much like the upper-middle-class suburban postwar abode occupied by Cathy in *Far from Heaven*. Both are grand and carefully set with period details that betray their owners' investment in 1950s material culture. However, whereas the cinematography renders the patriarchal oppression of *Far from Heaven*'s house palpable, this filter is missing in Haynes's later incarnation. Instead, images of Carol's (Cate Blanchett) home, especially at Christmas, are infused with warmth and are the place of tender interactions between Carol and her lover, Therese (Rooney Mara), as well as Carol and her daughter. Although the presence of her husband, Harge (Kyle Chandler), disrupts the serenity of this space, warmth returns with his absence. Harge's fiercest aggressions against Carol take place outside the home. As such, it is a space that seems to resist the tension his arrival introduces. It is not the site of the reproduction of patriarchal norms but an enclave that nurtures a different family structure and set of loving relationships. We witness Carol brushing her daughter's hair, carrying her tenderly upstairs to bed, and enlisting her in decorating the Christmas tree. We also see Therese serenading Carol at the piano as she wraps Christmas presents. These may be clichéd moments, but they are offered up with the utmost sincerity and as productive of authentic emotion. Likewise, Therese's apartment may be modest and somewhat bleak, but it is her refuge and a space where she develops (quite literally) her passion—photography.

The only thing that tempers the genuineness meant to adhere to scenes of home is their filming through a series of aesthetic tendencies borrowed from postwar photography. Rather than support a deconstructive agenda as it did in *Far from Heaven*, *Carol*'s deliberate archaism infuses its scenes with even greater sincerity and truth. That is, *Carol* may lean toward a postmodern sensibility in its borrowing of past media forms, but the ends to which its particular aesthetic archaisms are used tend toward a metamodern one. Indeed, as Alison Gibbons observes, a postmodern staple like irony may remain a key part of a metamodern text but be mobilized for a different purpose (85). Haynes shot *Carol* on Super 16 to give it a grainy feel, to mirror the grittiness of New York in the early 1950s and, especially, the photographs by Ruth Orkin, Esther Bubley, and Helen Levitt. He was interested in the photojournalism and art photography of the period that had a "patina of grit" and looked "nothing like the enameled polished look of studio filming in the Sirkian era" (Haynes). But he also replicates some of these photographers' framing strategies. The action often takes place in doorways, narrow corridors, or behind walls that partially obscure the action. In fact, the actors, who sometimes take up very little space on the screen, compete with the various sites—typically homes—described through multiple frames and planes. The space itself is thus privileged and, as in the postwar images that provide inspiration, we are made aware of the agency of place.

In hearkening back to these old images, the film also harnesses a particularly strong force with which these photographs are encoded: truth. These images are read as authentic historical records, a tendency that elides the more troubling elements that constitute the myth of photographic truth. Along with the grittiness or coded "realness" of Super 16, they do much to imbue the historical moment of *Carol* with a degree of authenticity and facticity too. And, as in *Hidden Figures*, history matters. Unlike *Far from Heaven*, *Carol* is not about deconstructing the problematic postwar identities shaped by toxic masculinity or passive femininity, though these do remain part of the lining of the film. Instead, it is about validating a set of experiences, processes of self-discovery, development of agency, and articulation of lesbian desires that have not been afforded much representation, cinematic or otherwise. The truthfulness and (emotional) sincerity of this, even in an otherwise fictionalized narrative, is thus deemed deserving of nostalgia.

So too are the commodified collectibles of Hollywood and jazz history that populate *La La Land*'s homes. Though less central to the development of the film than homes in *Hidden Figures* or *Carol*, Mia's and Sebastian's apartments are sites of encounter with cultural history and bastions of preservation for its paraphernalia. Posters of movie stars like Ingrid Bergman and memorabilia like Hoagy Carmichael's stool are prized possessions, deeply infused with meaning and emotion. They are set dressing, but repeatedly come in and out of narrative focus in ways that foreground their authenticity as conduits to history and instigators of personal and collective nostalgic longing. For instance, Sebastian implores his sister not to sit on Carmichael's stool, one of the few objects that managed to make it out of his many unpacked moving boxes. These objects render otherwise generic apartments meaningful to their inhabitants. But these spaces, carefully populated with such props, are also subjected to deliberate archaism. The cinematographic strategies deployed here, however, are not in the service of a flippant visual intertextuality. Instead they help underscore the emotional truths of the space's inhabitants as authentic. That is, Mia's apartment, shared with roommates, abounds with primary colors that recall the vibrancy of Technicolor as a way to give weight to her Hollywood dreams. Later in the film, Sebastian's apartment is bathed in *Vertigo*'s (1958) signature greenish glow. As Mia steps into the garish light wearing a complementary lilac dress, generating a ghostly effect reminiscent of Kim Novak's, cinema history is evoked not simply for the sake of homage, though that is part of it. Instead, the full emotional weight of Hitchcock's scene is harnessed here with the hope that the emotional reality of Judy/Madeleine and Scottie's relationship inform Mia and Sebastian's own doomed union.

In this way, *La La Land* and the recent films considered here reveal a metamodern oscillation between certain postmodern aesthetic modes—deliberate archaism in particular—and modern reinvestments in sincerity, reconstruction, authenticity, and meaning. Not home, nor history itself, is engaged with parodically or ironically. Instead there is a commitment to sharing important facets of the past that ought to be heralded or confronted, even yearned for nostalgically in some instances. As such, nostalgia is signaled not just aesthetically, as is often the case in postmodern representations of the postwar past, but emotively through figurations of home that recall nostalgia's origins as a sentiment predicated on genuine longing. But what purpose does a continued postmodern aesthetic serve? For one thing, it reminds us of the present and the mediated lenses through which we consume the images and histories on offer. Vermeulen and van der Akker may also have a contribution to make to this answer. They warn that the "modern" virtues being reintroduced should be framed by a Kantian as-if-ness. That is, our cultural expressions ought to proceed as if these things were possible, while filtering our efforts through a (postmodern) skepticism that recognizes the pitfalls of doing so. In other words, we ought to see the ideals and possibilities inherent in home, entrenched in important historical moments too long neglected, and ingrained in a genuine longing or nostalgia, but recognize the limitations that necessarily complicate our efforts to represent them.

Works Cited

Boym, Svetlana. *The Future of Nostalgia*. New York: Basic Books, 2002.
Cook, Pam. *Screening the Past: Memory and Nostalgia in Cinema*. London: Routledge, 2004.
Cross, Gary. *Consumed Nostalgia: Memory in the Age of Mass Capitalism*. New York: Columbia University Press, 2017.
Dika, Vera. *Recycled Culture in Contemporary Art and Film: The Uses of Nostalgia*. Cambridge: Cambridge University Press, 2003.
Dwyer, Michael. *Back to the Fifties: Nostalgia, Hollywood Film, and Popular Music of the Seventies and Eighties*. New York: Oxford University Press, 2015.
Dyer, Richard. *Pastiche*. London: Routledge, 2007.
Gibbons, Alison. "Metamodern Affect." *Metamodernism: Historicity, Affect and Depth After Postmodernism*. Ed. Robin van den Akker, Allison Gibbons, and Timotheus Vermeulen. Lanham, MD: Rowman and Littlefield, 2017. 83–86.
Grainge, Paul. *Monochrome Memories: Nostalgia and Style in Retro America*. Westport, CT: Praeger, 2002.
Guffey, Elizabeth. *Retro: The Culture of Revival*. London: Reaktion, 2006.
Haynes, Todd. "Director's Commentary." *Carol*. DVD. Film4 et al., 2016.
Hutcheon, Linda. *A Poetics of Postmodernism: History, Theory, Fiction*. London: Routledge, 1988.
Jameson, Fredric. *Postmodernism, or, the Cultural Logic of Late Capitalism*. Durham, NC: Duke University Press, 1990.
Kay, Jilly Boyce, Cat Mahoney, and Caitlin Shaw, eds. *The Past in Visual Culture: Essays on Memory, Nostalgia and the Media*. Jefferson, NC: McFarland, 2017.
Le Sueur, Marc. "Theory Number Five: Anatomy of Nostalgia Films." *Journal of Popular Film* 6.2 (1977): 187–97.
McDowell, James. "The Metamodern, the Quirky and Film Criticism." *Metamodernism: Historicity, Affect, and Depth after Postmodernism*. Ed. Robin van den Akker, Allison Gibbons, and Timotheus Vermeulen. London: Rowman and Littlefield, 2017. 25–40.
Morris, Tiyi M. "(Un) Learning Hollywood's Civil Rights Movement: A Scholar's Critique." *Journal of African American Studies* 22.4 (2018): 407–19.
Niemeyer, Katharina. *Memory and Nostalgia: Yearning for the Past, Present and Future*. London: Palgrave Macmillan, 2014.
Serres, Michel, with Bruno Latour. *Conversations on Science, Culture, and Time*. Trans. Roxanne Lapidus. Ann Arbor: University of Michigan Press, 1995.

Sperb, Jason. *Flickers of Film: Nostalgia in the Time of Digital Cinema*. Brunswick, NJ: Rutgers University Press, 2015.
Sprengler, Christine. *Screening Nostalgia: Populuxe Props and Technicolor Aesthetics in Contemporary American Film*. New York: Berghahn Books, 2009.
Toth, James. "Toni Morrison's *Beloved* and the Rise of Historioplastic Metafiction." *Metamodernism: Historicity, Affect, and Depth after Postmodernism*. Ed. Robin van den Akker, Allison Gibbons, and Timotheus Vermeulen. London: Rowman and Littlefield, 2017. 41–54.
Vermeulen, Timotheus, and Robin van den Akker. "Notes on Metamodernism." *Journal of Aesthetics and Culture* 2.1 (2010): 1–14.
Vesentini, Andrea. "Sheltering Time: The Containment of Everyday Life in Nuclear-Shelter Film Narratives." *Material Culture* 47.2 (2015): 41–58.
Wilson, Janelle. "An Exploration of Black Nostalgia for the 1950s." *Narrative Inquiry* 9.2 (1999): 303–25.

3

Touched by Time

Memories of the Faded Star

Daniel Varndell

> Touch us gently, Time!
> —Bryan Waller Procter,
> "A Petition to Time" (1832)

In an interview about her lost father, Hilary Mantel points out that generally asking someone to recount their childhood tends to "elicit a few bald and fumbling facts," whereas asking them to recollect an activity involving the senses (her Proustian example is eating) yields a quite different response: "The adult slips away and the child appears, wide-eyed and gleeful, reporting back to you with sensual precision." Memory of an

---

I thank Murray Pomerance for his generous suggestions on an early draft of this chapter.

event, much like the sight of an object, is diminished by distance. But as Thomas Hobbes argued in *Leviathan* (1651), imagination fills the gap and memory provides the means to "signifie that the Sense is fading, old, and past," that one's senses are in decay (167). Strong memories of the past therefore (1) temporarily reverse sensual decay—or, to put it another way, momentarily conquer the aging process; and (2) combine with powerful imaginative fancies to such an effect that—as the Greek philosophers already knew (Aristotle, for example, in *On Memory and Recollection*)—the "original" event to which memory returns is inaccessible without some present affectation powerful enough to stimulate its arousal.

When it comes to memory of cinema, however, distance in time from a moment so powerful and moving as to have indelibly imprinted on the mind some action or gesture, facial expression or vocal delivery, is complicated by the fact that such performative moments are literally available through repeat viewings, especially in the modern era. Hence, the moment can occasion its own reverie for past experiences of cinema; the pleasure of our present enjoyment commingles with the (often powerful) experience of that earlier encounter. In its timelessness, such images might cause us to slip back, wide-eyed and gleeful in their glowing presence, to the youthful viewer we once were.

A perfect example of this nostalgic disposition (I hesitate to use the word *mood*, not wanting to invoke Jameson's definition of postmodern nostalgia) can be found in *Sunset Blvd.* (1950), in which a faded silent-film star, Norma Desmond (played by real-life faded silent-film star Gloria Swanson), screens one of her old movies for her young houseguest, Joe Gillis (William Holden), more to stoke the embers in her own mind than convey something to him of her once-blazing fire as a screen icon. During the screening, Norma offers a running commentary on the qualities of the silent stars of yesteryear—qualities she argues are lacking in cinema's current emphasis on voice. In a famous moment, an agitated Norma stands, interrupting the projected image to turn her head (presenting a noble profile) and look away from the screen, silently bathing in the light of past glory. In a doubly ironic move, the silent film she screens for Joe is an excerpt from the incomplete (at that point unreleased) and infamously disastrous production of *Queen Kelly* (1932), the failure of which, despite being made at the height of Swanson's career at Paramount, hastened her decline (see Koller).

The moment (captured in figures 3.1 and 3.2) is complex. It hails a bygone era to which both Norma and Swanson belong via nostalgic reverie for a film that, strictly speaking, cannot have meant to others what it means to them. In one sense, the context of *Queen Kelly* is irrelevant

Figure 3.1 and 3.2. Gloria Swanson on-screen in *Queen Kelly* (Stroheim 1929) and "in the flesh" in *Sunset Blvd.* (Wilder 1950).

to the scene (which would have worked with any Swanson silent film); in another sense, it adds a wistful edge to Swanson's performance, knowing that this practically marked her fading as a star, a fate from which *Sunset Blvd.* promises to deliver Swanson if not Norma (whose final "close-up" propels her only toward infamy). The use of *Queen* is further heightened by the near presence of the film's director, Erich von Stroheim, who co-stars with Swanson playing Norma's butler/ex-husband (and resident in a suite above the garage).

As Norma stands (now in her early fifties) to strike that dignified pose, as the light of her former self (at the time in her late twenties) bounces off her half-closed eyes, she "slips away," to recall Mantel, to briefly let that young star shine once more. William Wordsworth described such moments as "spots of time," in which an individual, depressed by false opinions and contentious thoughts (or indeed, even heavier and more deadly weights), is vivified, her mind "nourished and invisibly repair'd" (qtd. in Raine 30). Yet if *Sunset Blvd.* details such moments of bliss, they are framed by an ultimate pathos: such slips into spots of time must fail. Despite the power of her illusory sense of grandeur, Norma's nostalgia is closer to what Milan Kundera describes as "the *suffering* caused by an unappeased yearning to return" (qtd. in Raine 31, emphasis added), unappeased not because of some failure of the imagination but because, instead of nourishing or repairing, the memories accentuate the decay and exacerbate the sense of loss/loss of sense.

To turn the screw, this chapter will explore nostalgic "spots of time" that extend to spectatorial encounters with faded stars today, those which have transported me back to an earlier spectatorial experience in my life, when I saw the same actor I am seeing now, but younger and in an earlier context. Such moments are more subjective for the spectator, more open to them making their own intertextual connections in noticing some of the same features, gestures, or vocal intonations, now faded with time's passage. Such a return reminds me not just of the aging of a performer but of my own relationship with that actor over time, an effect intensified in stars whose absence from the screen for a lengthy period marks a greater contrast between their appearance now, in this scene, and then, in that scene I am moved to recall. For example, having seen *To Have and Have Not* (1944) as a child in the early 1990s, I always thought of Lauren Bacall as belonging to a bygone era (not to say, like Bogie, actually gone). Her appearance in *Birth* (2004), therefore, seemed doubly anachronistic to me: first, the shock of seeing her now, looking older; and second, the shock of discovering that Bacall belonged to this time (my time), too (her performance, as in *Dogville* [2003], is doubly captivating for these effects). Conversely, sometimes the shock is the discovery that an actor from the past seems to have been so little affected by the "touch" of time on the body (Jodie Foster in *Inside Man*

[2006] compared with *Taxi Driver* [1976], for instance), that the uncanny effect is one of temporal *suspension*.

Such fading or suspension might be most acutely experienced in relation to female stars, whose shelf life in Hollywood is decidedly shorter than that of their male counterparts and who age on screen in ways the latter do not. As Jeanine Basinger points out of the studio era, "it was tough for a woman to last," and very few had what she calls the "indestructible bones" required to become legends (320). (As we all know, it was not her bones but the tautness of her skin that very typically mattered most.) This chapter looks at some faded female film stars from early to late classical (that is, up to 1967) Hollywood cinema who return in an era that seems to have forgotten them, or from which their absence has generated such a degree of friction between past and present that their present presence is able, even liable, to spark. First, in the final performances of Pola Negri and Gloria Stuart, who each return after a lengthy period of absence, I explore how some moments seem to recall the past, either indirectly (Negri) or even more obliquely (Stuart), revealing how the faded female star not only invokes her past performances through her present performative gestures but calls forth, through the aged body itself, historical weight in moments that otherwise might have been relatively weightless (even insubstantial). Second, the chapter looks at the return of Julie Andrews in *The Princess Diaries* films, specifically to her return to dancing and singing on screen as a star's triumph over aging. After suffering damage to her voice several years before and being told she might never sing again, Andrews returned with strong echoes of *The Sound of Music* (1965).

A Haunted Study

In *An Essay Concerning Human Understanding*, John Locke (a contemporary of Hobbes) wrote that "if it be possible for the same woman to have distinct incommunicable consciousness at different times, it is past doubt the same woman would at different times make different persons" (168, pronouns altered). There is no constant state of being to which the word *I* can be applied. One thinks of Wordsworth's famous 1798 composition about Tintern Abbey ("Lines"), in which he poeticized that the "coarser pleasures" of his "boyish days" (and their "glad animal movements") were received with a measure of loss as he approached his thirtieth year:

>   —I cannot paint
>   What then I was. The sounding cataract
>   Haunted me like a passion. ("Lines," 133)

That the rushing power of the waterfall failed to awake in him the same "aching joy" and "dizzy raptures" of his youthful appetite was not Wordsworth's point (nor was he simply lamenting its loss). By contrast, the haunting loss becomes "like a passion," one framed by what he called the "sad music of humanity." From youth's thoughtless appetite, then via adolescence's (chaotic) dawning perceptions, Wordsworth discovered his critical power as a poet dwelled in what framed the loss of youthful passion by a reflective facility previously inaccessible to him: a passion of and for return. Recollection, of course, is far from guaranteed.

In Disney's *The Moon-Spinners* (1964), a young holidaymaker in Greece, Nikky (Hayley Mills), becomes embroiled in a sinister plot orchestrated by a thief, Stratos (Eli Wallach), to steal expensive jewelry. She pleads with the mysterious owner of a yacht, Madame Habib, to whom Stratos intends to sell his ill-gotten gains. Madame Habib is played by Pola Negri (Swanson's biggest screen rival in the 1920s). As Habib listens suspiciously to shifty Stratos's sales pitch, she issues a sharp rebuke to her pet cheetah (!), abruptly silencing both cat and criminal. The moment perfectly captures Negri's famous head movement and smoky eyes bursting through heavy make-up from her silent pictures. One perhaps thinks of her rebuke of Holmes Herbert in *A Woman of the World* (1925) when, after mistaking her for a streetwalker, he is stilled by a slow turn of the head and self-assured glare. Aside from a brief return to the screen in 1943 (*Hi Diddle Diddle*), *Moon-Spinners* was Negri's first film in the United States since the late 1920s and her final screen role. During the film's denouement, the contextual significance of casting Negri is acknowledged when, the jewels recovered and Stratos arrested, Madame Habib turns and sits, seemingly overwhelmed, and stares into nothingness, noting: "I lived through two wars, four revolutions, and five marriages; but nothing, nothing like *this*." Whatever was intended by *this* (which, in diegetic terms, serves as a reflection on Nikky's incredible adventure), Negri's wistful delivery and vacant expression betray a sudden and acute sense of her own past, of pastness itself. Critics were likewise drunk on nostalgia at Negri's return, extolling the comeback of the "greatest vamp of them all" and noting that her presence "was in its fantastic, colossal, unbelievable way, a moment of utter glory . . . Miss Negri brought the dear, dead, golden days of Hollywood back for one sweet moment" (qtd. in Kotowski 195). It is a moment elevated by a faraway look on a face with a history, a history both personal (to Negri, but also to knowing viewers) and cinematic (the films themselves make for a stunning comparison, as seen in figures 3.3 and 3.4).

Figure 3.3 and 3.4. A haunted study: Negri in *A Woman of the World* (St. Clair 1925) and *The Moon-Spinners* (Neilson 1964).

On to a second example. In James Whale's *The Old Dark House* (1932), a young woman and her two friends seek refuge from a storm at a creepy old house in the Welsh countryside. The young woman, Margaret (Gloria Stuart), politely requests the use of a bedroom to change out of her wet clothes and is accompanied upstairs by a strange old woman, Rebecca (Eva Moore), the owner of the house. Despite being quite accommodating, Rebecca refuses to leave Margaret to change in peace, and her small talk soon takes an odd turn when she begins warning of the dangers posed by her "wicked, blasphemous" family. The old woman's warning becomes even more sinister when she suddenly rounds on Margaret (by this point stripped down to her undergarments) to issue an unprovoked barb: "You're wicked too. Young and handsome, silly and wicked. You think of nothing but your long, straight legs and your white body and how to please your man. You revel in the joys of fleshly love, *don't you?*" Then, clutching the fine fabric of Margaret's slip: "That's fine stuff, but it'll rot. [Touching Margaret's skin.] That's finer stuff still, but it'll rot too, in time." (Reminiscent of the Wicked Witch in *Snow White*) Margaret recoils and is saved by a knock on the door. With the old woman banished from the room (if not her thoughts), Margaret tries to dress in front of the mirror but is troubled by her distorted reflection in the uneven glass.

As she sits in front of that distorted mirror, it is clear that although old Rebecca had been speaking (as a spinster) of the religious virtues of chastity and uplifting the eternal spirit over ephemeral, mortal "flesh," Margaret is moved to contemplate her body (for perhaps the first time) as material that will rot. What was not immediately apparent to me in this scene (which has stayed with me over the years), but what I discovered later, is that Gloria Stuart (then in her early twenties) went on to star in films like *The Invisible Man* (1933), *Gold Diggers of 1935* (1935), and *The Three Musketeers* (1939) but abandoned Hollywood (and acting) in 1945. Despite doing some television work in the 1970s and 1980s, she was scarcely known in 1997 when, in her late eighties, she was cast in James Cameron's epic film *Titanic* (1997). Stuart's casting as 101-year-old Rose seemed calculated not just to invoke the 1910s (the *Titanic* sank in 1912) but the "Golden Era" of 1930s Hollywood for a cinematic and historical nostalgia. Stuart was perfect as old Rose, whose romantic reminiscing of her (somewhat fleshly) experiences on board the *Titanic* as a young woman (played by Kate Winslet) provides the frame narrative through which the disaster is experienced.

Like Negri, then, Stuart brings back the dear, dead, golden days of Hollywood just as old Rose brings back the *Titanic* (see figures 3.5 and 3.6). But when I now see her in *Titanic* as an elderly woman reflecting on

Figure 3.5 and 3.6. Reversing the rot: Gloria Stuart in *The Old Dark House* (Whale 1932) and *Titanic* (Cameron 1997).

her youthful moments of crisis regarding the future, I find it difficult not to think of Stuart, then in her early twenties, in *The Old Dark House* as she stares into that distorted mirror. To push the point further (perhaps to absurdity), I even see an echo of it in the moment Winslet (also in her early twenties) stares into a mirror vacantly contemplating her reflection while her vile fiancé (Billy Zane) gives her a terrifying insight into their miserable future together. At the very end of *Titanic*, old Rose finishes her nostalgic tale of romance and tragedy on board the ship and sneaks out to the bow of the research vessel. As she climbs the guard rail—the cold wind whipping her nightgown—Cameron cuts to a close-up of her bare foot (toenails painted red) finding a hold, a graphic match with an earlier scene when young Rose (wearing red shoes), similarly climbs the guard rail of the *Titanic* in an apparent suicide attempt. As she contemplates her youthful self-awakening and her brief lover, Jack (Leonardo DiCaprio)—the young man who stopped her from jumping and subsequently inspired her to leave her rotting aristocratic life—old Rose unveils a rare diamond she had kept from her engagement and casually tosses it into the ocean before retiring to her bed (to die, we presume). She is surrounded by photographs documenting her adventurous young life.

Perhaps it is a coincidence, but the moment echoes one in *The Moon-Spinners* in which Madame Habib, attempting to stall Stratos by examining the ill-gotten jewels he wishes to sell her, falls suddenly into a swoon. "What magnificence!" she gasps, holding them to her chest, before accusing Stratos of being interested only in their exchange value: "You don't even realize what you're holding do you? A thousand years of passion, plight and blood, crystallized into these perfect stones." The point is clear: diamonds don't bleed, but men do while fighting for their extraction and acquisition; they don't feel passion, but women have been wooed by the enduring value they add to young skin. And that skin will age. Negri and Stuart appear in these later films not just as enduring icons of the screen but as years of passion crystallized into perfect performances: gesture, movement, voice.

Speaking to Jean-Pierre Changeux, Paul Ricoeur stated that what is "called to mind" (re-membered) in nostalgia is ultimately oneself; not the reflexive self but the worldly self: oneself in a world passed. "It is a self of flesh and blood that we remember," he concludes, "with its moments of pleasure and suffering, its states, its actions, its feelings—which in their turn are situated in an environment, and particularly in places where we have been present with others and which we jointly remember" (145). When the faded star contemplates her past in a moment that seems to exceed (or at least enhances) her character's call to do so, it is her history, that is, the actress's history, that is recalled. Whether that reflective moment is marked as an explicit confrontation with the cinematic past (the Swanson case), or a more indirect reference to the historical gravity of a once-huge star now inhabiting a relatively minor role (Negri), or indeed, an oblique reference "charged" only in the mind of specific viewers (in this case, me) making intertextual connections (Stuart), still their twenty-something fleshy bodies are somehow invoked, riddlingly, through an expression connoting the existential weight of a past that bears down, suddenly (as if from nowhere), on a present, fleeting moment. Such "sweet moments"—irrespective of an audience's knowledge of the star's early work—demonstrate a momentary recall for the past on the faces of the aged stars. Although such faces might just as easily struggle as succeed in bringing back the "dear, dead, golden days of Hollywood," the "haunted study"—as we might call such contemplative moments—remains on the screen nonetheless.

She Sings Again!

Playing devil's advocate, one might raise E. Ann Kaplan's objection that despite the historical "weight" of such moments, they hardly trouble the films' overall valuation and celebration of youthful passion, plight, and blood. Kaplan describes old Rose in *Titanic* as "secretive and self-indulgent," and thus one of the many negative depictions of aging women on screen. For older women in cinema, Kaplan writes, only harridans and hags, eccentrics and possessive mothers seem to be available; they are "wicked old ladies" rather than "people trying to live reasonable lives under trying circumstances, in short, . . . real" (240). I am hardly arguing against this. What I am suggesting, however, is that by transporting us away from the text, nostalgic moments have the power to disrupt dominant generalizations about older women on screen, thereby unsettling those relations within the text.

For example, in *The Curtain* (2005), Milan Kundera differentiated between the weakness of everyday recollection and the indelibility of meaningful works of art: "Against our real world, which, by its very nature, is fleeting and worthy of forgetting, works of art stand as a different world, a world that is ideal, solid, where every detail has its importance, its meaning, where everything in it—every word, every phrase—deserves to be unforgettable and was conceived to be such" (149). Kundera's point is that unless we commit a poem or some such treasured moment in a work to heart, they will be no less prone to slipping out of the mind, decaying with the other senses. One cannot retain every aspect of a film, even while we are enjoying it. "It is presumptuous," even, writes Murray Pomerance, "to assume that any of us is capable of assimilating, then sustaining fully active memory of, the absolute entirety of any screen performance." However, what Pomerance calls the "riddle" of screen acting is that which stands out, the poetic "moment of performance as it influences the experience, feeling, and imagination of the viewer" (5), a moment so indelible in the mind that it is practically impervious of decay and can define how the rest of the performance is remembered. Such exceptional, indelible moments—however brief—can therefore disrupt or disturb generalizations about aging women in cinema—however true—inviting us to read "against the grain" and deconstruct the dominant interpretation.

The image of a star deconstructing her own image in this way is one that frames an example that, despite appearing at the end of the decade that saw the failure of nostalgia in movies with the rise of the "New Hollywood," marked the "tension between contemporaneity and nostalgia," as Leslie H. Abramson puts it, carried by the powerful central performance of its star, Julie Andrews (213). In *Star!* (1968) Andrews plays Gertrude Lawrence, a mercurial stage performer who headlined the West End and Broadway until her death in 1952. The film opens with footage documenting Lawrence's life, before—as the frame freezes and Andrews's voice interrupts—we realize that Lawrence is in a screening room watching a documentary of her life (screened by the director who nervously awaits her imprimatur). Wise returns to this framing device over the course of *Star!* as Lawrence regularly interjects to either dismiss or refute the veracity of the documentary, especially in relation to scenes depicting her early struggle as a chorus girl working for her shallow father (Bruce Forsyth), disastrous relationships with men and fellow performers, and heart-breaking estrangement from her daughter (Jenny Agutter). However, as the final scene plays, documenting her celebration as an actress and blossoming romance with and marriage to Richard Aldrich (Richard Crenna), the filmmaker is surprised as Andrews inhales deeply before letting out a luxurious "Mm," lost in her own happy ending. "Whatever else I've said," she tells him, "Forget it: don't change a thing. Leave it just the way it is. The way it *was*." In this moment, despite being generally unhappy with the way her life had been so starkly presented—depicting her as a poor mother and lover, all too ambitious for fame and glory—Lawrence finds solace in the film's happy ending, which marks a punctum in which she recognizes her own success. It is here, sitting before the screen, that she finally acknowledges her achievements.

This conflation of the present documentary and Lawrence's past life in *Star!* belies the film's conceit (that the film we've been watching is not a rendering of the past in the present but the past itself). Such a conflation of past and present is intrinsic to Andrews who, through her most iconic roles in *Mary Poppins* (1964)—a film described by Jürgen Müller as "the crowning achievement of producer Walt Disney's brilliant career," in which it takes just "one very special word [supercalifragilisticexpialidocious] to transport us back to a world of magical chalk drawing and enchanted penguins" (260)—and *The Sound of Music*—a film that declares itself as set in "the last golden days of the thirties"—past and present are deeply entwined, one almost always being used to read the other in Andrews's work. However, Andrews made fewer films after the box-office failure of *Star!* and the ensuing backlash against the family movies in which she had made her name. Notwithstanding her performance in the title role of Blake Edwards's *Victor Victoria* (1982) and minor roles in other films by Edwards (including the Pink Panther sequels and *The Man Who Loved Women* [1983]), by the mid-1980s Andrews had all but disappeared from the screen. Her return in Garry Marshall's *The Princess Diaries* (2001), followed by *The Princess Diaries 2: Royal Engagement* (2004), paired her with young Anne Hathaway (in her breakout role). These films marked a triumphant "comeback" for Andrews (then in her late sixties), especially for those who, as a child, fell in love with her in *Mary Poppins* or *Sound of Music* (as I did).

The Princess Diaries is a Cinderella story in which the leader of the fictional European country of Genovia, Clarisse (Julie Andrews), must convince her shy and gawkish teenage granddaughter, Mia (Hathaway), to leave the United States and rule as princess when Mia suddenly becomes heir to the throne. Clarisse arranges a series of disastrous "princess lessons," including a bungled etiquette class, fumbling formal dinner, and torturous makeover. In between these sessions, Mia is chauffeured by Clarisse's head of security, Joe (Héctor Elizondo), whom she quickly deduces is Clarisse's unrequited love. (An echo, perhaps, of Norma Desmond and her chauffeur/ex-husband in *Sunset Blvd.*). In a touching moment following one of Mia's princess lessons, Clarisse despairs at ever making her young protégée a princess. Joe, seizing the moment, takes Clarisse's hand and the pair begin to waltz. This is the first of the two (most delightful) ways Andrews punctuates her return to the screen, for it carries strong echoes of the moment in *The Sound of Music* in which Maria (Andrews) dances with the Captain (Christopher Plummer). In both scenes, the realization that they are in love coincides with the recognition that they cannot be together (as demonstrated in figures 3.7 and 3.8).

Figure 3.7 and 3.8. Enduring love: Maria (Julie Andrews) dancing with the Captain (Christopher Plummer) in *Sound of Music* (Wise 1965), and Clarisse dances with Joe (Héctor Elizondo) in *Princess Diaries* (Marshall 2001).

Princess Diaries 2 picks up on Mia and Clarisse as the new princess struggles to find a husband. At a slumber party thrown for local orphans, Mia encourages Clarisse to sing a song and, initially reluctant, she eventually concedes, performing "Your Crowning Glory." Taken by itself, the moment could be viewed as somewhat unremarkable (like the film in which it appears): Andrews's soprano voice lacks the power and range it once had, and she is joined by Raven-Symoné, who is needed to "fill out" her vocal. However, the moment is remarkable as being the first time Andrews had sung on screen since her voice was damaged after surgery in the 1990s to remove nodules on her vocal cords. She semi-retired from acting and feared she might never sing again. Linda Lister noted that "even the inimitable Julie Andrews has to age" (37), a reference to the fact that although Andrews seems not to have aged (her skin is breathtakingly flawless), in her voice the "wrinkles" of old age appear.

With this context, Andrews's performance was already framed as the triumphant return for a star synonymous with classic musical numbers like "A Spoonful of Sugar" and "Supercalifragilisticexpialidocious" in *Mary Poppins*, as well as "The Sound of Music" and "My Favorite Things" in *Sound of Music*, and "Someone to Watch over Me" and "The Saga of Jenny" in *Star!* (Andrews is, after all, the woman whose "heart wants to sing every song it hears" ["The Sound of Music"]). However, the nostalgic twist is provided by the presence of the children as they sit in their pajamas looking up adoringly at Clarisse. Here one finds (at least I do) a wonderful echo in the moment from *Sound of Music* in which Maria sings "My Favorite Things" for the Von Trapp children as she comforts them during a storm (see figures 3.9 and 3.10). Here, as in *Princess Diaries 2*, Maria is invited to sing but initially resists, relenting only at the behest of the children who spur her on and then sit likewise in adoring attention at this magical performer.

If the voice has indeed aged, what can they be so enchanted by if not being in the presence of such a precious star? Of course, one might object that these children are acting, have been instructed to look up at Andrews adoringly, yet reports from the set have documented how momentous and moving an occasion it was. Raven-Symoné described singing with Andrews "the biggest thrill of my career," and Garry Marshall stated that it was "very moving because y'know most of the crew . . . hadn't heard Julie sing [in a] long time. She started singing and, y'know, guys with tattoos got a little teary there, 'cause to see Julie Andrews singing again was quite something" ("Julie Andrews Singing"). What magnificence!—to recall Madame Habib once more—in which years of passion (screenwork),

Figure 3.9 and 3.10. Enchanting: Julie Andrews in *The Sound of Music* (Wise 1965) and *Princess Diaries 2* (Marshall 2004).

plight (loss of voice), and blood (strained vocal cords) are reified into a single performance that transcends the general work, elevating it purely through the effect of "nostalgia time."

Time touched by nostalgia, as it returns to me in these moments from the *Princess Diaries* films, recalls a wonderful poem by Elizabeth Barrett Browning from her *Sonnets from the Portuguese*, in which she reflects on the "sweet years, the dear and wished for years," but sees in her reflection only the "sweet, sad years, the melancholy years, / Those of my own life, who by turns had flung / A shadow across me." It is a shadow, however, not of death (as she suspected) but of love (7). That the dear, wished-for years might cede to sad, melancholy ones seem indicative of one's growth into old age, but it is striking that Browning regards both as "sweet." The moment Andrews and Elizondo waltz seems charged with memory, whether one sees it as a "spot of time" retaining the "taste" of love's early blossom from *The Sound of Music* or finds in it the melancholic suffering of an "unappeased yearning to return," one accentuating that this Andrews is no longer that Andrews. The moment is charged either way. Unless one simply sees two (old) people waltzing, or an old woman with a decent but unexceptional voice. Somehow, I doubt it, but at least these moments are touched in the minds of certain viewers whose nostalgic memory of earlier films is triggered, unsuspectingly, through such gestures, casting a shadow of sweeping love for Andrews's cinematic past to envelope her onscreen presence. A moment like the one where Maria dances with the Captain in *The Sound of Music* becomes the cinematic equivalent of a souvenir, which, as Emerson wrote, is a "token of love. *Remember me* means, Do not cease to love me" (76). And by returning to the faded star, we won't.

One cannot iron out the wrinkles of time, and no mortal being can reverse the inevitable march toward decay that life betokens in all its transience. Though inimitable, Andrews must age. But in this era of digital restoration and film preservation, one can always return to the film performances of the past—those of Swanson's and Negri's that have survived; Stuart's work with James Whale, and anything starring Andrews—and what is important is not how one always fails to recapture youth (either as performer or viewer) but how the moments that matter become charged once more in the present, iodized, as Emerson put it, by the nurture and care we give them. For him, the past has a new value every moment it is recalled to the mind: "Some fact," he wrote, "that has a childish significance to your childhood and was a type in the nursery, when riper intelligence recalls it means more and serves you better as an illustration; and perhaps in your age has new meaning" (64–65). When they return, such stars have a place (are not simply replaced). They form new connections which confirm and expand on those past moments we loved before. The broader insight of the return leads us (to paraphrase Emerson), to an even securer conviction that these are the moments that have made us.

The "touch" in these films is personal for me. As a young boy watching *The Sound of Music* and *Mary Poppins* on the television beside my mother, Andrews's maternal strength expressed through her powerful voice and graceful movement felt no less nurturing as a viewer than it seemed to feel for those adoring children on screen. Such nurture enables one to forge new bonds in a (patriarchal) world not often given to feelingful expression. Andrews was explicitly not the biological mother in these roles, tending instead to swoop down from the hills (or the sky) as an archetype of motherhood itself. It is the experience of this double embrace—in song and dance on screen, but also as a rapt young viewer ensconced in my own mother's arms—that I make a claim for the power of Andrews's performances in those films, and account for the power—in my adulthood—of her return to singing and dancing as the return of the sound of "Mother's Music," a music flushed with maternal memory.

For me, at least, Andrews's iconic roles in *Mary Poppins* and *Sound of Music* will never die or age, and while such moments as her dancing with the Captain or singing to the Von Trapp kids might not be with me at every moment, they arise and connect to other moments in cinema and life in ways that can't always be explained, much less anticipated. In *The World Viewed*, Stanley Cavell offered two examples of how such memories of film can have an impact: (1) that "memories of movies are strand over strand with memories of *my* life" (ixx, emphasis added) and (2) that "a few faulty memories will not themselves shake my conviction in what I've said, since I am as interested in how a memory went wrong as in why the memories that are right occur when they do" (x). Such memories might be triggered as easily by small gestures (Negri's look) as by large ones (Swanson's pose); bodily action (Stuart's climb) as vocal performance (Andrews's song), and their effectiveness at alighting nonetheless onto a past in which we (at least once) felt "at home," constitutes the magic of cinema. Even if we might not always be able to go back, the suffering that registers this loss can itself remind us of how important these past moments have been in our lives; crucial, even, to defining who we are. The return of a faded star might elicit no recognition in young filmgoers, who, impervious to the material fact of aging, tend to see only the long, straight legs and smooth bodies of youth on screen. But the magical pasts of faded stars await their discovery; for in the light of their return, while dimmed, one is reminded that we, too, are alive—alive to the sweetness, whether wishful or melancholic, of time's gentle touch.

> What though the radiance which was once so bright
> Be now for ever taken from my sight,
> Though nothing can bring back the hour
> Of splendour in the grass, of glory in the flower;
> We will grieve not, rather find
> Strength in what remains behind. (Wordsworth, "Ode")

Works Cited

Abramson, Leslie H. "1968: Movies and the Failure of Nostalgia." *American Cinema of the 1960s: Themes and Variations*. Ed. Barry Keith Grant. New Brunswick, NJ: Rutgers University Press, 2008. 193–216.

Aristotle. *On Memory and Recollection* (c. 345 BC). Trans. W. S. Hett. *Memory: An Anthology*. Ed. Harriet Harvey Wood and A. S. Byatt. London: Chatto and Windus, 2008. 159–60.

Basinger, Jeanine. *The Star Machine*. New York: Vintage Books, 2009.

Browning, Elizabeth Barrett. *Sonnets from the Portuguese: And Other Treasured Poems*. London: Roger Schlesinger, 1969.

Cavell, Stanley. *The World Viewed: Reflections on the Ontology of Film*. Enlarged ed. Cambridge, MA: Harvard University Press, 1979.

Changeux, Jean-Pierre, and Paul Ricoeur. *What Makes Us Think?: A Neuroscientist and a Philosopher Argue about Ethics, Human Nature, and the Brain*. Trans. M. B. DeBevoise. Princeton, NJ: Princeton University Press, 2000.

Emerson, Ralph Waldo Emerson. "Memory." *The Works of Ralph Waldo Emerson*, vol. 12 *(Natural History of the Intellect and Other Papers)* (1909). https://oll.libertyfund.org/titles/emerson-the-works-of-ralph-waldo-emerson-vol-12-natural-history-of-intellect-and-other-papers. 63–83.

Hobbes, Thomas. *Leviathan*, I, II (1651). *Memory: An Anthology*. Ed. Harriet Harvey Wood and A. S. Byatt. London: Chatto and Windus, 2008. 167.

"Julie Andrews Singing in Princess Diaries 2." RoseLippedMaiden, YouTube, October 7, 2010. https://www.youtube.com/watch?v=6dEKS4lMTfs&t=1s.

Kaplan, E. Ann. "Wicked Old Ladies from Europe: Jeanne Moreau and Marlene Dietrich on the Screen and Live." *Bad: Infamy, Darkness, Evil, and Slime on Screen*. Ed. Murray Pomerance. Albany: State University of New York Press, 2004. 238–53.

Koller, Michael. "Erich von Stroheim's Damned Queen: *Queen Kelly*." *Senses of Cinema* no. 78 (August 2007). http://sensesofcinema.com/2007/cteq/queen-kelly/.

Kotowski, Mariusz. *Pola Negri: Hollywood's First Femme Fatale*. Lexington: University Press of Kentucky, 2014.

Kundera, Milan. *The Curtain: An Essay in Seven Parts*. Trans. Linda Asher. New York: Harper Perennial, 2008.

Lister, Linda. "The Broadway Soprano: The Lineage and Evolution from Julie Andrews to Kristin Chenoweth." *American Music Teacher* 62.5 (2013): 37–39.

Locke, John. *An Essay Concerning Human Understanding* (1690). *Memory: An Anthology*. Ed. Harriet Harvey Wood and A. S. Byatt. London: Chatto and Windus, 2008. 168.

Mantel, Hilary. "Father Figured." *Telegraph*, April 24, 2005. https://www.telegraph.co.uk/culture/books/3640930/Father-figured.html.

Müller, Jürgen. *Movies of the 60s*. Cologne: Taschen, 2004.

Pomerance, Murray. *Moment of Action: Riddles of Cinematic Performance*. New Brunswick, NJ: Rutgers University Press, 2016.

Proctor, Bryan Waller. "A Petition to Time." *Poet's Corner* (1832). https://www.theotherpages.org/poems/2001/cornwall0105.html.

Raine, Craig. "Memory in Literature." *Memory: An Anthology*. Ed. Harriet Harvey Wood and A. S. Byatt. London: Chatto and Windus, 2008. 28–39.

Wordsworth, William. "Lines Composed a Few Miles above Tintern Abbey, On Revisiting the Banks of the Wye during a Tour. July 13, 1798." *The Norton Anthology of English Literature: The Major Authors*. Ed. Stephen Greenblatt. New York: Norton, 2013. 131–35.

Wordsworth, William. "Ode: Intimations of Immortality from Recollections of Early Childhood" (1807). https://www.poetryfoundation.org/poems/45536/ode-intimations-of-immortality-from-recollections-of-early-childhood.

4

Mimetic Tangible Nostalgia and Spatial Cosplay

Replica Merchandise and Place in Fandom's Material Cultures

Ross P. Garner

The websites of cult-oriented retailers like Forbidden Planet and Firebox present fans with a range of officially licensed merchandise depicting characters, props and elements of set iconography that use a variety of aesthetic modes, ranging from screen-accurate replicas to the stylized renderings of Funko's Pop! Vinyl range. This choice of merchandise covers multiple price points and spans myriad franchises. Regarding replica items, consumers can buy a life-size reproduction of the infinity gauntlet from *Avengers: Infinity War* (2018) produced under license by Hot Toys for just under £1,000 (figure 4.1) or, at the other end of the spectrum, a mug depicting the same item for £12.99. If browsing extends to sites specializing in selling fan-produced and -targeted items (like Etsy), the range of available merchandise expands to include items reproducing franchise iconography with a variety of materials and aesthetic styles (Cherry). Despite the range of available commodities, conceptual distinctions between items must be retained. Commodities on Etsy repre-

Figure 4.1. Hot Toys' life-size replica of the Infinity Gauntlet from *Avengers: Infinity War*.

sent fans' "textual productivity" and occupy different positions in systems of cultural classification, manufacture, and value to those listed by online cult retailers (Fiske, "Cultural Economy" 39). Following Walter Benjamin's writings, a mass-produced infinity gauntlet replica—whether high-end, limited edition, or otherwise—generates an aura that "is jeopardized by reproduction" because of that item's origins in industrial manufacturing processes ("Work of Art" para. 8).

The trends identified in officially licensed and mass-produced replicas are arguably unsurprising. They reflect the increasingly "mainstream cult" status of commodities derived from (cult) media properties (Hills, "Mainstream Cult") as well as speaking to the ubiquity and centrality of branding practices in maintaining the visibility of screen franchises (Johnson). As Avi Santo argues, fans inhabit a historical moment where "IP management has become central to how the contemporary entertainment industry operates," resulting in objects depicting iconography from screen properties—both retro and contemporary—being available for consumption (*Selling the Silver Bullet* 206). However, as Nicolle Lamerichs posits, "few scholars pay attention to the merchandise . . . which . . . mediates . . . existing stories and characters" with even less attention dedicated to the appeal and significance of officially licensed merchandise in fan cultures ("Fan Fashion" 176). In this chapter, I offer reflections on this absence by arguing that a specific discourse of nostalgia, named here as mimetic tangible nostalgia, underpins how these items appeal to fans as desirable commodities. If, as Santo has argued elsewhere, media-derived merchandise can "elicit affect tied to nostalgia" ("Fans and Merchandise" 330), the chapter assists in advancing the acknowledged but underdeveloped role that nostalgia plays in the place and production of fandom's material cultures (also Woo).

Little consideration has been afforded to the precise ways that contemporary mass-produced replicas may be read as nostalgic by niche (fan) consumer groups. In the cases when this topic has been broached, scholars have employed narrow interpretive parameters. Lincoln Geraghty has accounted for the nostalgic potential of mass-produced and media-associated objects as souvenirs of previous experiences ("It's Not All About"); this account mirrors interpretations offered of non–media-derived artifacts as reminders of previous leisure-coded activities (Stewart). Alternatively, nostalgia and media merchandise has been discussed in relation to their role in supporting and maintaining fan identities (Geraghty, *Cult Collectors* and "Nostalgia, Fandom"). Although this work is insightful, what has been overlooked is analysis of how the aesthetic strategies of replicas encourage nostalgic responses among consumer groups and the relevance of nostalgia to the contexts and environments where fans display such objects.

Alternatively, scholars of material culture have developed limited understandings by linking nostalgia solely to old objects, like heirlooms (Csikszentmihalyi; McCracken) or only making allusions to an item's nostalgic potential in the latter stages of its "biography" (Kopytoff). Although these arguments are useful in understanding the nostalgic affordances of objects from previous historical moments, this chapter examines the more challenging matter of how the aesthetic properties of contemporary mass-produced replicas like a replica of the DeLorean from *Back to the Future* (1985) or a character's helmet from *Mighty Morphin Power Rangers* (1993–1996) motivate consumption among fans by encouraging nostalgic affect.

This chapter therefore asks how the aesthetics of manufactured replicas can work as nostalgic stimuli for fans. The first section argues that the significant differential between my intervention and preceding work is my suggestion that the mimetic aesthetic of such objects enhances their nostalgic appeal. Mimetic reproduction, combined with how replica merchandise grants tangibility to onscreen referents, leads to positing that these commodities articulate discourses of mimetic tangible nostalgia. Mimetic tangible nostalgia covers how affective longing becomes encouraged in fans through the style and design of objects that imitate onscreen (or, in a wider context, mediated) referents, bringing physical form to either previously intangible or ephemeral items. The chapter's use of the word *tangible* is therefore indebted to how Jonathan Gray's study of media paratexts uses the term. Gray argues that interpretive frames constructed through promotional material sitting alongside the text itself can include "intangible entities," such as genre categories, while also taking on "a tangible form, as with posters, videogames, podcasts, reviews, or merchandise" (6; see also Peters), which connect consumers to the media property's storyworld.

The second section of the chapter deepens understanding of the appeals, pleasures, and significance of mimetic tangible nostalgia by considering what I call spatial cosplay. Spatial cosplay conceptually advances academic discourses concerning cosplay by addressing the hitherto overlooked relationship between mimetic objects and the environments in which fans display these (Lamerichs, "Stranger than Fiction"; Rahman, Wing-sun, and Cheung). The term refers to how exhibiting replica items assists in transforming personal and semi-personal spaces into sites where fandom is performed. By teasing out the differences between spatial cosplay and its bodily equivalent, the discussion refines Susan Stewart's arguments concerning nostalgia and collecting to recognize that mimetic tangible nostalgia subsumes to a higher-level form of media-oriented nostalgia, which provides coherence to the private context(s) where spatial cosplay occurs. If "consideration of the relationship between materiality and fandom is relatively underdeveloped, and fan studies is poorer for its neglect" (Woo, para. 2.11), this chapter engages this absence by exploring why consuming collectibles that are mass-produced in the present moment—and the environments in which fans display these—generate, negotiate, and sustain particular inflections of nostalgia.

Mimetic Tangible Nostalgia

Mimesis is a loaded term that carries a history of debate across disciplines, including literary studies (Auerbach) and cultural studies (Benjamin, "Doctrine of the Similar" and "Work of Art"). In the latter, foundational positions have linked mimesis to debates regarding identity and embodied experience within the sociohistorical conditions of (post)modernity (Nicoll and Nansen). These perspectives would overlook mass-produced objects intended for private economic gain, like collectible merchandise, by understanding mass-produced replicas as Other. For example, summarizing Benjamin's arguments on film as a modernist storytelling technology, Michael Taussig positions the cinematic apparatus as "mighty mimetic machinery" through which "the ability to communicate experience is diminished" (35). Benjamin's arguments allude to how objects that provide or enable mimetic reproductions are frequently negatively evaluated, partly because of their associations with the sacrifice of Romantic ideas concerning individual expression to standardization, replication, and frequently commodification (Baudrillard).

My understanding of mimesis in mimetic tangible nostalgia builds conceptually from Matt Hills's arguments concerning mimetic fandom. Hills ("Dalek Half Balls" para. 1.3) defines mimetic fandom as "the fannish object practices of replica building" and argues that this is "a specialized fan activity" ("Dalek Half Balls" para. 1.6) due to the practical knowledges concerning construction, measurement, and materials that participation requires. Analytically, the value of exploring mimetic fan practices lies in "fandom's predominantly material cultures," which, according to Hills, "seem to have gone missing in much scholarship, perhaps because they are assumed to be too close to the commodity fetish of merchandise, but also perhaps because these communities tend to be thought of as culturally gendered as masculine or dominated by male fans" ("Dalek Half Balls" para. 1.3). Similar sentiments regarding why fandom's material cultures have remained an analytical absence have been offered elsewhere (Geraghty, *Cult Collectors* 2). Analyzing collectible replicas (whether mass-produced or limited edition) further addresses these scholarly omissions by shifting the focus on to official (rather than fan-made) commodities. What's more, focusing on mimetic replicas like reproductions of the baseball bat Lucille from *The Walking Dead* (2010–) extends these discussions as theorizing mimetic tangible nostalgia requires taking the design of these objects on their own terms and considering the affective responses these encourage for fans due to their mimetic aesthetic.

Replica items produced for capitalist exchange modes nevertheless fall heavily on the devalued side of the cultural hierarchies that Hills outlines. Consuming replicas represents "bad" fan identities and practices, equated, as they are, with fans' passive absorption into exploitative industrial practices (Stanfill). Rather than complicating value judgments separating production and consumption, assumed audience passivity and activity, and "affirmational" and "transformational" fan practices (Hills, "Dalek Half Balls"; obsession_inc), constructions of mimetic tangible nostalgia articulated through the style of items like replica wands from the

Harry Potter franchise or weaponry from *Game of Thrones* (2011–2019) epitomize the commodity fetishism that Marxist-indebted cultural studies has consistently critiqued. Replica items exhibit little opportunity for individual agency when being acquired by fans other than the exchange of capital for goods. Moreover, these items demonstrate little use value other than as aspects of the acquirer's habitus (Bourdieu), such as class position (via the disposable income required for purchasing) and levels of (popular; Fiske, "Cultural Economy") cultural capital. Owning a replica of a communicator from the original *Star Trek* (1966–1969) series (retailing at £120) demonstrates the owner's levels of economic capital alongside their investment in popular culture franchises over traditionally respected cultural works.

Although they are embedded in structures of consumerism, I nevertheless argue that Marxist critiques should not represent the endpoint of discussing replica merchandise. These perspectives overlook analysis of how and why objects are designed and manufactured to articulate nostalgia by combining tangibility with mimetic qualities. Developing this theory first requires recognizing that

> economic objects, in particular, exist in the space between pure desire and immediate enjoyment, with some distance between them and the person who desires them, which is a distance that can be overcome. This distance is overcome in and through economic exchange, in which the value of objects is determined reciprocally. That is, one's desire for an object is fulfilled by the sacrifice of some other object, which is the focus of the desire of another. Such exchange of sacrifices is what economic life is all about. (Appadurai 3–4)

Where a replica of a model skull or arm from the Terminator might represent a desire for extracting economic capital by media organizations and licensees, this commercial interpretation contrasts with a desire for nostalgic attachment to the media property on behalf of the fan-consumer. Stewart supports this argument by addressing the link between souvenirs as material objects and nostalgia: "The souvenir speaks to a context of origin through a language of longing, for it is not an object arising out of need or use value; it is an object arising out of the necessarily insatiable demands of nostalgia. The souvenir generates a narrative which reaches only 'behind,' spiraling in a continually inward movement rather than outward toward the future" (135). While Stewart directs hostility toward popular culture objects acting as nostalgic stimuli due in part to their mass-produced nature (167–68), overlaps between her arguments linking nostalgia and tangibility with others pertaining to mimesis are observable. Hills ("Dalek Half Balls" para. 2.17) argues that "Mimetic fandom can thus be defined as a matter of oscillatory distinctions," including "an ontological bridging of the branded story world or hyperdiegesis and the fan's everyday life" (Hills, "Dalek Half Balls" para. 3.3). By extension, although individual objects can construct a narrated bridge between past and present by providing fans with tangible links to nostalgic past experiences, such as (re)viewing favorite screen media texts, their mimetic qualities assist in linking reality and fiction. What's more, in contrast to Stewart's dismissals of mass-produced items, Catherine Johnson has argued that officially licensed merchandise also "offers a fantasy space akin to that offered by the series overall" (18). Combining these positions, the mimetic style of collectibles not only ontologically bridges between fantasy and reality but also past and present to provide nostalgic pleasures to specific consumer groups. Rather than representing exploitation of fans by media conglomerates, shifting attention to the design of replicas and how their imitative look targets fans offers an alternative, less dismissive understanding of replicas that recognizes their commodity status alongside the affective affordances generated by encodings of mimetic tangible nostalgia.

Having demonstrated the overlaps between existing theories of mimetic fandom, licensed merchandising, and material objects as nostalgic stimuli, it is necessary to address points of fissure to provide a comprehensive theorization of mimetic tangible nostalgia. Despite reproducing likenesses of character, sets, or props, the mimetic design of some items—especially at the cheaper or more functional end of the spectrum—can result in their warping of size, scale, or the level of detail. There is a significant difference between the levels of mimesis identifiable on a replica of the thirteenth Doctor's sonic screwdriver from *Doctor Who* (1963–1989, 1996, 2005–) produced by Character Options for retail at £16.99 and an equivalent made by Rubbertoe Replicas that retails at £375.

Hills's fan-produced examples, such as life-size replica Daleks, constitute exact re-creations of the dimensions and size of their mediated referents ("Dalek Half Balls"). In contrast, and depending on the examples selected, mass-produced replicas complicate a style of to-scale likeness in different ways. First, as a 3D character mug of Rick Sanchez or Mr. Meeseeks from *Rick and Morty* (2013–) suggests, the mimetic representation of the onscreen referent might become altered to incorporate new functionality. Second, items like plush dolls of *Pokémon* or *The Simpsons* (1989–) characters might provide concrete measurements or proportions to animated equivalents that either demonstrate plasticity on screen or variances across different licensing contexts. Third, miniatures like the PKE meter from *Ghostbusters* or the Xenomorph skull from the *Alien* franchise produced by Running Press (retailing at approximately £9.99) sacrifice detail for affordability in their visual style. Rather than being dimensionally accurate and arising out of "forensic" fan research, officially produced replicas can instead involve warping, locking, or miniaturizing the dimensions of onscreen referents (Mittell 52).

The complications to mimetic reproduction outlined might, on one hand, undermine the nostalgic potential of a replica item's design for fan consumers. Colin B. Harvey supports this position as, writing anecdotally on his childhood memories of *Star Wars* toys, he identifies how a "lack of fidelity with regard to the spaceships and other vehicles depicted on screen always proved faintly irksome" (151). On the other hand, strategies including miniaturization might assist in articulating nostalgia:

> once the miniature becomes souvenir, it speaks not so much to the time of production as to the time of consumption. For example, a traditional basket-maker might make miniatures of his [sic] goods to sell as toys just as he [sic] makes full-sized baskets for carrying wood or eggs. But as the market for his full-sized baskets decreases because of changes in the economic system, such miniature baskets increase in demand. They are no longer models; rather, they are souvenirs of a mode of consumption which is now extinct. They have moved from the domain of use value to the domain of *gift*, where exchange is abstracted to the level of social relations and away from the level of materials and processes. (Stewart 144)

Iconography encoded into replica items linked to canceled or out-of-production media properties could be read as representing an extinct mode of consumption due to being associated with past ways of accessing audiovisual content, such as linear television delivery via scheduled slots on satellite and cable. Alternatively, adapting characters and set likenesses to new forms and functionalities, such as a paperweight modeled on the *Game of Thrones* Iron Throne, suggests the movement of the original referent into a new historical domain of consumption as licensed merchandise. Irrespective of whether the distinction between past and present relating to replicas concerns old or contemporary media franchises, then, it is arguable that processes of miniaturization or adapted functionality do not necessarily lessen mimetic tangible nostalgia's appeal. Instead, the item's encoding practices arguably heighten the nostalgic pleasures articulated through the object's design to fans by communicating the pastness of the original context and mode of media consumption.

The theory of mimetic tangible nostalgia lends itself to consideration beyond this chapter's parameters. For example, discussing mimetic tangible nostalgia in relation to action figures represents an immediate area for further exploration of the concept. Existing research has explored both action figures' historical development in response to changes in commercial media culture as well as noting the tendency for contemporary examples targeting adult consumers to accentuate mimesis through design and molding (Bainbridge; Santo, *Selling* 232). Building on these insights, a theory of mimetic tangible nostalgia developed in relation to action figures could further refine the concept by recognizing how it responds to historical and industrial trends in manufacturing and consumer cultures. Maintaining a broader focus on a wider range of mimetic collectibles, however, the popularity of replicas with fans links to "the art toy movement coming out of Japan in the late 1990s" (Bainbridge 838) where "emphasis [is] placed less on play than display" (Santo, *Selling* 232). This argument points toward the need for better understanding of the relationship between replicas, mimetic tangible nostalgia, and the environments where fans exhibit these.

Mimetic Tangible Nostalgia and Spatial Cosplay

Replica items exhibiting mimetic tangible nostalgia are encoded for multiple purposes, depending on their pricing, intended audience, and primary functionality. While an electronic lightsaber replica from the *Star Wars* universe might be played with by a child or used by an adult cosplayer, a bottle opener replicating a velociraptor claw from *Jurassic Park* (1993) could also become integrated into a fan's everyday routines. However, fans may defy the intended meanings of replicas using an aesthetic of mimetic tangible nostalgia by displaying them in spaces like bedrooms, sitting rooms, or offices. Understood in this way, the items' fan-ascribed meanings—as well as the mimetic tangible nostalgia articulated through the object's production—function as markers of identity and taste. Supporting this interpretation, John Fiske argues that displaying acquired items in personal areas represents an "enunciation of a systemic social resource" where the artifacts communicate the owner's situatedness in structures of class-derived taste, economics, gender, race, and beyond ("Ethnosemiotics" 86). Despite infrequent allusions to the topic (Godwin; Woo), little academic knowledge concerning how fans construct and organize their personal spaces and environments is available—even less regarding how practices of domestic display generate spatial dimensions linked to nostalgia. First, these absences point to the need for greater empirical research with audiences regarding the meanings they attach to private places of fan dwelling and how these become subjectively meaningful by being populated with merchandise. Second, and specific to this chapter's themes, gaps emerge in academic knowledge concerning the significance of mimetic tangible nostalgia in the spatial dimensions of fandom's material cultures and the structural constraints with which this form of nostalgia intersects.

I would argue that insights into mimetic tangible nostalgia's relationship with personal spaces can be found by turning to academic positions on cosplay and extending these to theorize what I have called spatial cosplay. Originating in Japan, "Cosplay or *kosupure* is a term that represents the combining of the words for 'costume' and 'play' or 'role-play'" (Rahman, Wing-sun, and Cheung 318) and "is about simulation, role-playing, and performance" (Rahman, Wing-sun, and Cheung 324). As Suzanne Scott makes explicit, cosplay is "a form of mimetic fan production" (147), but one where analysis of its bodily dimensions has taken precedence over the construction of spaces inhabited by fans. For example, Nicolle Lamerichs argues that cosplay "involve[s] four elements: a narrative, a set of clothing, a play or performance before spectators, and a subject or player" ("Stranger than Fiction" para. 1.2). Despite space representing an integral part of cosplay as a social practice, the primacy afforded to bodily dimensions has bound understanding of cosplay's spatiality primarily to convention halls (Bainbridge and Norris para. 12; Kirkpatrick para. 3.2; Lamerichs, "Cultural Dynamic" 157; Affuso has challenged these associations). While space is vital to cosplay, focusing on cosplay-as-embodiment overlooks fans' agency in "dressing up" (Kirkpatrick para. 4.5) domestic and occupied spaces as an alternative form of cosplay. Recognizing that mimetic tangible nostalgia contributes toward spatial cosplay reverses this trend by focusing on how physical personal spaces become "dressed" with merchandise replicating the iconography of fan brands for the purpose of performing attachments and identities. If dressing the fan body "allow[s] fans to visualize their affect for certain texts" (Lamerichs, "Fan Fashion"

176), then by extension, spatial cosplayers express their affect through mimetic tangible nostalgia's potential to ontologically bridge between discursively bounded notions of reality and fiction and past and present.

However, just as cosplay has been theorized as being unable to offer "a literal transformation" of the performer's body as the individual's "material reality ultimately limits and bounds their transformation" (Kirkpatrick para. 4.5), the materiality of a location where a fan performs spatial cosplay also demonstrates structural constraints. Although there are infrequent exceptions, as in the case of Anthony Alleyne, who transformed his entire flat into a replica of a *Star Trek* spaceship (Sehmer), sites used for spatial cosplay performances can rarely (if ever) directly or continually mimic the exact aesthetic of the onscreen referent. This is partly a pragmatic limitation: as Joanne Hollows argues, "Few people in the West build their own houses or apartments and so our primary relationship to the places we rent or buy is established through consumption rather than production" (74). Spatial cosplayers must therefore work within constraints arising out of nationally—and historically—specific discourses of domestic architecture when constructing personal spaces that communicate mimetic tangible nostalgia.

Additional points of divergence in spatial cosplay's mimetic potential further distinguish this practice from its bodily equivalent. Fan-occupied spaces will rarely have singular meanings or uses, resulting in their status as sites of spatial cosplay existing alongside others (which may or may not gain greater legitimacy). Hollows argues against considering "domestic consumption . . . as a self-reflexive and individualistic activity" (79) because these spaces construct shared, rather than personalized, identities (Reimer and Leslie 192–93). Spatially cosplaying a living room or bedroom as a site of fandom would sit alongside the agency demonstrated by others (e.g., partners, flatmates) who occupy and make use of that space, creating competition between its status as a location for communicating fan affect and other shared meanings (Woo paras. 5.14–19). Homemaking has been analyzed as a practice in which "lifestyle discourses compete with other discourses of home that associate domestic culture with ideas such as privacy, morality, family and care" (Hollows 81). Because spatial cosplay is a practice linked to consumption-based lifestyle choices, reconciliation with other more conventional meanings of domestic space may generate tension among residents. Similarly, while a fan-occupier may decorate an office (cubicle) with replica items to perform their fan attachments, these demonstrations of individual agency may exist in tension with other structuring discourses, such as the expectations of professional identities or management policies. Such concerns speak to how, as Mark Duffett argues, "each person adopts or disowns his or her status ... as a fan depending on an estimation of the immediate social context." (29) These considerations indicate that mimetic tangible nostalgia articulated by displaying replica objects must negotiate with other discursive meanings of space that may discourage using these as sites where affective ties to media franchises are performed. Further investigation is required into how mimetic tangible nostalgia sits alongside discourses structuring (potential) spatial cosplay sites.

Another difference between spatial cosplay and its bodily equivalent concerns the former's deployment of a transfandom aesthetic. Lamerichs argues that "As a fan practice, cosplay is centrally concerned with embodying a character accurately" as precise imitation assists the performance in being positively evaluated as 'authentic' by the consuming audience ("Stranger than Fiction" para. 4.4). The assumption underpinning this and other understandings (see Bainbridge and Norris) of bodily cosplay is that despite being a cultural practice that covers content arising from myriad genres, franchises, and media platforms (Rahman, Wing-sun, and Cheung 318), the cosplayer is generally only able to imitate one character at a time.

Adapting this consideration to how fans construct their spatial environments, it is arguable that positions linked to what Hills has called transfandom ("Interview") are more applicable. As Lori Morimoto argues, a "transfandom approach ... brings to fan studies conversations ... a greater awareness of the extent to which such discrete categorization is in fact antithetical to the ways that fandoms emerge and evolve" (286). In other words, just as "being a fan" is not a singular set of practices (Lamerichs, "Stranger than Fiction" para. 1.2), fans' affective attachments span multiple media texts and franchises simultaneously. Thus, while bodily cosplayers demonstrate transfandom attachments by either imitating many favorite characters (Rahman, Wing-sun, and Cheung 320)—sometimes at the same event—or producing character mash-ups, these must occur as discrete iterations.

In contrast, spatial cosplay demonstrates a transfandom aesthetic as fans display multiple franchise attachments alongside each other. Exhibitions of a transfandom aesthetic consequently subsume mimetic tangible nostalgia to a generalized, metalevel form of media-oriented nostalgia. Transfandom perspectives are absent from existing discussions of fandom's material cultures, though, as case study methodologies focusing on individual franchises or fan texts prevail (see Geraghty *Cult Collectors*; "It's

Not All About"; Lamerichs, "Fan Fashion"). Consequently, while Woo mentions material goods' centrality to multiple fan practices (para. 4.1), academic discourse has implied that fans' consumption habits circulate around discrete fan texts or objects when purchasing and displaying merchandise. This is despite analyses of popular representations of fandom's material cultures in shows like *The Big Bang Theory* (2007–2019) and *The Simpsons* depicting collecting as a transfandom practice spanning multiple franchises (Geraghty, *Cult Collectors* 20, 28).

Consequently, spatial cosplay diverges from its bodily equivalent by foregrounding transfandom performativity over monofandom iterations. Stewart argues that collecting involves "the invention of a classification scheme which will define space and time in such a way that the world is accounted for by the elements of the collection" (162). Regarding spatial cosplay, nostalgic affect may serve as one organizational principle among other intertexts that assists in legitimating the transfandom aesthetic. From this perspective, while mimetic tangible nostalgia is a significant factor in the appeal of individual replicas through the ontological bridging that this offers fans, this form of nostalgia must continually interact with a higher-level form of media-oriented nostalgia that brings coherence to a transfandom collection of objects. Stewart offers additional support for this argument by stating that "the collection presents a hermetic world: to have a representative collection is to have both the minimum and the complete number of elements necessary for an autonomous world—a world which is both full and singular, which has banished repetition and achieved authority" (152). Thus, unlike bodily cosplay's emphasis on singular iterative expressions of fan attachment(s), spatial cosplay demonstrates a fragmentary aesthetic where fans performatively move across media franchises through the items that they incorporate into personal spaces. While the aesthetic of replicas articulate affective affordances linked to mimetic tangible nostalgia, the cumulative range of items owned, displayed, and used by spatial cosplayers alludes to the wider "textual environments" (Couldry 67) that stimulate affective remembrance and attachments on a daily basis.

Conclusion

The relationship between nostalgia and contemporary-produced replica merchandise is complex, and more research is needed to better understand how commodities encourage such emotions among niche consumer groups (as well as how they are understood and discussed by their target markets). This chapter explored only a small area of this relationship by offering an initial theorization of mimetic tangible nostalgia and spatial cosplay. It has been argued that affective longing for screen media becomes articulated through the mimetic aesthetic encoded into replicas by producers and that these strategies assist in ontologically bridging between real and fictive spaces as well as past and present temporalities. Rather than dismissing these items and the audiences who consume them as exploited by media industries, I argued that the value of these items should instead be understood in the ability of commodities to provide affective bridges across spatial and temporal parameters in a way that raises their significance beyond debates concerning exchange and use value. In addition, I argued for exploring practices of displaying replicas within (semi-) personal spaces as a form of spatial cosplay where fan-dwellers use material objects to imaginatively transform such spaces into arenas for performing fan identities and affective attachments through the circulation and intersection of different levels of nostalgic classification. As understood in this chapter, and unlike its bodily equivalent, spatial cosplay is not a wholly mimetic practice as multiple factors, including architectural, social, and domestic-organizational elements, constrain how fans perform their (nostalgic) affection for media properties. Spatial cosplay might therefore be best thought of as a quasi-mimetic practice where items and the nostalgic readings they encourage compete with others operating in environments of fan identity performance.

Both (mimetic) tangible nostalgia and spatial cosplay require further scholarly engagement. This chapter focused on the nostalgic articulation of mimetic items. However, many merchandise producers forsake or combine mimetic reproductions of likenesses in favor of providing alternative takes on characters or scenarios linked to myriad issues, including branding and licensing. These indicate different modes of tangible nostalgia that also need in-depth theorization. In addition, the relationship between different modes of tangible nostalgia and industrial circumstances (including product differentiation) remain overlooked. Addressing this absence requires, as I have argued elsewhere (Garner), contextualizing individual forms of media-derived nostalgia in the industrial circumstances from which they arise. Moreover, future empirical work with consumers of different forms of material culture could contribute to understandings of how such groups negotiate the status of (replica) merchandise as simultaneously commodity forms and nostalgic stimuli. Such studies would test, refine, and develop this chapter's arguments concerning spatial cosplay by investigating how, why, and whether audiences construct and arrange the spaces they occupy as sites for performing fandom. Addressing these points clearly requires moving beyond singular dismissals of merchandise as commercially exploiting fans or "affirmational fandom" to instead understand how affective forms like nostalgia structure and circulate among the material objects fans consume and the role of such emotions in the everyday spaces they occupy.

Works Cited

Affuso, Elizabeth. "Everyday Costume: Feminized Fandom, Retail, and Beauty Culture." *The Routledge Companion to Media Fandom*. Ed. Melissa A. Click and Suzanne Scott. London: Routledge, 2018. 184–92.

Appadurai, Arjun. "Introduction: Commodities and the Politics of Value." *The Social Life of Things: Commodities in Cultural Perspective*. Ed. Arjan Appadurai. Cambridge: Cambridge University Press, 1986. 3–63.

Auerbach, Erich. *Mimesis: The Representation of Reality in Western Literature*. New York: Doubleday, 1957.

Bainbridge, Jason. "Fully Articulated: The Rise of the Action Figure and the Changing Face of Children's Entertainment." *Continuum: Journal of Media and Cultural Studies* 24.6 (2010): 829–42.

Bainbridge, Jason, and Craig Norris. "Posthuman Drag: Understanding Cosplay as Social Networking in a Material Culture." *Intersections: Gender and Sexuality in Asia and the Pacific* 32 (2013). http://intersections.anu.edu.au/issue32/bainbridge_norris.htm.

Baudrillard, Jean. *Simulacra and Simulation*. Ann Arbor: University of Michigan Press, 1994.

Benjamin, Walter. "Doctrine of the Similar" (1933). *New German Critique* 17 (Spring 1979): 65–69.

Benjamin, Walter. "The Work of Art in the Age of Mechanical Reproduction" (1935). Trans. Harry Zohn. *Illuminations*. Ed. Hannah Arendt. New York: Schocken Books, 1969.

Bourdieu, Pierre. *Distinction: A Social Critique of the Judgement of Taste*. London: Routledge, 1984.

Cherry, Brigid. *Cult Media, Fandom and Textiles: Handcrafting as Fan Art*. London: Bloomsbury, 2016.

Couldry, Nick. *Inside Culture: Re-imagining the Method of Cultural Studies*. London: Sage, 2000.

Csikszentmihalyi, Mihalyi. "Why We Need Things." *History from Things: Essays on Material Culture*. Ed. Steven Lubar and W. David Kingery. Washington: Smithsonian Institution Press, 1993. 20–29.

Duffett, Mark. *Understanding Fandom: An Introduction to the Study of Media Fan Culture*. London: Bloomsbury, 2013.
Fiske, John. "The Cultural Economy of Fandom." *The Adoring Audience: Fan Culture and Popular Media*. Ed. Lisa A. Lewis. London: Routledge, 1992. 30–49.
Fiske, John. "Ethnosemiotics: Some Personal and Theoretical Reflections." *Cultural Studies* 4.1 (1990): 85–98.
Garner, Ross P. "Celebrating and Critiquing 'Past' and 'Present'? The Intersection between Nostalgia and Public Service Discourses in BBC1's *Ashes to Ashes*." *Visual Communication*. Ed. David Machin. Berlin: De Gruyter, 2014. 405–25.
Geraghty, Lincoln. *Cult Collectors: Nostalgia, Fandom and Collecting Popular Culture*. London: Routledge, 2014.
Geraghty, Lincoln. "It's Not All about the Music: Online Fan Communities and Collecting Hard Rock Café Pins." *Transformative Works and Cultures* 16 (2014). https://doi.org/10.3983/twc.2014.0492.
Geraghty, Lincoln. "Nostalgia, Fandom and the Remediation of Children's Culture." *A Companion to Media Fandom and Fan Studies*. Ed. Paul Booth. Oxford: Wiley-Blackwell, 2018. 161–74.
Godwin, Victoria. "Hogwarts House Merchandise, Liminal Play, and Fan Identities." *Film Criticism* 42.4 (2018). https://doi.org/10.3998/fc.13761232.0042.206.
Gray, Jonathan. *Show Sold Separately: Promos, Spoilers, and Other Media Paratexts*. New York: New York University Press, 2010.
Harvey, Colin B. *Fantastic Transmedia: Narrative, Play and Memory across Science Fiction and Fantasy Storyworlds*. Basingstoke: Palgrave Macmillan, 2015.
Hills, Matt. "From Dalek Half Balls to Daft Punk Helmets: Mimetic Fandom and the Crafting of Replicas." *Transformative Works and Cultures* 16 (2014). https://doi.org/10.3983/twc.2014.0531
Hills, Matt. "Interview: Fandom as Object and the Objects of Fandom." *MATRIZes* 9.1 (2015): 147–62.
Hills, Matt. "Mainstream Cult." *The Cult TV Book*. Ed. Stacey Abbott. London: I. B. Tauris, 2010. 67–73.
Hollows, Joanne. *Domestic Cultures*. Maidenhead: Open University Press, 2008.
Johnson, Catherine. "Tele-Branding in TVIII." *New Review of Film and Television Studies* 5.1 (2007): 5–24.
Kirkpatrick, Ellen. "Toward New Horizons: Cosplay (Re)Imagined through the Superhero Genre, Authenticity, and Transformation." *Transformative Works and Cultures* 18 (2015). https://doi.org/10.3983/twc.2015.0613.
Kopytoff, Igor. "The Cultural Biography of Things: Commoditization as Process." *The Social Life of Things: Commodities in Cultural Perspective*. Ed. Arjun Appadurai. Cambridge: Cambridge University Press, 1986. 64–91.
Lamerichs, Nicolle. "The Cultural Dynamic of Doujinshi and Cosplay: Local Anime Fandom in Japan, USA and Europe." *Participations: Journal of Audience and Reception Studies* 10.1 (2013): 154–76.

Lamerichs, Nicolle. "Fan Fashion: Re-enacting *Hunger Games* through Clothing and Design." *A Companion to Media Fandom and Fan Studies*. Ed. Paul Booth. Oxford: Wiley, 2018. 175–88.

Lamerichs, Nicolle. "Stranger than Fiction: Fan Identity in Cosplay." *Transformative Works and Cultures* 7 (2011). https://doi.org/10.3983/twc.2011.0246.

McCracken, Grant. *Culture and Consumption*. Bloomington: University of Indiana Press, 1988.

Mittell, Jason. *Complex TV: The Poetics of Contemporary Television Storytelling*. New York: New York University Press, 2015.

Morimoto, Lori. "Transnational Media Fan Studies." *The Routledge Companion to Media Fandom*. Ed. Melissa A. Click and Suzanne Scott. London: Routledge, 2018. 280–88.

Nicoll, Benjamin, and Bjorn Nansen. "Mimetic Production in YouTube Toy Unboxing Videos." *Social Media + Society* 4.3 (2018): 1–12.

obsession_inc. "Affirmational Fandom vs. Transformational Fandom." Dreamwidth. org, June 1, 2009. https://obsession-inc.dreamwidth.org/82589.html.

Peters, Ian M. "Peril-Sensitive Sunglasses, Superheroes in Miniature, and Pink Polka-Dot Boxers: Artifact and Collectible Video Game Feelies, Play, and the Paratextual Gaming Experience." *Transformative Works and Cultures* 16 (2014). https://doi.org/10.3983/twc.2014.0509.

Rahman, Osmand, Liu Wing-Sun, and Brittany Hei-man Cheung. "'Cosplay': Imaginative Self and Performing Identity." *Fashion Theory: The Journal of Dress, Body and Culture* 16.3 (2012): 317–41.

Reimer, Suzanne, and Deborah Leslie. "Identity, Consumption and the Home." *Home Cultures* 1.2 (2004): 187–210.

Santo, Avi. "Fans and Merchandise." *The Routledge Companion to Media Fandom*. Ed. Melissa A. Click and Suzanne Scott. London: Routledge, 2018. 329–36.

Santo, Avi. *Selling the Silver Bullet: The Lone Ranger and Transmedia Brand Licensing*. Austin: University of Texas Press, 2015.

Scott, Suzanne. "'Cosplay Is Serious Business': Gendering Material Fan Labor on *Heroes of Cosplay*." *Cinema Journal* 54.3 (2015): 146–54.

Sehmer, Alexander. "Star Trek–Themed Flat Is Up for Sale after Owner Is Jailed for Sex Offences." *Independent*, May 15, 2015. http://www.independent.co.uk/news/uk/home-news/star-trek-themed-flat-up-for-sale-after-owner-is-jailed-for-sex-offences-10253445.html.

Stanfill, Mel. *Exploiting Fandom: How the Media Industry Seeks to Manipulate Fans*. Iowa City: University of Iowa Press, 2019.

Stewart, Susan. *On Longing: Narratives of the Miniature, the Gigantic, the Souvenir, the Collection*. Durham, NC: Duke University Press, 1993.

Taussig, Michael T. *Mimesis and Alterity: A Particular History of the Senses*. New York: Routledge, 1993.

Woo, Benjamin. "A Pragmatics of Things: Materiality and Constraint in Fan Practices." *Transformative Works and Cultures* 16 (2014). https://doi.org/10.3983/twc.2014.0495.

Part 2

When Is Nostalgia?

5

A Nostalgic Exception

Warren Beatty's Star Performance in *Rules Don't Apply*

STEVEN RYBIN

"WATER. FROM MAINE." ASPIRING starlet Marla Mabrey (Lily Collins) intones these words as she sits patiently in a bungalow, awaiting her big break in show business. Her attention and inquisitiveness are momentarily fixed on several meticulously arranged bottles. These bottles are among the unusual details Marla will note about the man for whom she is waiting: Howard Hughes—aviator, film director, industrialist, and maker of young celebrity. Hughes is the man who might "bottle" Marla up in a star image and market her in a prospective RKO Studios musical, *Stella Starlight*. Levar Mathis (Matthew Broderick), who works security for Hughes, satisfies Marla's curiosity by telling her the bottles contain water imported from Maine, water for which Hughes has an inexplicable longing. At his response, she contemplates these words, turning them over in her speech—"Water. From Maine"—with a charming sing-song chirp that we will hear again and again when her words are repeated a little later, after it is revealed that Hughes has recorded and is listening unseen to everything she says in this room. Without knowing it yet, Marla is becoming a little like these bottles, but not because she will become a Hollywood commodity; she wins a screen test from Hughes, but *Stella Starlight* never materializes. Rather, her words and her way of speaking them—"Water. From Maine"—are being bottled up and recorded offscreen on audiotape as a memory of a past Hughes will hold onto with fixation and obsession.

This Hughes is incarnated, when he finally does appear on screen a few moments later, by Warren Beatty, writer, director, and star of this long-gestating Howard Hughes movie, *Rules Don't Apply* (2016). Where the reimagined Hollywood of 1958 in Beatty's film is sun-kissed and radiant (most of the first act takes place outdoors or in rooms with glass doors and windows that let in generous light), this small bungalow where Marla waits for Hughes is sparse and dark, a re-creation of what the interior of a Los Angeles bungalow in 1958 might have looked like. The real Hughes no doubt met many actresses in rooms like this—but he never met Marla, who is a fictional creation of Beatty and coscreenwriter Bo Goldman and who is not directly based on any historically existing figure. Hughes would have been fifty-three years old in 1958 (and just shy of sixty in 1964, the year the film begins and ends); that Beatty, aged seventy-six at the time of making *Rules Don't Apply*, is playing a man more than two decades his junior did not go unnoticed in the film's initial reception. "There was a moment," David Thomson reminisces, remembering the actor at just under forty, "when Beatty looked like the Hughes who sat for Senate committees and told them to get lost" ("Lost Lord" 47). But those are not the moments of life (the Hughes of history or the younger Beatty) that *Rules Don't Apply* imagines. That Beatty intends this film to be at all about the historical Hughes is questionable. Although he first had the idea for a Hughes movie in the 1970s, in press junkets for *Rules Don't Apply* he claims that the film is not a biopic at all, but rather about the Hollywood of the late 1950s, the Hollywood he first encountered in his youth (Lindsay 10).

Nevertheless, certain aspects of *Rules Don't Apply* are clearly rooted in the myth of Hughes: the industrialist-aviator-film director really did "drink only Poland mineral water bottled at the spring in Maine" and in the quart-sized bottles Marla wonders about ("he refused to drink from pint bottles," it is recorded) ("Tycoons"); he really did once obsess over purchasing bulk stock of Baskin-Robbins banana nut ice cream, after learning it was no longer in production. He really did repeatedly relish, via his portable 16mm projector, scenes from his cherished pet project *Hell's Angels* (1930), which Beatty's Hughes keeps beside him throughout *Rules Don't Apply*. To this list of "really dids," we might add Hughes's obsession with the concept of DNA, expressed by the Beatty character as a kind of spiritual tether to the haunting memory of a deceased father.

Perhaps Beatty views the mythical Hughes as a kind of Hollywood father figure. In any case, the notoriously private Beatty plays his cards close to the vest, meaning that any reference to his own autobiography or personal life is kept oblique in the film. Fittingly, *Rules Don't Apply* emphasizes the character's private, reclusive nostalgia, set in relation to a more expansive vision of a bygone moment in Hollywood history. The story Beatty tells in this film offers some indication that his nostalgic vision of Hollywood goes beyond Hughes. The narrative involves two eager young people, Frank Forbes (Alden Ehrenreich) and Marla Mabrey, who arrive in Hollywood with similar dreams. Frank wants to arrange (with Hughes's help) the purchase of vast swaths of undeveloped Mulholland Canyon to capitalize on the growing demand for suburban real estate (he dreams of living in a large house himself). Marla wants to act and sing—she is a smart and charming songwriter and at one point in the film pens a tune, "Rules Don't Apply." She writes this song as a memento of words Frank shares with her early in the film, words suggesting that the usual conventions of accepted stardom—the ability to sing, to become famous, to conform to the beauty standards of the era, and to achieve all this while still young—do not or should not apply to her. Marla and Frank will eventually leave Hollywood once Hughes's surface charm wears away and once the two of them are no longer able to project their fantasies of the future onto a figure who, no matter how much Beatty's performance makes him comically amusing, is mentally unstable and professionally abusive.

Collins and Ehrenreich, as stars, evoke certain associations in their roles as two fictional amalgams of hopeful young people who might have inhabited Hollywood in the late 1950s and early 1960s. Beatty is on record saying that he cast the two actors because they "shared these characteristics of intelligence, beauty, comedic talent, and a level of integrity—a highly principled, strong-willed industriousness" (Lindsay). They also look like people who might have done in 1958 the things they do in the film. In her personality and presence, Collins is reminiscent of Maggie McNamara, or a McNamara who might have existed had her career not declined after her appearance in Otto Preminger's *The Moon Is Blue* (1953). Ehrenreich evokes the physical presence of a young Beatty, playing a character handsome enough, despite Frank's modest dreams of real estate, to be a star himself, and at about the age Beatty would have been in 1958, upon his arrival to Los Angeles.

Given the film's focus on the love story between these hopefuls who look at 1958 Hollywood with virginal eyes, and the fact that Hughes, as a character, does not appear on screen until nearly thirty minutes into the film, we should take Beatty seriously when he claims that *Rules Don't Apply* is primarily about Hollywood and only secondarily about Hughes. The film is infused with nostalgia for a Hollywood that never existed quite as Beatty presents it here: this is a 1958 (and, in a handful of scenes, a 1964) that is thoroughly processed—both literally, through the color grading that represents the Hollywood landscape as if it were a picture postcard, and metaphorically, through Beatty's imagination and memory. In this way, *Rules Don't Apply* is in keeping with "the inherently reflexive nature" of the films analyzed in Jason Sperb's study of nostalgia in cinema, films that "reflect a self-awareness of an industry in a period of transition" (12). This reflection is especially vivid in Beatty's film given that the years fictionalized in *Rules Don't Apply* were themselves crucial years of transition in a Hollywood that was beginning to leave its golden age behind. Furthermore, *Rules Don't Apply*—in the lineage of Jonathan Demme's *Melvin and Howard* (1980; also written by Bo Goldman)—presents Hughes as a screwball figure, a character whose nostalgic fixations serve as a comic mechanism for the film's reflexive sentiment. Beatty's departure from any intention to make a serious Hughes biopic is comically licensed by the possibly apocryphal quote from Hughes himself—"Never check an interesting fact"—which the film presents on a title card before its narrative begins.

But in order to figure out what kind of film about Hollywood this is, it is necessary to think about what kind of film about Hughes it is, what kind of star Beatty himself is and was, and what kinds of stylistic choices he makes as director. Beatty's celebrity persona, dormant for fifteen years prior to his taking the lead in this film—his previous appearance as a performer was in *Town & Country* (2001) and his previous film as director *Bulworth* (1998)—is now itself historical, with Beatty's very presence in *Rules Don't Apply* perhaps sparking nostalgia for viewers who remember his rise to the leading ranks of Hollywood men. This is a sentiment attached to the younger Beatty as well as the ideals associated with his image in the 1960s and 1970s, when he was part of a certain generation of young, famous liberals associated with the Kennedy dynasty. Beatty's own nostalgia for this particular political and cultural moment in *Rules Don't Apply* is carefully shaped by his filmmaking choices, including how he orchestrates his own performance in the frame. Also at play here is the idea that the Hughes character in the film has his own nostalgic longings for 1930s Hollywood, in particular for *Hell's Angels*, a synecdoche for a studio-era Hollywood that never quite existed as he imagines. The world Hughes longs for ultimately stands at some distance from the love story involving Marla and Frank, a couple whose relatively progressive union at the end of the film (discarding as it does the fixation on biological inheritance with which Beatty's Hughes is obsessed) relies on forgetting both Hughes and the Hollywood this film imagines through him (see Hutchinson for an example of a review that makes a similar point about the progressive nature of the film's ending). That this Hollywood exists in the film as something still possible to imagine and then forget and leave behind is at the heart of its sentimental, reflexive nostalgia.

Beatty as Hughes: Star Persona

Howard Hughes is an infamous figure whose life has been reimagined in a number of films, ranging from relatively straightforward biopics to more stylized and mythological variations on the Hughes legend. Several significant films contain figures who seem to recall or are loosely based on the figure of Hughes, such as Willard Whyte (Jimmy Dean) in *Diamonds Are Forever* (1971) or the less thinly veiled Howard Stark (Dominic Cooper) of *Captain America: The First Avenger* (2011). In this group we also find a character like Smith Ohlrig (Robert Ryan) in *Caught* (1949), purportedly, as one reviewer describes this characterization in the Max Ophüls film, a "barely concealed portrait" (Lane) of the Howard Hughes who would go on to fire Ophüls one year later from the set of *Vendetta* (1950). And, of course, there are many figures on screen with whom Hughes may have identified, in films Hughes himself produced, such as the daring aviators of *Hell's Angels* or the hero played by John Wayne in *Jet Pilot* (1957). Beatty's film certainly suggests a kind of identification between Hughes and these mythical figures on whom Hughes seems to project his desires and fantasies. There are finally several films in which Hughes is taken as a central subject of interest, a historical personage channeled into myth, and Beatty's film may most belong in this category with *Melvin and Howard*, with Jason Robards as Hughes; *Tucker: The Man and His Dream* (1988), with Dean Stockwell; *The Rocketeer* (1991), a fantasy film that casts Terry O'Quinn as Hughes; and *The Aviator* (2004), Martin Scorsese's biopic with Leonardo DiCaprio in the title role. Of these films, which are (if only loosely) works of creative fiction based on Hughes's life and work, Beatty's is the most unusual, a strange and oddly endearing film about an eccentric figure.

Beatty's presence in the leading role gives *Rules Don't Apply* an additional intertextual resonance. If Hughes is a mythical figure, Beatty is himself something of a legend in the New Hollywood cinema of the late 1960s and 1970s, a key member of an artistically adventurous crop of male Hollywood stars who predate the rise of the blockbuster mentality of the late 1970s. For Beatty the star, the figure of Hughes he plays in *Rules Don't Apply* is tethered to the memory of Beatty's past film roles. As Thomson notes in his adventurous book on the star, Beatty's character Nicky Wilson in *The Fortune* (1975) is best described as "an aging dude . . . with such a tidy, stuck-on mustache that, for the first time, Beatty looks like Howard Hughes" (*Warren Beatty* 368). And there is the added intrigue of treating *Rules Don't Apply* as a belated but significant entry into the work of Beatty as a director, perhaps finally impossible to fully distinguish from the star persona (given that Beatty appears centrally in all his works as director), and which now consists of five films: *Heaven Can Wait* (1978, codirected with Buck Henry), *Reds* (1981), *Dick Tracy* (1990), *Bulworth*, and *Rules Don't Apply*.

Chris Cagle argues that Beatty's star persona in the 1960s and 1970s, held in balance a matinee idol desirability with "its countercultural alternative," which, in Beatty's films, sometimes took the form of an engagement with US politics (40). Although this political aspect to Beatty's work often takes the form of romanticizing political history (in *Reds*) or contemporary party politics (in his skewering of the US political climate of the late 1990s in *Bulworth*), Cagle reminds us that Beatty's sexual appeal itself contains implicit political connotations. Cagle writes that "Sexual appeal frequently forms the basis of stars' popularity; what distinguished [the Beatty image was its] representation of sex appeal in an age of sexual liberation and shifting gender politics" (44). In this sense, what Cagle describes as Beatty's famous "potent bachelor sexuality"—a key aspect of his star image and the popular myths about his personal life as propagated in trade books such as Peter Biskind's 2010 biography *Star*—is also a carrier of political meanings in its implicit rejection of repression in favor of a liberated lifestyle linked to a larger counterculture politics.

It is notable, then, that the surface appeal of *Rules Don't Apply* serves partly as a vehicle for Beatty's continued autobiographical interest, as both star and director, in the idea that personal sexual freedom is also potentially a political gesture. This theme winds its way throughout his work as a filmmaker, from the romance of *Reds* to the subplot involving Beatty and Halle Berry in *Bulworth*, narratives in which political plots are weaved into romantic entanglements. Even certain films in which Beatty appears only as an actor, and not as director—Hal Ashby's *Shampoo* (1975) is central among these—connect a liberated libido to what Hollywood is able to imagine as leftist, unrepressed politics. And yet part of the fascination of *Rules Don't Apply* is that in reiterating Beatty's personal theme of finding one's way out of a conservative lifestyle and sexual modesty, it joins this motif to a representation of Hughes, whose relationships with actresses (at least during the time period depicted in the film) seem more an example of frustrated desire and abusive power than liberated and politically aware feeling. Many notable books on Hughes reinforce the image of a man whose relationships with contract actresses in the 1950s, for example, are not exactly the picture of progressive politics. Donald L. Barlett and James B. Steele write on Hughes's propensity to sign actresses to long-term contracts bound in stultifying and in some cases career-ending terms: "With visions of the fame that lay ahead, the young women submitted to drama and singing lessons, designed, they were told, to turn them into polished actresses" (244). Pointing to the case of Gail Ganley, a singer and dancer pegged by Hughes as a potential star for RKO Studios, the authors tell a story of a contract that seems less like signed papers and more like the steel bars of a prison window: "The terms were strict—she would refrain from appearing as a singer, dancer, or actress during the training period, she would keep her arrangement with Hughes a secret from all but her immediate family, and 'hold herself' ready to meet with Hughes at any time to discuss her career" (244). Hughes's sexuality, meanwhile, is often framed by his biographers—at least those writing about him later in his life—as one manifest in displacements and projections onto curvaceous screen goddesses rather than in real relationships with flesh-and-blood women. We see other kinds of projections and displacements throughout *Rules Don't Apply*, too, such as the bottled water from Maine and the fetishized 16mm film print of *Hell's Angels*, objects that are eroticized displacements of the desire for screen actresses that remain Hughes's chief obsession. One biographer, amplifying this aspect of the Hughes myth, regales us with descriptions of a hall in Hughes's home, in which we see "eight or ten pictures of Jane Russell, oil paintings on wood four feet tall, one depicting the buxom actress nearly nude" (Drosnin 10). Although Beatty's film avoids reference to these particular paintings, it clearly suggests that many of the character's obsessions and projections are of a sexual nature.

Rules Don't Apply plays with these inherent links and contrasts between Beatty, movie star of famous and unapologetic libido, but also public citizen engaged in the politics of a democratic republic and, after his marriage to Annette Bening in the early 1990s, relatively domesticated and modestly private family man; and Howard Hughes, aviator and film producer who became more and more obsessively reclusive and whose thoughts of marriage often seemed inextricable from his Hollywood ambitions (and later his paranoia). Where Beatty's sexual proclivities in the 1960s and 1970s stood then for a certain expression of sexual freedom (even if Beatty, like his character puts it in *Shampoo*, is ultimately not "anti-establishment"), Hughes's treatment of women in his profession seems today largely damaging. That Beatty's star persona also involves a frequently avowed desire for privacy suggests, however, one area of intersection between the two quasi-mythical celebrity personalities at the center of *Rules Don't Apply* and one possible source of the film's wistfulness. These tensions play out in the body of Beatty's performance in the film, in which the star-auteur physically inscribes himself into the role of a Hughes with whom he has long been fascinated but whose public reputation is significantly different from the one Beatty has established.

The Star Director's Nostalgic Performance

In *Rules Don't Apply*, Beatty's Hughes lingers in the margins of the frame, sometimes entirely off screen, rarely seen under light of day. When he finally appears in the flesh, in the scene in which Marla waits in the bungalow, his arrival characterizes Hughes as hesitant, unsure. He is first a shadow, cast on the wall, and then a figure who lurks in an interior doorway, tentatively stepping out only after Marla greets him with anxious, silly patter: "I recognize you from your photos!," she exclaims, even though Hughes here stands in shadow. Beatty's editing in this scene, as it is for several other stretches of the film, is oddly syncopated, often missing what in other films would be key movements or gestures. The cutting rhythms throughout this film, without ever departing from Hollywood continuity, are often unusual, swiftly moving through stretches of emotional development on which other films would linger, while extending shots and moments other films might elide. In this particular scene, the viewer never quite sees Beatty-as-Hughes walk into the room: his movements are broken up by the cutting patterns, and his movement toward Marla is not even represented by Beatty-the-actor: instead Beatty-the-director uses a forward tracking shot to suggest the movement toward Marla.

These choices Beatty makes as director, with the movement of the camera and with the cutting, create a neat conjunction of a star's performance and a star director's stylistic gesture behind the camera. The film's construction links the expressions of the film itself (camera, staging, editing, and music) to the physical movements of his character as well as the eccentricity of his personality. In this way, the eccentric style of the film matches the peculiarity of the fictional Hughes who inhabits it. This intimate connection between Beatty's choices as director and his own presence on the screen parallels Hughes's relationship with his own movie, *Hell's Angels*, clips from which are seen throughout *Rules Don't Apply* as Hughes brings with him a 16mm projector always equipped with a reel from the film. In one scene, Hughes—unshaven and disheveled, hiding from creditors, and looking more like Beatty's nearly eight decades of life than the six Hughes would have lived at this point—stares in wonder at the aviation derring-do represented in shots from *Hell's Angels*, astonishing glimpses into an imagined past to which he can never return. In another moment, burrowed away in a hotel in Nicaragua, Beatty has Hughes mimic the gestures and movements of his *Hell's Angels* characters, as if trying to bring the past back through performance. And when Hughes is charmed enough by Marla to offer marriage to her, shots of planes being downed in *Hell's Angels* flicker behind him. Beatty's orchestration of this proposal scene is emblematic of how the film links Hughes's nostalgic eccentricity with the oddball style of *Rules Don't Apply*. Prior to the beginning of the scene, Hughes has been quarreling with potential investors about the future of TWA. Marla, meanwhile, waiting for Hughes in another of his bungalows, drowns in drink, intoxicated for the first time in her life after a spat with Frank. When Hughes arrives to meet her (he expects another "M.M.," Marilyn Monroe), she is drunk, asking Hughes if he has watched her screen test for *Stella Starlight*. Characteristically, Hughes does not answer her question but instead turns on his projector, *Hell's Angels* again unfolding on a screen that emerges, as if by magic, behind Marla. Hughes prefers to talk about his company, and when Marla asks if he has children, he speaks about his father. He tells Marla about his new foundation, devoted to the study of DNA, the genetic material that in his mind keeps his father alive inside of him ("I'm still more of a son than a father," Hughes says). "You have no choice," Hughes goes on to explain; the DNA and the past will continue to "replicate and replicate." Here, as *Hell's Angels* flickers in the room, Beatty's Hughes tethers his nostalgic sentiment for the past, for his own achievements, to a kind of biological determinism.

Marla is fascinated by this, but she does not directly respond to it. Instead, after a comic pause (such pauses shape the otherwise sprightly exchange between Marla and Hughes in the scene), she begins weaving together, in her lilting, lightly intoxicated speech, a series of observations and questions that implicitly and drunkenly tie her possible future in Hollywood to Hughes's failure to produce progeny: "What if Stella Starlight sang? . . . You know, make the movie a musical. [*in an inebriated chirp*]: *I can sing*! Well, but nobody should have children if they don't want to, [*chirpy again*]: *that's for sure.*"

Marla's sing-song intonation, her light and lyrical way of speaking these words, bends the movie slightly to the genre of the musical. She makes references to an earlier dialogue she shared with Frank, in which he told her that the conventional rules of Hollywood stardom did not apply to her. "You're an exception," she tells Hughes, after he shares his worry that others find him insane; the moment amounts to something of an intoxicated, unintentional betrayal of Frank, whose sentimental words toward Marla are refashioned by her as something charming to say in the presence of one of the most powerful men in the world. This idea is underscored a moment later when Marla, moving over to a piano that has appeared in Hughes's bungalow as magically as the screen on which *Hell's Angels* flickers, gives a tipsy performance of the film's title song, written for Frank but now sung for Hughes (see figure 5.1). As she drunkenly coos the song's lyrics, which express a wistfulness for lost

Figure 5.1. Marla Mabrey (Lily Collins) sings a song as *Hell's Angels* (1930) flickers behind her in *Rules Don't Apply* (Warren Beatty, 2016). Digital frame enlargement.

opportunities while still assuring the listener that the conventional rules do not apply to those who yearn to achieve something new, *Hell's Angels* continues its projection behind her. A cut to Beatty, his face lit only by the flickering frames of the 1930 film. Hughes is crying.

Shortly after this moment, Hughes proposes to Marla with a green emerald ring, and then Marla and Hughes have impulsive sex, from which Marla later bears Hughes's son.

Beatty's Adagietto

Because screen performance is bound up with at least some of the biological determinants that so fascinate the Hughes of this film, it is difficult to extricate Hughes's tears from Beatty's own. Actor and character (if not the historical person the character is based on) do share DNA and at times possibly even an emotional state. If I end here by thinking about *Rules Don't Apply* as a movie about Howard Hughes that may ultimately be more substantially about Beatty, what does this mean for the film's reflexive nostalgia? Beatty's tears in the proposal scene remind us that this is a sentimental sort of filmic nostalgia indulged in by *Rules Don't Apply*, not ultimately an ironic or cynical one. As if to underscore this, the fourth part of Gustav Mahler's Symphony No. 5 (Adagietto) occasionally floats into the film, a piece of music that in the context of cinema will be most familiar to cinephiles from Luchino Visconti's *Death in Venice* (1971). Beatty uses it in ways that often serve to longingly punctuate the sweet, earnest love story between Marla and Frank. And it is suitable for this purpose because we know that Mahler "wrote the Adagietto during his first summer with Alma, and even commentators disinclined to adopt a straightforwardly biographical approach may abandon their reservations here: it is a musical declaration of love" (Fischer 390). The relationship between Marla and Frank may begin with a kind of shared virtuousness and earnest glee for the coming future, but it ends, after the revelation of Hughes's unfeeling treatment of Marla on learning of her pregnancy, with a sense of innocence lost. In that context, the Adagietto as Beatty uses it contains a wisp of regret.

In the larger frame of Beatty's history as an actor, a director, and a celebrity figure, there is another implication in the use of this piece of music in *Rules Don't Apply*: the Adagietto also scored the funeral of Robert Kennedy in 1968, when Beatty spent the better part of his time as a public figure campaigning for Democratic presidential candidate

George McGovern (as he would again during McGovern's next campaign for president in 1972). As he reminded journalists during his press junket for *Rules Don't Apply*, Beatty was also with Kennedy the day before he was shot (see Newman). If this suggests on Beatty's part a wistful longing for a lost moment in US politics (a pre-Nixon moment that is also eulogized, in a different way, in *Shampoo*), this does not prevent *Rules Don't Apply* from ultimately encouraging us to move beyond the lost fragments from the past even as we sentimentalize them. At the end of the film, Beatty's Hughes, hiding away in Acapulco, is briefly brought out of his shell, sparked to life again by Marla's return—this time with her son, Matt (Evan O'Toole). Hughes, according to the historical record, had no known son; but in Beatty's fiction, Matt is the son of Hughes who will never inherit his biological father's fortune. Frank, spotting the engagement ring given to Marla by Hughes, which she has left in the room (her final gesture to the eccentric billionaire, and a sign that she is permanently leaving behind the part of her past that he represents), and looking on at Matt, finally realizes what Hughes and Marla once did, a drunken night long ago. As Mahler's Adagietto drifts into the world of *Rules Don't Apply* once more, Frank leaves the ring behind and severs his working relationship with Hughes. So too does he leave behind the idea of an inheritance of the past based on biology. In the final sequence of the film, Frank and Marla will form a makeshift, partly nonbiological formation of a family with Matt, countering Hughes's insistence on the overwhelming determinism of genetic material.

The final time Beatty appears in the film—which may prove to be his final moment on the Hollywood screen (at the time of my writing, Beatty is still alive)—is when Hughes, tape recorder nestled next to him in bed, listens quietly to Marla's effervescent words, now memories from a past he was never quite present for but which are bottled up, to be repeated again and again, as the audiotape is rewound perpetually: "Water. From Maine." Beatty, lying down, raises his right hand in the air, as if conducting the sound of Marla's voice as a conductor might Mahler's Fifth. A cut to the film's final image: Marla, Frank, and Matt in a taxi, leaving Acapulco, toward a future beyond the frame of the film and beyond anything that Beatty's Hughes, too tethered to a past both biological and sentimental, can quite conceive. *Rules Don't Apply* is as eccentric a film, and as odd in its mannerisms, as the fictional Hughes it conjures. But it is also a remarkable star text, an effort by Beatty as director and performer to sweetly and reflexively imagine a past of which he was never a part, or at least not quite like this.

Works Cited

Barlett, Donald L., and James B. Steele. *Empire: The Life, Legend, and Madness of Howard Hughes*. London: Deutsch, 1979.
Biskind, Peter. *Star: How Warren Beatty Seduced America*. London: Pocket, 2011.
Cagle, Chris. "Robert Redford and Warren Beatty: Consensus Stars for a Post-Consensus Age." *Hollywood Reborn: Movie Stars of the 1970s*. Ed. James Morrison. New Brunswick, NJ: Rutgers University Press, 2010. 39–60.
Drosnin, Michael. *Citizen Hughes*. New York: Holt, Rinehart and Winston, 1985.
Fischer, Jens Malte. *Gustav Mahler*. New Haven, CT: Yale University Press, 2014.
Hutchinson, Pamela. "*Rules Don't Apply*." *Sight and Sound* 27.4 (April 2017): 91.
Lane, Anthony. "Master of Ceremonies: The Films of Max Ophuls." *New Yorker*, July 8, 2002. https://www.newyorker.com/magazine/2002/07/08/master-of-ceremonies-4.
Lindsay, Benjamin. "Warren Beatty, *Rules Don't Apply*." *Back Stage* 58.5 (February 2, 2017): 10.
Newman, Judith. "Where Have You Been, Warren Beatty?" *AARP the Magazine* (October/November 2016). https://www.aarp.org/entertainment/movies-for-grownups/info-2016/warren-beatty-interview.html.
Sperb, Jason. *Flickers of Film: Nostalgia in the Time of Digital Cinema*. New Brunswick, NJ: Rutgers University Press, 2016.
Thomson, David. "The Lost Lord of Romaine." *Sight and Sound* 27.2 (February 2017): 44–47.
Thomson, David. *Warren Beatty and Desert Eyes: A Life and Story*. New York: Vintage, 1988.
"Tycoons: The Secret Life of Howard Hughes." *Time* 108.24 (December 13, 1976). http://content.time.com/time/subscriber/article/0,33009,918526-1,00.html.

6

The Past as a Temporal Free-Zone

The Nostalgic 1970s in Contemporary Crime Film and Television

FRAN MASON

IN CONTEMPORARY CINEMA, THE 1970s has become a popular backdrop for historical or nostalgia films in the crime genre, including a number of gangster biopics such as *American Gangster* (2007), *Kill the Irishman* (2011), *Black Mass* (2015) and *The Irishman* (2019), as well as *American Hustle* (2013), *The Nice Guys* (2016), and *Free Fire* (2016), which form the focus here alongside the retro crime television of *Fargo*, season 2 (2015). Revisiting the 1970s involves a return to a decade that Fredric Jameson characterized as already nostalgic because of a shift in the approach of historical fictions from an emphasis on historicity to the empty style of postmodernist nostalgia. In the latter mode, 1970s films such as *Chinatown* (1974), *American Graffiti* (1973), *The Conformist* (1970), and, in the early 1980s, *Body Heat* (1981) communicate "'pastness' by the glossy qualities of the image, and '1930s-ness' or '1950s-ness' by the attributes of fashion" (Jameson, "Postmodernism" 67). These films supplement the first *Star Wars* film (1977) and *Raiders of the Lost Ark* (1981), which Jameson identified in an earlier article ("Postmodernism and Consumer Society" 116–17) as part of *le mode retro* and its reconfiguration of history as style. For Jameson there is something qualitatively different in the 1970s nostalgia film's shaping of the past in contrast to prior historical fictions because, as he clarified in an interview, nostalgia films are never about the "real" past, merely textual re-presentation or simulation: "Nostalgia art gives us the image of various generations of the past as fashion-plate images that entertain no determinable ideological relationship to other moments of time: they are not the outcome of anything, nor are they the antecedents of our present; they are simply images" ("Interview" 60).

The return to a 1970s that is, in Jameson's account, already nostalgic for signs of cultural cohesion, authenticity, originality, or individuality, the loss of which are part of the wider constellation of postmodernism, prompts a consideration of what exactly the contemporary crime genre is nostalgic for in looking back to this period. Tony Judt, for example, says that the 1970s was "the most dispiriting decade of the twentieth century" because "the sharp and sustained economic downturn, together with widespread political violence encouraged the sentiment that Europe's 'good times' had gone" (477). A more global perspective provided by Duco Hellema notes the first major postwar economic recession following the 1973 energy crisis, terrorism, confrontations between left and right in nations and internationally, anti-Western assertions of power by countries newly independent after decolonization, and the social atomization of the "Me Decade" (ix–xiv). To these we can add paranoia about the activities of the state prompted by Watergate and aggressive responses to countercultural protest, increased corporatization of life, and anxieties over crime and failing cities in the United States and Europe as signs of wider social instability. However, this "dispiriting decade" is not the 1970s portrayed in the texts discussed here, despite the background of terrorism in *Free Fire*, corporate corruption in *The Nice Guys*, and political graft (and passing mention of "the oil embargo, gasoline crisis, the hijackings, the Olympics") in *American Hustle*. Nor is Jameson's postmodernist loss on show because the 1970s is portrayed as a decade of possibility and freedom.

How the texts discussed here can map the 1970s this way requires some consideration of the function of nostalgia and the present's response to and use of the past. In a discussion of the confusion of responses to the past in the postwar period, Peter Middleton and Tim Woods note that "there is a widespread sense that the past has changed, but considerable disagreement as to whether it has mutated, become foreign, dangerous, been murdered or lost all its power and become a treasury of souvenirs, a heritage park and a spectacle for the time travel of modern knowledge" (50). Multiple approaches to history are present in one of Jameson's examples, *Chinatown*, which is a nostalgia film and a revisionist investigation of the ideologies of the detective film that reflects on the present, particularly the critique of masculine individuality, and an archaeology revealing a hidden history of the corrupt power structures of Los Angeles before the war. Nor are nostalgic revisitings of the past reducible to the empty miming of signs of the past that Jameson identifies. Nostalgia can use the past to invoke a sense of loss in the present, or in a related move, as Svetlana Boym argues, it can recall the past as a form of longing to engender "an affective yearning for a community with a collective memory, a longing for continuity in a fragmented world" (xiv). Zygmunt Bauman proposes a different position in seeing nostalgia in sociological terms as a way to renew the present to move into the future in the "'back to the future' tendencies inside the emergent 'retrotopian' phase in utopia's history" (9), which recover the past by reviving discarded models of the social contract or versions of individuality.

Finally, nostalgia can have a revisionist impulse, as Vera Dika contends in her examination of "works of film and art that use past images and genres in oppositional ways" (20). These include films analyzed by Jameson to define the postmodernist retro mode (*American Graffiti* and *The Conformist*), which Dika reappraises to argue that they "do not render an experience of nostalgia as much as a direct confrontation, serving to indict the historical or societal conditions of those eras" (89). Dika's view that nostalgia indicts past social conditions, however, entails censure of a dead past that serves no purpose unless it has relevance for the present. She argues that this is the case in the films she analyzes but only in the meanings created by viewers willing to make connections between the films' historical context and the present. *American Graffiti*'s past is still dead and gone and can offer no comment on the present, except, as Dika argues, in the audience's responses. However, this locates the meanings of history and confrontations with it not in the nostalgia text but externally in its reception. Bauman's "retrotopia" goes some way to addressing this issue in his concept of the "undead past" (5), where the past can walk again in the present as a reminder of its continued efficacy. This nevertheless suggests that when the past is represented or textualized, rather than lived in the social, cultural, and everyday modes that Bauman outlines, it takes the form of zombie nostalgia by reawakening history in the text but without consciousness of its own signification. While Jameson's analysis of the 1970s retro mode accords with such a position, this is not necessarily the case with twenty-first-century renditions of the 1970s, which offer the kind of self-consciousness in their use of history that Jameson overlooks in his account of 1970s nostalgia texts because it does not comply with his view of them as empty or failed renditions of "real" history. *American Hustle*, *The Nice Guys*, *Free Fire*, and *Fargo* season 2 are less concerned with real history, however, than they are with nostalgia as a mode of historical representation that allows the text access to the past as a space for its fictionalization as a temporal-free zone.

Paul Ricoeur considers how the past is rendered by and in relation to the present when he proposes two accounts of the past, one that is "simply passed and gone, abolished" (*Time and Narrative III* 220) and another, "tradition, formally conceived of as traditionality," that mediates a still active past in the present that "signifies that the temporal distance separating us from the past is not a dead interval but a transmission that is generative of meaning" (*Time and Narrative III* 221). The first version of history can be characterized as the-past-that-is-gone, whereas "traditionality" can be thought of as the past-in-the-now (the past's continued relevance in the present). For Ricoeur, all narratives (historical and fictional) are rendered through "emplotment," a narrative organization of time that creates patterns of signification for temporality so that "the world unfolded by every narrative work is always a temporal world" (*Time and Narrative I* 3). When applied to historical fictions that render traditionality to satirize the cultural or ideological dominants of the past within a frame of revisionism that reflects on the present, such as *The Wolf of Wall Street*'s (2013) critique of the excesses of rampant capitalism or *The Nice Guys*' representation of undiluted corporate power, the past is rendered in the nostalgic evocations that circulate in the text as the-past-that-is-gone. Moreover, their reflections on the present are not primarily a product of the continued valency of the past in the present but a teleological reading by the present in reframing the past according to contemporary values and ideas. Although this might be said to be historical understanding granted by a reflection on the past by its future, it is still an imagined past, or what might be referred to as the past-that-could-have-been imagined by contemporary sensibilities. An amplified version of such a process occurs in nostalgic texts where the past functions simply as a space (rather than a time) for events to occur. This entails a synchronic freezing of pastness where there may be a diachronic flow of narrative (in the form of emplotment) but no comparable diachronic flow of history.

This is the situation in the nostalgia films discussed here, which exist both within and outside of their history because they are inside a historical space opened up by framing narrative action in the 1970s, but as textualized temporal free-zones unburdened by the demands of historical authenticity. They serve therefore as versions of Ricoeur's "abolished" past, not as the past that has irrecoverably gone but as possible forms of the past in their reimagining as fiction. Despite occurring in history as the past-that-is-gone, "emplotment" in *Free Fire* is bound within an internal narrative that occurs in a version of real time. However, there is no real time in *Free Fire* in a historical sense because history does not exist for its 1970s referents, such as the diegetic use of music, which suggests it is set in 1974; the clothes, hairstyles, and facial hair of the characters; the vehicles; and its political context. The latter emerges from comments that frame events by reference to the Troubles in Northern Ireland, such as the guns being bought by IRA members Chris (Cillian Murphy) and Frank (Michael Smiley) in an arms deal with Vernon (Sharlto Copley) and his associate, Martin (Babou Ceesay), through two intermediaries, Justine (Brie Larson) and Ord (Armie Hammer), being referred to as the "key to victory for you and the Irish." The hour-long gunfight that follows a dispute between the different groups has nothing to do with any political or historical frame, but arises out of the backstory of two of the hired henchmen when Harry (muscle for the arms dealers) shoots Stevo (muscle for the IRA members) because of an assault on his cousin the evening before. It escalates because of already existing tensions between the groups, partly from general dislike on each side and partly because Vernon has delivered different rifles than those ordered, but the emergence of a story of betrayal by Justine and Martin, who have hired outside gunmen to steal the money, deepens the antagonisms and extends the conflict.

The self-enclosed world of the disused factory where the gunfight occurs isolates the narrative events and actants from the outside world that hypothetically exists beyond the screen and from historical reality. The screen world is the only reality in the film and the dispute is entirely a matter of the film's internal narrative and spatial choreography as people are pinned down and wounded or crawl and stagger to new positions under fire, during which allegiances shift as characters begin to suspect others' motives or fight over the money. Finally, Justine is the only one left alive, but when she tries to leave, she is greeted by the sound of police sirens, which prevent her return to the world outside. Despite its reference to a major anxiety of the 1970s, terrorism and its destabilization of national and global politics, *Free Fire* is a nostalgia film outside the flow of history that represents a past that is not part of a historical continuity with the present. Its extended gunfight is separated from the present because the film portrays the IRA as part of an "abolished" past while abstracting violence involving terrorists from historical context so that it becomes simply a textual ballet of gunfire and killing. This is not the past-that-is-gone or even a past-that-could-have-been because the film's version of the 1970s is effectively a temporal free-zone where terrorism is just the motor for narrative events unrelated to the politics or history of terrorism of the time. Instead, this is a past-that-could-be, an imagined version of the past made possible through its fictionalization as a textual (rather than historical) space. Nostalgia in *Free Fire* is simply for a historical time separated from the present: nostalgia for nostalgia, which is nostalgia for the past (any past) simply because it is not the present and can be reimagined as a space of fictional possibility.

Nostalgia for nostalgia might apply to any time period, but the 1970s seems to offer rich possibilities for the past as an imagined space in postwar narratives of the United States in the texts examined here. In part this is because the 1970s is a decade without the kind of popular cultural metanarrative that attaches to, for example, the 1950s and its associations with conformism, Cold War politics, suburban living, and postwar consumer society, the countercultural "swinging sixties," or the materialistic Reaganite 1980s. According to Bruce Schulman, the 1960s and 1980s invoke in popular imagination "a whole set of political, social, and cultural associations" (xii), but the 1970s is for "most Americans an eminently forgettable decade" that produces only empty signs of "bad clothes, bad hair, and bad music" (xi). The absence of a metanarrative, except perhaps "the decade that style forgot," makes the 1970s an open field for reinterpretation in a way that the decades on either side of it are not because their popular images are more clearly fixed as decadal paradigms. It is not that the 1970s is empty of signs of itself but that there are too many signifying systems in the popular imagination for them to cohere into a dominant narrative, as Shelton Waldrep comments in surveying the cultural variety and innovation of the decade: "The unstable nature of the seventies era—its very ambiguity—provides the period with its generative and disruptive influences" (4). The only paradigm of the 1970s is paradigm shift from countercultural values and lifestyles at the beginning of the decade, through class and labor struggles in the early years, disaffection and nihilism in the mid- to late period, before the emergence of the monetarist and materialist values that became dominant in the 1980s. For Hellema, "the story of the 1970s" is therefore one of upheaval and transition in which occurred "the most radical political and ideological transformation of the post–World War II period" (12).

This means that there are multiple 1970s available for contemporary revisitings, including fictional versions of the 1970s as an "abolished" past outside of history, as in *Free Fire*, or texts that attempt to deny the flow of history itself, such as *Fargo* season 2 which hints at the future to come in Reagan's 1980s but seems to want to freeze the past (at least fictionally) before this occurs. Reagan makes occasional appearances during the series as an out-of-touch comedic figure, either on the campaign trail or in clips from invented films; although the series is aware that he will become president, it denies his representation as such. Its desire to stop history before his presidency is suggested in the first episode ("Waiting for Dutch"), which opens with a scene set sometime in the black-and-white past in which Reagan, as a Godot figure, fails to arrive on the set of a western called *Massacre at Sioux Falls*. One of the major narratives of *Fargo* season 2 is the victory of the corporatized Kansas City crime syndicate over the local Gerhardt family mob, which serves as a metonymy for the triumph of the values of the impending Reagan presidency, but the series leaves this as an absent future by focusing instead on the 1970s as a past-that-could-be, a postmodernist nostalgic textualization after historicity has been evaporated. *Fargo* season 2 is very similar to the imagined past of *Inglourious Basterds* (2009) in its creation of an alternate reality akin to the alternative realities of science fiction, albeit without a modified timeline that creates a projected or revised present. Instead, the nostalgic alternate reality of *Fargo* season 2 is a spatialized past, a landscape or country that exists as a self-contained textual reality, a time capsule of the past in which events are imagined differently to the past as it happened. While mob activity occurred in Minnesota (controlled by Isadore "Kid Cann" Blumenfeld until 1959), *Fargo*'s 1979 rural gang war in the upper Midwest between the Gerhardt family and the corporate Kansas City Mob is history reimagined as a textual fantasy of the past, a past-that-could-be in the spatial history of the text. Following the model of the Coen Brothers' film *Fargo* (1996), each episode begins with the claim: "This is a true story. The events depicted took place in Minnesota in 1979. At the request of the survivors, the names have been changed. Out of respect for the dead, the rest has been told exactly as it occurred." This self-reflexive device is supplemented by the use of split-screen and wipes that foreground technique across the series, along with the voice-over narration of episode 9 ("The Castle"), which tells the story of the fictional massacre of Sioux Falls in the style of a book called *The History of True Crime in the Mid West*. Instead of tying *Fargo* to historical reality such strategies self-consciously produce a fictionality of the 1970s where anything can happen. "1979" is merely the fictional landscape for *Fargo*'s temporal free-zone of events outside of historical reality, particularly the intensification of violence in the carnage of multiple mob gunfights in an area not associated with such and in fictional referents (a head in a box, alluding to *Se7en* [1995]) and the stylization of a match-cut montage of violence (a spoon dipped into sugar matched with a shovel digging a grave and milk swirling in a cup of coffee matched with someone being drowned in a toilet bowl) at the beginning of episode 7 ("Did You Do This? No, You Did It!").

The signs of pastness that characterize the nostalgia text are all present in *Fargo*, in the cars, clothes, and kitschy beige and magnolia decor of 1970s homes, but this is not the pastness Jameson identifies in *American Graffiti* or *Chinatown*, whose narrative events are possible to imagine according to their historical frame world, because so many of the events and characters of *Fargo* season 2 belong to a self-consciously fictional textworld. The textual reality is driven by the familiarities of crime genre codes, which form its main axis of reference, so that its variations are all imaginable in the fictional system of signification it traverses. These include the rural gang war; Mike Milligan's erudite literature-quoting gangster; a Native American mob hitman called Hanzee; Floyd Gerhardt's matriarch gang boss; the accidental couple of Ed and Peggy caught up in mob affairs by a bizarre twist of fate that sees Rye Gerhardt lodged in Peggy's windscreen to be taken off to her home as if abducted by the UFO that distracted him from noticing Peggy's car; and Peggy's transformation from frustrated beautician and wife to affectless torturer when she stabs a captive Gerhardt son, Dodd, in the chest with a kitchen knife to teach him manners (episode 8, "Loplop"). Even minor characters such as Noreen, the cheerful teenage nihilist who reads works of existentialism, and Karl Weathers, a blustering white lawyer fictionally named after black actor Carl Weathers, who pronounces himself to be "the Breakfast King of Loyala" as if this were his major life achievement, are plausible because of the origins of the series' absurdist world of crime in the work of the Coen Brothers. The latter also provide numerous intertextual moments such as references to *Miller's Crossing* (1990) when Simone Gerhardt is killed in the woods by her uncle, Hanzee's affinities with Chigurh from *No Country for Old Men* (2007) in terrifying a gas station owner and mending his injuries with peroxide and glue, and the

UFO from *The Man Who Wasn't There* (2001), which makes two appearances, one to set off the events in episode 1 as noted and then at the final shootout in Sioux Falls that wipes out the Gerhardts, but which Peggy takes in stride as part of the textual normality of *Fargo*'s temporal free-zone by telling Ed "It's just a flyin' saucer, Ed, we gotta go" as the pair make their escape.

Fargo season 2 nevertheless gestures to the 1970s as a nostalgic period when, in episode 4 ("Fear and Trembling"), Simone looks back nostalgically to the freedoms of the 1960s and Mike Milligan replies by referring to the 1970s as "a hangover." It also refers to the 1970s in America as a failed decade in the use of footage from Jimmy Carter's famous Crisis of Confidence speech of July 15, 1979, shortly after the beginning of the first episode, albeit anachronistically because the narrative events take place in March 1979. *Fargo* is also aware of what is coming in the narrative and historical future, even if this is partly presented self-consciously in the final episode in the vision of the future dreamed by Betsy, wife of Lou, the state trooper who pursues the crimes, in which she remains in the *Fargo* fictional world by seeing the future of season 1 (the husband and daughter who survive her death from cancer) while stepping outside of it by imagining a historical future of megastores (such as Costco) and pervasive technology. In the specific narrative future, Hanzee, despite demonstrating the self-sufficiency of an expert assassin, has the chronicle of his future death foretold in the final episode when he gains a new identity as Moses Tripoli, the future boss of the Fargo crime syndicate killed by the hitman Lorne Malvo in season 1. The futility of Hanzee's apparent individuality also applies to Mike Milligan who, despite overseeing the Kansas City mob's victory (indirectly), finds that his promotion is to become a corporate drone in the mob's accounting department to advance the story into a future of the death of individuality under 1980s corporatism.

Although sustaining a synchronic spatialized pastness, because it connects to its future, *Fargo* season 2 has more of a sense of historicity than *American Hustle* (2013) despite the latter's historical basis in the FBI's Abscam investigation of political corruption in the late 1970s. Set in 1978, the backdrop of the film is the economic crisis of New York in the 1970s, which led the city to the verge of bankruptcy in 1975 and whose paradigmatic moment is the collapse of law during the rioting and looting that occurred in the blackout of July 13–14, 1977. However, *American Hustle* also evokes (as an absent context) the 1970s urban dystopia film that represented New York falling apart in a variety of ways as a metonymy to outline crisis in society as a whole. In such films, New York loses the status it had achieved in the American imagination for much of the twentieth century as the locus for aspiration and individual success in becoming the city of broken dreams in the economic deprivation of *Across 110th Street* (1972), the rampant criminality of *The French Connection* (1971), the meaningless disorder of *Taxi Driver* (1976), and its futuristic vision in *The Warriors* (1979), or the general sense of the dilapidation of litter, dirt, and rundown infrastructure. The fragmented unruly city of the urban dystopia film, which Stephen Paul Miller refers to as "the rubble of the city" (84) by reference to *The French Connection*, is nowhere evident in the New York of *American Hustle* because here the city is reframed to become a stage on which to perform the play of identity by dressing up the self as a masquerade in the con game.

American Hustle ignores the crisis of 1970s New York and, indeed, the vestiges of nostalgia for the older story of New York already circulating in 1970s film in, for example, *Saturday Night Fever* (1977), which retained a semblance of the dreams of possibility represented by the city, or *Manhattan* (1979), which is more overtly nostalgic in its romanticization of the cultural history of New York in contrast to the consumerist and narcissistic present that Richard Blake identifies in the film (127–28). New York in *American Hustle* is the locus for the play of self and style derived from the cultural freedoms allowed by a city where the negligible structures and apparent lack of rules associated with the urban dystopia film are reframed to promote the city as a cultural playground rather than a precarious place or dead-end city of failure. The New York of 1978 is merely a textual place and time, a fictionalized past that serves as an imagined historical mirror of the present because of the apparent affinity between the decade's perceived propensity for the reinvention of self through fashion, style, and contemporary performance of identity. The reimagination of New York as a "historical" zone of possibility and freedom for the textual re-creation of self is properly nostalgia for nostalgia. The city is a brighter, more colorful, and cleaned-up version of 1970s New York, and the appearance of the Mafia in the film is not to reflect on 1970s urban crime because this is a very safe New York where the mob is only ever a textual threat to provide a narrative of jeopardy for Irving Rosenfeld (Christian Bale), a fictionalized version of the con artist used by the FBI in the Abscam operation, and his accomplice, Sydney Prosser (Amy Adams).

Instead, the emphasis is on the fictional con artists, Irving and Sydney, under the direction of FBI agent Richie DiMaso (Bradley Cooper), and the identities they adopt to escape their existing lives. The scams orchestrated by Irving and Sydney necessarily entail the adoption of masks, but these are more than just fake selves for the purpose of the con games because they are "lived" identities for both characters. Before their co-optation into Abscam, Sydney remakes her life in a montage of reinvented identities in which Irving is also shown to adopt a more flamboyant persona in the clothes Sydney chooses for him. Sydney transforms from stripper to English aristocrat ("to become anyone else other than who I was") by adopting the persona of Lady Edith Greensly, an identity that endows her with confidence. Irving does the same by adding masculine power and independence to his existing downbeat self, with his main anxiety being the possibility that his wife, Rosalyn (Jennifer Lawrence), will prevent the achievement of his desired identity by dragging him back to the disorganized domestic life his new self is designed to escape. Indeed, it is Irving's attempts to escape Rosalyn that provides the narrative impetus for his fashioning of a new life with Sydney. Although on the side of the law, Richie is also part of the games of identity, remaking himself in image by curling his hair and in persona by adopting the mask of a spontaneous and all-action maverick. There are also intertextual gestures to the 1970s in his *Saturday Night Fever* narrative of frustration and desire to be somebody, most obviously when he becomes a dark-suited version of Tony Manero to go dancing with Sydney in the open shirt that reveals a medallion underneath and in the invocation of the pleasure and freedom of the dance floor.

Richie's story lacks the grime and hard life of Tony Manero because his home, where he lives with his mother, is dingy in a slovenly way and primarily operates, like Irving and Rosalyn's similarly untidy house, to signify the home as an unhappy place containing unfulfilled lives, rather than as a sign of the dilapidated or impoverished city of the urban dystopia film. The frustration of the home is nevertheless the reality of everyday life to be displaced by the pursuit of new identities in the game of masquerade. Although Richie fails, because he is outscammed by Irving, the film ends not with the narrative of civic corruption that forms its *telos*, which is hurried over in a brief montage of arrests, but with the confirmation of new selves (Irving and Sydney) or escape from frustration (Rosalyn). However, the film wavers over the value of faking new selves in its constant references to the need or desire to be real. The most significant of these is at the casino party, when Sydney tells Rosalyn that the love she and Irving once felt was "beautiful and it was real," the purpose of which is to insinuate that Rosalyn's renewed love for Irving is fake and, worse, that it has disrupted the real "love" Sydney and Irving forged in making their new identities. While Sydney achieves her desire of returning to the real with Irving, the real is also destructive. Carmine Polito (Jeremy Renner), the mayor of Camden, who is presented as a man of authenticity (as a loyal friend and helper of the working class and the underprivileged), is destroyed by the return of the real when he discovers that he has been treated as a stooge to be entrapped by Irving. Nevertheless, *American Hustle* still wants to partake of a nostalgia for the real of the 1970s as a period of authenticity because this allows remaking the self to move beyond the masquerade into the authentic.

The Nice Guys, which is set in 1977 Los Angeles, is another film that uses the 1970s to outline nostalgia for the real, although it prevaricates over whether the 1970s is marked by authenticity because its concern, as a review by A. O. Scott points out, "is less historical accuracy than pop-cultural period riffing." It could easily have been set in the present because the narrative, involving two detectives looking for Amelia (whose mother is the Head of the Justice Department in Los Angeles), who has made a pornographic film with associates who are being killed off, connects with contemporary environmental issues and corporate practices when it is revealed that Amelia is an activist who used the porn film as a means to disclose details of governmental collusion with the car industry to suppress technology that will make cars cleaner. Setting the narrative in the 1970s, however, allows the film to double-code its meanings in hinting toward contemporary political relevance to incarnate revisionism, as noted above, while operating as postmodernist nostalgia. The film is perhaps best defined by its pastiche of the hard-boiled detective form, similar in style to Robert Altman's *The Long Goodbye* (1973) but in the form of an action comedy romp through generic tropes. *The Nice Guys* is not even particularly nostalgic for the 1970s version of Los Angeles it imagines as a city of smog, corporate malfeasance, and political corruption even if these are also just clue tracks to be mapped by the plot. The same might be said for the narrative world of sleaze inhabited by the two detectives, Jackson Healy (Russell Crowe) and Holland March (Ryan Gosling), which involves men preying on underage girls and the "cesspool" of "sex, more sex," which is Holland's description of his world of work.

The Nice Guys does, nevertheless, hark back to the 1970s as a time of apparent authenticity and freedom, particularly the freedom available to the male protagonists, even if they fail to use this very effectively. However, the film also doubles its nostalgic impulses in the invocation of older detective noir through its play with the convoluted hard-boiled narrative in which a seemingly simple case (the search for Amelia) reveals a Chandleresque web of connections incorporating corporate crime, political corruption, and underworld criminals. Though this might be said to be part of a longer detective narrative of corruption tracked back to the 1930s and forward to the present, it is also a sign of the 1970s itself as a period of nostalgia. This involves simple nostalgia such as the child-like pleasure of Yoo-hoo or the brief appearance of *The Waltons* on a television screen, but also incorporates Holland's lament that "the days of ladies and gentlemen are over" after a precocious young boy has asked the two detectives: "Do you want to see my dick?" The film's nostalgia for a time before its own setting applies to Jackson and Holland, who are measured against the classic hard-boiled detective. Jackson is a bruiser who is paid to beat people up, and Holland is an incompetent alcoholic who manages to slash his own wrist by accident when breaking a window. Both are hapless figures who, when they throw a body that Holland discovers over a fence, manage to land it right in the middle of a marriage party to provide the bride and groom with a perfect memory for their wedding day. They also fail according to the codes of hard-boiled detective masculinity when they duck out of their intended rescue of Amelia after witnessing John Boy, a hitman on her trail, killing the men she was due to meet, which is then brought into relief when Holly (Angourie Rice), Holland's thirteen-year old daughter, stands up to John Boy and holds him off with a gun when he appears at March's home.

Although the two detectives ultimately manage to solve the case, they fail to save Amelia, while the arraignment of her mother, who is complicit in the killing of her daughter and of collusion with the car industry, is ultimately futile because the car companies escape punishment. This hardly seems to matter and only goes to confirm Holland's description of the pointlessness of the detective's work: "You drive around like an asshole. You're going to spend half the time interviewing the fucking Chets of the world. You spend the other half trying to translate Fuckwit to English and when it's over, the only thing that's changed is that the sun went down twice." This may indeed be the point of the film's nostalgia and the reason for setting it in the 1970s rather than in the present or in another time period. The failure to administer justice to civic corruption in the 1930s of *Chinatown* involves a revisionist revisiting of the origins of the hard-boiled form to indicate that nothing has changed between past and present, while the failure to punish corporate crime in a film set in the present would more likely be either a matter of injustice or an examination of the operations of power.

The 1970s setting, however, allows a comic rendition of events in a fictional past where the protagonists can drive around like assholes, make a mess of many things, and stumble their way to a solution that makes no difference, but without this really mattering because it is only a fictional past-that-could-be instead of a version of the past that might inform either an understanding of history or the present. The nostalgic 1970s becomes an escape zone where nostalgia's usual longing for a meaning located in the past is absent. Instead, this is more like Boym's "reflective nostalgia," which is a longing for the longing for the past, not the past itself, because this version of "the past opens up a multitude of potentialities, nonteleological possibilities of historic development" (50). Like *Free Fire*, *Fargo*, and *American Hustle*, *The Nice Guys*, in its use of the nostalgic 1970s, thereby isolates how nostalgia is always about the past at a distance from its historical reality, an imagined time and space or a temporal free-zone—or perhaps, more properly, a temporal-free zone.

Works Cited

Bauman, Zygmunt. *Retrotopia*. Cambridge, MA: Polity, 2017.
Blake, Richard A. *Street Smart: The New York of Lumet, Allen, Scorsese, and Lee*. Lexington: University Press of Kentucky, 2005.
Boym, Svetlana. *The Future of Nostalgia*. New York: Basic Books, 2001.
Dika, Vera. *Recycled Culture in Contemporary Art and Film: The Uses of Nostalgia*. Cambridge: Cambridge University Press, 2003.
Hellema, Duco. *The Global 1970s: Radicalism, Reform, and Crisis*. London: Routledge, 2019.
Jameson, Fredric. "Interview with Anders Stephenson." *Jameson on Jameson: Conversations on Cultural Marxism*. Ed. Ian Buchanan. Durham, NC: Duke University Press, 2007. 44–73.
Jameson, Fredric. "Postmodernism and Consumer Society." *The Anti-Aesthetic: Essays on Postmodern Culture*. Ed. Hal Foster. Seattle: Bay Press, 1983. 111–25.
Jameson, Fredric. "Postmodernism, or the Cultural Logic of Late Capitalism." *New Left Review*, no. 146 (1984): 53–92.
Judt, Tony. *Postwar: A History of Europe since 1945*. London: Heinemann, 2005.
Middleton, Peter, and Tim Woods. *Literatures of Memory: History, Time and Space in Postwar Writing*. Manchester: Manchester University Press, 2000.
Miller, Stephen Paul. *The Seventies Now: Culture as Surveillance*. Durham, NC: Duke University Press, 1999.
Ricoeur, Paul. *Time and Narrative: Volume I*. Trans. Kathleen McLaughlin and David Pellauer. Chicago: University of Chicago Press, 1984.

Ricoeur, Paul. *Time and Narrative: Volume III*. Trans. Kathleen Blamey and David Pellauer. Chicago: University of Chicago Press, 1988.

Schulman, Bruce J. *The Seventies: The Great Shift in American Culture, Society, and Politics*. New York: Free Press, 2001.

Scott, A. O. "Review: *The Nice Guys* Pairs Gosling and Crowe as Slapstick Detectives." *New York Times*, May 19, 2016. http://www.nytimes.com/2016/05/20/movies/the-nice-guys-review-ryan-gosling-russell-crowe.html.

Waldrep, Shelton. "Introducing the Seventies." *The Seventies: The Age of Glitter in Popular Culture*. Ed. Shelton Waldrep. New York: Routledge, 2000. 1–15.

7

On the Limits of Nostalgia

Understanding the Marketplace for Remaking and Rebooting the Hollywood Musical

JUSTIN WYATT

THE FAMILIAR HOLLYWOOD PITCH of "the same, but different" resonates for much of mainstream entertainment. This adage is never truer than in the case of a remake or reboot, which instantly recall times past and the pleasures of the original movie, TV show, or other entertainment form. Traditionally, nostalgia has been invoked as a marketplace rationale for remaking, rebooting, or repurposing forms of entertainment (Neale and Hall). The audience of the original can ensure at least some revenue for the new version. In our contemporary media environment, however, this pathway is more circuitous and the financial rewards less obvious. Indeed, many 1980s nostalgia reboots have failed to connect with audiences across movie genres (think of such underperforming remakes of 1980s hits as *Arthur* [2011], *Fright Night* [2011], *Endless Love* [2014], and *Robocop* [2014]). Setting aside any consideration of critical or aesthetic value, the demise of these reboots could be viewed as evidence of an exhausted marketing strategy that has not responded to the rapidly changing marketplace for entertainment in the digital era. Their failure could also reflect a different set of commercial rules in the digital era for the financial success of the remake. The traditional understanding that a remake will capitalize on both those who knew the original film and those who are fresh to the experience has been considerably complicated in our current era. By characterizing this marketplace and, more specifically, the opportunities for transmedia storytelling in the digital age, I analyze three cases of nostalgia reframed as a marketing strategy for past music-oriented blockbusters. The lessons of these cases illustrate how under certain circumstances nostalgia can still be a potent marketing strategy for media. The key provision though for the success is activating multiple transmedia storytelling entry points; without these, nostalgia alone rarely translates into long-term success or a sustained presence in the marketplace.

Nostalgia as Appeal and Marketing Force

To understand the long-standing appeal of nostalgia as a marketing element, look no further than the *Mad Men* episode titled "The Wheel" (season 1, episode 13). In a stroke of creative genius, advertising executive Don Draper anoints Kodak's new slide wheel as a "carousel." This suggests not just the fun of the carnival but also the promise of time travel through assorted pictures of family, younger and older, across a wide span of years. While Draper's own family is tested and splintered, the imagination of an all-encompassing happiness from the slides of years past hits a nerve for the adman and, of course, for his clients too. As Brandon Nowalk suggests, Draper sees the Kodak slide projector as a "portable nostalgia generator," tapping into the notion of a simple, happy nuclear family.

In the marketing and business literature, the concept of nostalgia is well covered as an important driver for consumer interest and purchase. Defined as "a positively valenced complex feeling, emotion, or mood produced by reflection on things (objects, persons, experiences, ideas) associated with the past," nostalgia from the consumer side is seen as a primarily positive affect, although wistful and bittersweet at times (Shields and Johnson 713). In terms of cognitive psychology, nostalgia is credited with improving a negative mood, reducing feelings of loneliness, increasing prosocial behavior, and inducing an overall sense of psychological well-being (Sedikides et al. 304).

Although these conceptions of nostalgia appear to depend on connecting to one's past, David Shumway makes the useful distinction between personal nostalgia and commodified nostalgia. Personal nostalgia is indeed a longing for one's own past. Commodified nostalgia though is a construction of the culture industry, invoking certain fashions and styles of an era (Shumway 39). Commodified nostalgia opens the door to a much wider audience, in effect evoking a positive affect of the past even among those who have no memory of the period being represented (Shumway 40).

This affective appeal of film, TV, and media has been viewed through several different lenses over the years. In *High Concept: Movies and Marketing in Hollywood*, I considered the notion of presold elements, including remakes, sequels, and series films, as a key way to ensure a minimum marketing base for a new project (Wyatt 129). The points of nostalgic reference could be seen as an easy marker for potential viewers familiar with the original property or franchise. More recently, Derek Johnson and Henry Jenkins offer a more flexible and nuanced way to understand nostalgia as a key textual and marketing element for entertainment. Discussing the *Transformers* franchise, Johnson identifies nostalgia as a key aspect for the launch of the 2007 film. As Johnson notes, nostalgia is played out across a span of time rather than directly at the time of the new film's release: "The nostalgic gloss of 2007 did not emerge fully formed at the release of the *Transformers* film, but had instead cohered as a discourse over the course of the decade" (183). In that sense, the nostalgia in the online and offline articles, commentaries, and think pieces add a layer that augments the paid advertising for the new film.

In "'The Reign of the Mothership': Transmedia's Past, Present and Possible Futures," Jenkins charts the meaning of transmedia as a coordinated relationship among multiple media platforms and practices. Nostalgia informs much of his analyses. Jenkins's own insights and observations are crucial though for locating a turning point for transmedia and nostalgia. He recounts his experience talking with millennials (and thirtysomethings) about transmedia storytelling. He suggests that they see the stories "less in terms of plots than in terms of clusters of characters and world building" (244). This claim has implications for understanding nostalgia in remakes and reboots. Nostalgia in remakes and reboots had been marked by a general valorizing of the original text, with analysts accounting for the differences and variations between the original and a remake. Jenkins's work suggests a more flexible means of accounting for the impact of nostalgia, and it also returns agency to the viewer or audience member. The viewer is actively engaged with creating meaning and purpose from various iterations of the property rather than merely being the target of an industry intent on mobilizing the positive glow of nostalgia for marketing and promotional purposes.

The Limits of Nostalgia

Jenkins readily admits that transmedia storytelling is a "mode of promotion designed to intensify audience engagement" (260). He posits that this function may conflict with a producer's desire for richer content and greater creativity in the transmedia experience. The limits of transmedia storytelling are suggested by Anna Westerstahl Stenport and Garrett Traylor in "The Eradication of Memory: Film Adaptations and Algorithms of the Digital." Stenport and Traylor identify two main factors affecting the reception of remakes and reboots: accelerated transhistorical forgetfulness and database logic (74). Both are a consequence of the explosion of media—especially the increased opportunity for remakes, reboots, and new iterations—in the current digital era. Their first argument (transhistorical forgetfulness) is based on the increasing proliferation of media versions, each having a shorter half-life in the marketplace. They argue that "cultural currency and attention" is more and more fleeting; as we produce more information, we are also able to preserve more. The authors cite both "information overload" and "filter failure" as reasons for the lack of market "stickiness" in adaptations and remakes across genres (82). Drawing on Lev Manovich's theories of database logic, the authors' second hypothesis outlines the shift in spatial and associative organization in digital/database culture. Search culture depends on the particular search algorithm, the query terms, and the relevant metadata. Stenport and Traylor posit that the database search yields results that are nonhierarchical. They possess a mutability dependent on a wide variety of inputs (87).

The authors link both tendencies to the remake. The first tendency leads to the shorter shelf life of the remade film, the second to a nonhierarchical view of the remake (i.e., the search function privileges components searched for, leading to a leveling of the different versions and significantly a nonhierarchical listing of all the versions). *The Girl with the Dragon Tattoo* (2009 and 2011) is used by Stenport and Traylor to illustrate these factors, leading to key changes in narrative, character, marketing, and focus from the original to the remake only two years later. The authors stress that these influences apply far beyond just the recent example of this film. For instance, they reference how selecting the search terms "Nosferatu" and "vampire" would yield many results, but would privilege the Murnau and Herzog versions of *Nosferatu* (1922 and 1979). Searching for just the single term "vampire" would yield many largely undifferentiated options (92).

The Stenport and Traylor argument links to Jenkins's anecdotal observation on the twenty- or thirtysomething's view of the stories dependent on clusters of characters and world building. The building blocks of the intellectual property hold the key for these viewers. Valorizing an original property and searching for points of difference between the original and the remake/reboot are much less significant. Taken together, this theorizing suggests that nostalgia no longer carries the same cultural or commercial weight in our digital era. Nostalgia, by itself, is inflected as a marketing and production strategy by such factors as the length of time from original, character functions, paratexts, the creation of alternative narratives, and a host of other issues.

Adding the factor of music to these films, however, complicates the relationship between viewer and the remake in an interesting way. As David Shumway reminds us, nostalgia and music are deeply connected: "Music is the most important ingredient in the production of the affect of nostalgia or the recollection of such affective experiences in the viewer" (40). The ways music and nostalgia intersect are numerous. Philip Drake argues that nostalgic music in a film can suggest a retro cool attitude both to those who remember the original musical cues and those who merely associate the songs with an earlier time period (193). For Drake, this evocation of pastness functions as both a stylistic feature and a means of marketing the film (195). Drake cites *Jackie Brown* (1997) as a film heavily invested in 1970s nostalgia with music as a key element driving this function. In addition to setting and reinforcing the 1970s nostalgia, the songs are used to comment on the action, as "an ironic counterpoint to action onscreen" (194). Thinking about the connection between music and nostalgia more broadly, outside of film, a considerable body of literature argues that nostalgic music can aid in building both a positive sense of identity and connection with others. Specifically examining the power of lyrics from older songs to evoke emotion, Krystine Irene Batcho sees nostalgia as a positive, prosocial force; as she comments on the process of nostalgia, "Nostalgia promotes psychological well-being by countering alienation and strengthening community" (363). So, considering that the evocation of nostalgia through music is highly charged, it should be no surprise that the building blocks of the movie musical remake have traditionally been a key means to evoke nostalgia and hopefully a built-in appeal for a remake or a reboot of the property.

Three Cases: Nostalgia, Multiplication, and Transmedia Storytelling

Is nostalgia more or less irrelevant as a commercial media imperative in the current times? I want to follow these theories through three case studies from the world of nostalgic movie musicals: the reboots of *Fame* (2009), *Footloose* (2011), and the broadcast of *Grease Live!* (2016). In all three cases, many concerns about the remake hypothesized by Stenport and Traylor are realized. These issues are, in fact, tempered and sometimes reversed by the role of transmedia storytelling. Stenport and Traylor allude to transmedia storytelling through their use of the term *multiplication* ("a marketing strategy that connects institutions, and their audiences, beyond textual and national boundaries via adjacent discursive fields"; 85). Whether we call this multiplication or transmedia storytelling, I want to suggest that while nostalgia is still an active and viable marketing strategy, it requires activation via multiple entry points across media, versions, and points of audience or viewer contact to be successful.

The remakes of *Fame* and *Footloose* follow a similar trajectory. Both properties started in the early 1980s as films with simple premises, best-selling soundtracks and singles, and an afterlife in home entertainment across the decades. *Fame* morphed into a TV show (network for two years followed by first-run syndication for four years), the formation of a music group (The Kids from "Fame"), and, starting in 1988, a variety of different stage musicals. In light of the success of *American Idol*, NBC also produced a reality show of *Fame* focused on those able to sing, dance, and act. The series lasted for ten episodes only. The formal 2009 remake of the 1980 original film similarly focused on a handful of students at New York's High School of Performing Arts, following them from audition year by year through graduation. Elements from the original film are scattered in the remake: the song "Out Here on My Own,"; the subplot of a professional actor duping a student, one student almost committing suicide by jumping on the subway track, a "Hot Lunch" jam with all the students creating music and merriment in the cafeteria. There does not appear to be any internal logic to what is included, what is excluded, and what is transformed as an element. The connection between original and remake is decidedly loose. The structure and chronology are similar, but most other elements are discarded from the original. Among original cast members, only Debbie Allen, a dance teacher in the original film and now the principal, returns for the remake. Even with the similar structure, the characters are largely novel and have only a remote connection to the original *Fame*. The timid, sheltered acting student Doris Finsecker (Maureen Teefy) in the first film is echoed by another shy student, Jenny (Kay Panabaker), waiting to mature emotionally. The process and story points for these characters' development are unique, however. The similarities relate to certain types of characters only, rather than holding closely to the characters' original motivation and story line. Furthermore, in Alan Parker's original film, the characters and their ambitions were anchored solidly by the social, class, and racial divides present in the New York City of that era. The remake, though still set in New York, does not contextualize the characters in their environment in the way that Parker's original did so effectively.

Most tellingly, while the original was rated R by the Motion Picture Association of America in 1980, the remake was given merely a PG rating. The "grittier" elements of the first film (Coco's topless scene, profanity, the gay character of Montgomery) are elided in the remake. As several reviews mentioned, the new version seemed to be filtered through *High School Musical* rather than the first *Fame*. As critic Roger Ebert commented on the remake, "The new 'Fame' is a sad reflection of the new Hollywood, where material is sanitized and dumbed down for a hypothetical teen market that is way too sophisticated for it." Clearly, the new version was counting on the value of the *Fame* franchise across the decades. This failed to deliver a strong audience for the remake, which earned a domestic gross of only $22 million.

Although the building blocks of the original film are retained, albeit loosely, the new *Fame* suffers because so many of these blocks have been usurped by the culture industries. In the three decades between original and remake, American culture has embraced the talent competition genre. Reality TV competitions *American Idol, Dancing with the Stars, America's Got Talent*, and the other variants are all based on the same concept as *Fame*—the transformative power of talent for the individual and for the culture. The practice of reaching for stardom and fame has become accepted and commonplace in contemporary culture. Even in the context of a dramatic portrayal of teenagers learning their artistic craft, the new *Fame* entered the marketplace about four months after the debut of the livelier, acerbic, and more relevant TV show *Glee*. Arguably, *Glee* could be regarded as a better remake of the original *Fame*, placing the drama (and comedy) of ambition, talent, and adolescence in the new context of the show choir. The *Fame* remake simply does not capitalize on the original's elements and dramas in anything but the most superficial way. Nostalgia is missing as both a marketing and textual element in the new film.

Director Paul Verhoeven, in characterizing the remakes of his hits *Robocop* (1987) and *Total Recall* (1990), claimed that the remakes took themselves and their source material much too seriously. Verhoeven considered both originals "absurd," needing the distance provided by comedy or satire (Child). The remakes failed to give them this space. A similar issue plagued the 2011 remake of *Footloose*. The premise of the original—a teen lobbying to dance in a small Midwestern town that outlawed it—was almost ludicrous to begin with. The original transformed into a stage musical in 1998, first on Broadway and later in London's West End. The remake sticks remarkably close to the original film, even to the extent of using many of the same lines of dialogue.

The difference in the new film is the tone. This is evident even in the opening scenes. The close-up of the various dancing shoes of the original are repeated against the *Footloose* theme. With certain shots re-creating the original almost perfectly, the opening promises the fun and energy of the first film. However, in a significant structural change from the original, the remake immediately proceeds with a shot of the dancing teens being massacred in a fiery car crash. The driver turns out to be Reverend Shaw Moore's only son. This incident is never dramatized in the original film. It occurs as part of an anecdote about two-thirds through the original.

Right after this opening, we learn that Ren has moved to Bomont alone. In the original *Footloose*, Ren and his mother move to the small town of Bomont together from big-city Chicago. To add to the "feel bad" of the opening scenes, in the remake, Ren's mother has recently died of leukemia, and Ren has no other family to stay with. The light mother/son banter and support of the first film are completely missing in the new version. He arrives in Bomont to live with his aunt and uncle and their family. With no room inside the home, Ren is forced to live in the converted garage, which his uncle had been using as a makeshift office. Throughout the film, viewers are reminded of these sad plot points: a memorial to the dead teens is enacted in the school, and in several moments, Ren discusses helping support his mother in her fight against leukemia. In fact, Ren and the stern Reverend Moore bond in part over the shared loss of family members. Reverend Moore concludes the conversation with the cheery insight, "Death is on its own clock." These initial changes reflect the general shift in the remake: more graphic realism, clearer social context and social divisions, and, to echo Verhoeven, a step away from the absurd.

This tonal adjustment admittedly is a large change in the film. In so many other ways, the remake reflects the first film directly, even to the extent of repeating original lines of dialogue. The story development and arc are exactly the same in the two films. Director Craig Brewer also gestures to the first film by employing visual icons and elements: the yellow VW bug driven by Ren, Ren's narrow tie and jacket on the first day of school, Ariel's rebellious red cowboy boots, and the same costumes for Ren and Ariel for the final dance. The other substantive difference between the films is Brewer's identifying the location for Bomont in the South. This leads to a heavier emphasis on country songs, including Blake Shelton's version of the classic theme song.

The *Footloose* remake, it would seem, does not supply the needed fantasy or positive emotion to be deemed truly nostalgic. The premise (a town outlaws dancing to safeguard its youth) requires a leap of faith to begin with. In highlighting the more serious aspects of the story, the remake offers a different emotional experience from the original. The audience for the remake skewed older (60 percent over twenty-five, 46 percent over thirty-five), indicating that some might have connected with the original in theaters or at home (Finke). Still, younger audiences failed to connect with the remake. Although reviews were mostly favorable, the film underperformed at the box office, yielding revenue far below the level of the 1984 original.

So far, we have seen two 1980s musicals, supported by franchises and spin-offs through the decades, fail to make an impact as remakes. The argument for their commercial failure would seem to underscore the Stenport and Traylor argument on "trans-historical forgetfulness," the shorter half-life for entertainment remakes and reboots in our era. In addition, the argument could be made that the remakes failed to make sufficient—or strategic—use of the building blocks (characters, drama, music) from the original, leaving the remake unanchored in the commercial space. These conclusions might be valid, but the third case study—*Grease Live!*—complicates the equation considerably.

Starting as a stage musical in 1971, *Grease* has the greatest longevity of the three musical franchises. As with the others, the property lived across the decades through stage, movies (original and a sequel), and various iterations (*Grease Sing-a-Long*, the twentieth anniversary rerelease). The difference in how *Grease Live!* engages with nostalgia can be appreciated first through the casting of the live show. Strategically, the show was cast to appeal to a range of generations with stars, actors, and singers attached from different time periods. Most obviously Didi Conn, Frenchie in the original and waitress Vi in the remake, and Barry Pearl, Doody in the original and Bandstand executive Stan Weaver in the remake, connect the new version to the original film, recasting beloved stars in roles now more age appropriate. These connections are augmented by a cast whose popularity links to a range of time periods after the original. Mario Lopez, first known as a teen idol in *Saved by the Bell* in the late 1980s and early 1990s and later an entertainment news journalist, fits perfectly as loquacious Bandstand host Vince Fontaine. Ana Gasteyer, most associated with *Saturday Night Live* in the late 1990s and early 2000s, replaces Eve Arden as Principal McGee. Vanessa Hudgens, from *High School Musical*, enjoys a costarring role as Pink Lady Rizzo. Finally, singers Joe Jonas and Carly Rae Jepsen, famous since 2010, round out the cast. In this way, the "stunt casting" of pop culture figures through the decades gives an easy nostalgic entry point for the potential viewer of the live show.

Unlike the remakes of *Fame* and *Footloose*, however, the 2016 *Grease Live!* was designed to be a live "event" on Fox. With the rise of time-shifted viewing and DVR usage, traditionally two kinds of events—sports matches and awards shows—can withstand the time shifting. Viewers make a point of watching these programs live. Rather than being reborn in the motion picture theater, *Grease Live!* reimagined the show through two specific lenses: a live musical broadcast for television and as immersive theater. Following the huge audience (18 million) for NBC's live broadcast of *The Sound of Music* (2013) with Carrie Underwood, the live musical on TV appears to have been resurrected as a genre. Promotional efforts for *Grease Live!* stressed the live component above all else. As director Thomas Kail commented, "The nature of theater is that it has to be experienced live" ("Without a Net"). In effect, the show was marketed as "live theater from the comfort of your living room." Although some cast members mentioned the stress of performing live to a national TV audience, others emphasized the vitality and energy of seeing a live performance ("Without a Net").

Liveness is underscored powerfully through the show's use of space. Shot on the Warner Bros. lot with two soundstages and a substantial portion of the outdoor lot, *Grease Live!* made the viewer more aware of the live quality by having characters continually walking through space, with a moving camera capturing the action. The opening establishes the model (see figure 7.1). Perfectly re-creating the summer beach opening of the 1978 film, the TV remake finishes with Danny telling Sandy, "Just be here in the moment. All that matters is right now." The camera pulls back to reveal the set (the actors standing on a prop, the beach and waves simply green screen imagery), the logo for the show, and Jessie J singing

Figure 7.1. Danny (Aaron Tveit) and Sandy (Julianne Hough) at the beach, the opening of *Grease Live!*

the familiar theme song. She wanders through the studio, interacting with the dancers and carefully placed audience members, making connections between old and new (taking selfies with Rizzo, hugging Didi Conn, the original Frenchie). Walking outside the soundstage, Jessie J is greeted by rain, the huge audience, various cast members, and a tour of the production space. The divisions between viewer and cast, fantasy and reality, and even past and present are dissolved. The opening insists on the value of the immediate experience, even as it manufactures a double take on nostalgia (a 2016 interpretation of a 1978 film set in the late 1950s).

Even more, *Grease Live!* aims to make the production transparent. This is done through several other strategies as well. The show pivots continually on the use of space, with temporal and narrative movement coming through this strategy. Some sets, for example, miraculously open up to reveal completely different scenes: the high school hallway revealing Principal McGee's office; more dramatically, the slumber party bedroom opening up to an imaginary USO cat walk where Keke Palmer, playing Marty, serenades an audience of real servicemen by singing "Freddy, My Love." The effect is so seamless and unexpected that the production suggests an endless world of *Grease Live!* with spaces, interiors and exteriors, blending into each other to reveal character and drama. These tricks continue through the show's blocking and camera placement. For instance, the "Summer Nights" number is played by cutting between two supposedly separate spaces: Danny and the T-Birds on the bleachers and Sandy and the Pink Ladies eating lunch outside. This cutting between the separate spaces continues through the song. The ending shows Danny and Sandy in split screen, until the camera moves out a touch: the split screen is actually the two actors standing inches from each other. Space is configured as connecting the characters, creating an all-encompassing world for the show. This strategy is amplified in the finale. Starting with a carnival constructed within the gym, as the final number ("We Go Together") begins, the cast runs from the gym, jumps into trams, and careens over to the backlot. Another carnival is waiting there, but this time the rides and carnival booths are real and fully functional. An artificial setting is replaced by a real setting. The suggestion is that the world of *Grease* may seem false and artificial, but it plays out just as much in the real world as in the dramatic one.

Other strategies emphasize the live nature of the show. After going to commercials, Mario Lopez hosted several behind-the-scenes moments showing how the requirements of a live show create great demands on the actors and crew. In an unexpected marketing benefit, the work of associate director Carrie Havel calling the shot list for the "Greased Lightning" number from the control booth became a viral sensation as a YouTube clip. Online, the show's viewers praised Havel's intricate work controlling the sequence from the booth ("Grease Live Control Room Split Screen"). These additional elements help create a space in which the live experience is multiplied, with viewers implicated in the production of the show.

Grease Live!, however, adds another dimension by being staged with an audience on studio backlot and soundstages. Producer Marc Platt deliberately wanted to make the experience an immersive one; as he commented, "We started thinking, maybe the audience [is] not just for purposes of energy and comedy, but maybe the audience becomes part of the experience" (Catton). A total of 650 audience members were placed throughout the locations, from bleachers for cheerleading tryouts to the gym for a dance and so on. The producers purposefully blur the distinction between audience and cast. For example, while the bleachers are filled with people watching Sandy's cheerleading tryout, some are clearly cast members (wearing distinctly 1950s clothing) and others are not in period clothing (although this difference is minimized by having the audience extras wear Rydell red scarves, giving them just a touch of authenticity). In this way, *Grease Live!* echoes the experiments with immersive theater of recent years. In 2011, for instance, *Sleep No More*, performed by the Punchdrunk Company, offered a loose staging of Macbeth in a Chelsea warehouse with audience members wandering through the space, observing and interacting with the cast and the audience. While *Grease Live!* operates in a different register, it is worth noting that immersive theater and the televised special event both operate around deviations in space from the normal parameters of theater (Sakellaridou 28). Shared space is more important than theatrical versus audience space.

While a vast majority of television shows and events push social media hashtags, *Grease Live!* benefited significantly by making the social media request while the event was actually happening. Viewers were reminded to access behind-the-scenes footage on the show's Facebook page. In addition, viewers were asked to tweet using the hashtag #GreaseLive, resulting in more than two million tweets. By fostering social media in real time for *Grease Live!*, the team was able to marshal social media as a direct marketing force for viewer engagement.

Nostalgia and Transmedia Storytelling Revisited

Unlike the *Fame* and *Footloose* remakes, the broadcast of *Grease Live!* garnered a strong viewership (12.2 million viewers). We are left with two cases of musical remake failure and one of strong success. Some potential hypotheses on marketing, commerce, and media are worth considering. The discrepancy between these cases suggests that nostalgia plays out as a marketing strategy quite differently given context. With *Fame* and *Footloose*, the traditional route of a cinematic remake proved unappealing, whether pitched at a younger audience (*Fame*) or infused with more realism and serious purpose (*Footloose*). Reframing the original text, either closely (*Footloose*) or loosely (*Fame*), was not sufficient as a commercial approach. The franchises built throughout the decades were also unable to create a base of support for either project. Clearly, *Grease Live!* did activate nostalgia as a key marketing and textual element. To invoke Stenport and Traylor's terminology, in this case, the lesson is that transmedia storytelling can transcend transhistorical forgetfulness.

Nostalgia needs not only multiple versions across a span of years, but different entry points to be activated successfully. Transmedia storytelling is a crucial part of this approach, but there are other key components. The immersive experience, the transparency of the production, and the ability to bring the viewer into the musical through the trope of liveness all affect the building blocks of the creative property. These entry points also suggest that nostalgia may work best when made explicit, with the difference between the now (the live moment) and the past (the media property) underscored. Nostalgia needs to be laid bare, and the differences between past and present reiterated by stressing the immersive, live media experience that can now be offered to us. Nostalgia has developed far beyond the emotional buttons of Don Draper's carousel moment, but it can be just as effective as a commercial force.

Works Cited

Batcho, Krystine Irene. "Nostalgia and the Emotional Tone and Content of Song Lyrics." *American Journal of Psychology* 120.3 (Fall 2007): 361–81.

Catton, Pia. "'Grease' Is the Word for a New Kind of Live TV Audience Experience." *Wall Street Journal*, January 15, 2016. https://www.wsj.com/articles/grease-is-the-word-for-a-new-kind-of-live-tv-audience-experience-1453758439.

Child, Ben. "How Dare You Remake My Classic! When Directors Revolt." *Guardian*, September 16, 2016. https://www.theguardian.com/film/filmblog/2016/sep/16/how-dare-you-remake-my-classic-when-directors-attack.

Drake, Philip. "'Mortgaged to Music': New Retro Movies in 1990s Hollywood Cinema." *Memory and Popular Film*. Ed. Paul Grainge. Manchester: Manchester University Press, 2003. 183–201.

Ebert, Roger. "This One Ain't Gonna Live Forever." Review of *Fame* (2009). Roger ebert.com, September 23, 2009. https://www.rogerebert.com/reviews/fame-2009.

Finke, Nikki. "Hollywood Worries about Weak Box Office: 'Real Steel' #1 after 'Footloose' Stumbles; 'The Thing' #3; 'The Big Year' Comics Bomb." Deadline.com, October 15, 2011. https://deadline.com/2011/10/hollywood-worries-about-weak-box-office-footloose-reboot-1-real-steel-2-the-thing-3-big-comedy-stars-bomb-in-the-big-year-183334/.

"Grease Live Control Room Split Screen." Charbs20, YouTube, February 2, 2016. https://www.youtube.com/watch?v=DP2QOmN57iU.

Jenkins, Henry. "The Reign of the 'Mothership': Transmedia's Past, Present and Possible Futures." *Wired TV: Laboring over an Interactive Future*. Ed. Denise Mann. New Brunswick, NJ: Rutgers University Press, 2014. 244–68.

Johnson, Derek. *Media Franchising: Creative License and Collaboration in the Culture Industries*. New York: New York University Press, 2013.
Neale, Steve, and Sheldon Hall. *Epics, Spectacles and Blockbusters*. Detroit: Wayne State University Press, 2010.
Nowalk, Brandon. "The Seven Defining Pitches of Mad Men." *AV Club*, April 1, 2015. http://www.avclub.com/article/seven-defining-pitches-mad-men-216671.
Sakellaridou, Elizabeth. "'Oh My God, Audience Participation!': Some Twenty-First-Century Reflections." *Comparative Drama* 48.1/2 (Spring and Summer 2014): 13–38.
Sedikides, Constantine, Tim Wildschut, Jamie Arndt, and Clay Routledge. "Nostalgia: Past, Present, and Future." *Current Directions in Psychological Science* 17.5 (2008): 304–7.
Shields, Alison B., and Jennifer Wiggins Johnson. "What Did You Do to My Brand? The Moderating Effects of Nostalgia on Consumer Responses to Changes in a Brand." *Psychology and Marketing* 33.9 (2016): 713–28.
Shumway, David R. "Rock 'n' Roll Sound Tracks and the Production of Nostalgia." *Cinema Journal* 38.2 (Winter 1999): 36–51.
Stenport, Anna Westerstahl, and Garrett Traylor. "The Eradication of Memory: Film Adaptations and Algorithms of the Digital." *Cinema Journal* 55.1 (Fall 2015): 74–94.
"Without a Net, Performing Grease *Live!*" Feature documentary. *Grease Live!* Universal Pictures. DVD. March 2016.
Wyatt, Justin. *High Concept: Movies and Marketing in Hollywood*. Austin: University of Texas Press, 1994.

8

"I'm Going to My Friends . . . I'm Going Home"

Contingent Nostalgia in Netflix's *Stranger Things*

TRACEY MOLLET

In *Stranger Things*, season 2, episode 7, after a brief foray in Chicago, the show's young female protagonist, Eleven (Millie Bobby Brown), announces, "I'm going to my friends . . . I'm going home." Eleven's decision to return to the series's hometown of Hawkins holds a special significance in the narrative of the show, given her nomadic wanderings in seasons 1 and 2. Prior to stumbling across high-school Dungeons & Dragons nerds Mike (Finn Wolfhard), Dustin (Gaten Matarazzo), and Lucas (Caleb McLaughlin) in their quest to find their missing friend, Will (Noah Schnapp), Eleven was raised in near captivity by her "Papa," Dr. Brenner (Matthew Modine) in Hawkins National Laboratory and used as a weapon in his Cold War experiments. Eleven's "home" is in the comfort of her friends, as they offer an inclusive, safe space away from Brenner and his "bad men," and are an important part of a surrogate family who accept her as she is.

Eleven's choice of home is also important in terms of its location: 1980s suburbia. Just as this is a source of comfort for Eleven, Hawkins, Indiana, operates as the nostalgic setting for the series due to its association with the 1980s sci-fi, fantasy, and horror narratives of Steven Spielberg and Stephen King. Notably, season 2's outing in the big city received less favorable reviews than all other episodes of the show, indicative of the audience's explicit preference for *Stranger Things* to remain in the comforting backdrop of "home" (Power).

The concept of home is central to scholarly understanding of nostalgia. Derived from the word *nostos*, "to return home," and *algia*, indicative of a yearning or a longing, nostalgia literally means "homesickness" (Hofer). Today nostalgia is conceptualized more broadly, shifting from a focus on spatial dislocation to a temporal dislocation: a longing for a specific time (Higson). One of the important characteristics of nostalgia, relevant to this discussion, is its tendency to elevate the positive elements of the period under reflection (Jameson). One finds a certain comfort in the certainties of the past and escapes to them as part of the nostalgic contemplation. However, this does not and should not reduce the individual to a passive or escapist relationship with the past. Rather, as Andrew Bergman recalls, "people do not escape into something they cannot relate to" (xii). Nostalgia is a process through which one deliberates on the present situation and uses this to reconstruct the past. As Kimberly Smith reminds us, it is an "ideologically charged construct," a "lens" and not a label (510–15). Nostalgia thus allows us to forge a specific narrative out of memories, which, given the nature of postmodern life, are often dominated by popular media products. Katharina Niemeyer and Daniela Wentz suggest that there is an "indivisible connection between one's own past and the media that accompanied the past" (134) and thus, that nostalgia is often experienced through popular culture: films, music, television, and media celebrities (Davis 125).

Popular media products have recently harnessed their potential as platforms for nostalgia narratives, as seen in AMC's *Mad Men* (2007–2015) and HBO's *Boardwalk Empire* (2010–2015). More specifically, however, *Stranger Things* follows a general trend toward nostalgizing 1980s popular culture seen since about 2010. There has been a desire to recapture this decade, to "go home" to the synergistic roots of the postmodern media age. As Kevin Wetmore illuminates, "Pop culture embraced the 1980s significantly after 9/11, especially in genre film and television. . . . Since the millennium, American culture has called a 'do over' and run straight back to the 80s" (2). Films such as *Super 8* (2011), *Guardians of the Galaxy*

(2014), and *Ready Player One* (2018) all seek out cultural touchstones of the 1980s for their inspiration, while the proliferation of reboots of 1980s horror narratives such as *Friday the 13th* (2009), *It* (2017), *Nightmare: Return to Elm Street* (2018), and *Halloween* (2018) are also indicative of the lucrative nature of nostalgia (Hamilton et al.; Jameson).

Stranger Things has been enormously successful since its release onto the popular streaming platform of Netflix in summer 2016. The show has attracted critical attention for its nostalgic channeling of "the spirits of the celluloid storytellers" of the era (Mangan) and its extensive use of intertextuality, as it obsessively references visual cues from the sci-fi, horror, fantasy and coming-of-age films of the 1980s. In its postmodern awareness and "commodified aesthetic style," the show strongly evokes Paul Grainge's "nostalgia mode." Indeed, the Duffer Brothers shot the series on a RED Dragon camera and added film grain to create its 1980s look. Given the show's quick renewal for future series (season 2 was released in October 2017 and season 3 in July 2019), *Stranger Things* has become an international phenomenon, spawning comic books, video games, retro merchandise, and even theme park attractions (Sollosi). The show thus invites us to choose a number of different ways to go home to the 1980s, evidence of its inherent transmediality (Mollet, "Looking" 58).

In the text itself, when contemplating her return home, Eleven thinks of Mike and her surrogate father, Jim Hopper (David Harbour), navigating her journey home through her positive memories of friends and her adopted surrogate family. She also uses her mind to visit them in the present, entering a lonely one-way ethereal plane between dimensions where she can see and hear them but where they are (largely) unaware of her presence. The nature of this interaction only intensifies her feeling of homesickness as ultimately, her home is only accessible in her mind. In reality, she is very much alone. Eleven's contemplation is reflective of Svetlana Boym's description of the experience of home, as a knowing "that things are in their places and so are you; it is a state of mind that doesn't depend on an actual location" (251).

The show's deployment of nostalgia is centered on 1980s childhood: the home comforts that the audience (and Eleven) seek in the bonds of friendship and the feeling of belonging. However, as *Stranger Things* navigates its veneration of the past through problematic, exclusionary 1980s source texts and ideologies, it adds conditions to its narrative, transforming the nature of its nostalgia. In this chapter, I suggest that *Stranger Things* evokes a contingent nostalgia, applying liberal twenty-first-century values to its 1980s recollections. Owing to the current neoconservative sociopolitical climate, reminding viewers that the "pain of the past is not entirely resolved" (Spigel 276), *Stranger Things* "corrects" the 1980s through reflection and critique of its source texts. The ideology of its narrative thus functions as an atemporal inclusive safe space or a home for both our past and present selves.

Stranger Things: Making America Great . . . Again?

Stranger Things complicates traditional notions of nostalgia in a number of ways. First, the show is a Netflix series that accentuates the intensity of its reflection on the past. As Niemeyer and Wentz highlight, "series can never *not* evoke a feeling of nostalgia, because they are based on the imperative to always fill a void" (134). The platform releases all episodes of new seasons at the same time and many fans 'binge watch' the show's episodes (Baker; Otterson). The show's specific deployment of 1980s nostalgia is also ironic given its hyperawareness of the "Easter egg hunting tendencies of the web 2.0 audience" and the way Netflix opens the text "fully to this very activity" (Mollet, "Looking" 60; Dunleavy 149). The immersive nature of this viewing experience, providing audiences with an eight- or nine-hour "injection" of nostalgia, subsequently heightens the feeling on the narrative's close. As Justin Grandinetti has underscored, the advent of sites such as Netflix "allows audiences to transcend physical barriers and watch television 'together'" (17), creating a new virtual surrogate family environment that they choose for themselves.

This also draws attention to the centrality of context in a viewing of *Stranger Things*. Although some audience members will be old enough to remember Ronald Reagan's 1980s Star Wars initiative, landline telephones, and VCRs, the show also attracted many Millennials, growing up in the 1990s and early 2000s. Such audience members may experience what Tom Vanderbilt has called a "displaced nostalgia": nostalgia for a time not known firsthand (152–57). This in turn illuminates the importance of the present in our understanding of nostalgia and accentuates its inherent activism. Nostalgia constitutes an "active reconstruction of the past" (Wilson 25) and signals the need to "transform the present and secure a desirable future" (Kalinina 7).

The focus on the 1980s in *Stranger Things* thus forces us to draw important connections between that era and the current sociopolitical climate. In an era through which significant cultural upheavals have been experienced, nostalgia's use in the media is further problematized.

Donald Trump was elected on the basis of nostalgia, in his infamous pronouncements to "Make America Great *Again*" (emphasis mine). Many people in Britain voted to leave the European Union largely under the guise of taking back control of its borders from a perceived influx of immigrants and thus a loss of national identity. The polarization of politics on the current global landscape is reminiscent of developments in the mid-twentieth century, when totalitarian regimes rose to power largely on the back of exclusionary nostalgic sentiment. Thus, because of the sociopolitical moment of its release (and the liberal position of the film and television industry), *Stranger Things* distances its protagonists from the neoconservatism of America's past. The characters are all outcasts in some way, struggling against the hegemonic social order through appearance, race, sensitivity, loss, or social isolation. Their characterization enables us to empathize with and appreciate their difference. This explicit critique of exclusionary sentiment and glorification of the inclusivity of otherness enforces the show's distance from the discomforts of home in the present and the past. These discomforts, however, are explored in *Stranger Things* in other ways.

Production designer Chris Trujillo describes the show's dangerous Upside Down dimension as "a shadow world, [a] murky dark reflection of reality that feels infected" (quoted in McIntyre 132). Its very existence challenges the nostalgic foundations on which the show is built. Wilson even argues that nostalgia cannot be negative (27). However, the way *Stranger Things*' protagonists interact with the Upside Down can be read as a damning critique on Reagan's military-industrial complex and neoconservative ideology. From the very first precredits sequence, the Demogorgon monster (named after the boys' primary foe in their game of Dungeons & Dragons) is shown as the principal threat to the series' ensemble of tween, teen, and adult protagonists. Similarly in season 2, the Mind Flayer monster, its creation of dangerous tunnels, and packs of Demodog monsters threaten the stability of Hawkins.

While the monsters in the Upside Down are the site of the show's horror, they are "reflective of larger impersonal forces" (Weinstock 3). The Upside Down, discovered by the bad men of Reagan's industrial complex, operates as a dark reflection of the show's nostalgic home of Hawkins, threatening to "disrupt the dream world of national myth" (Goddu 10). Despite her obvious terror, Eleven is forced to visit the Upside Down and its monsters by the 'bad men.' Similarly, to attempt to cover their horrifying mistakes, Brenner and his team fake Will's death, devastating his family and friends. The dimension is both exclusionary and isolating; a place where the unbridled forces of neoconservatism and dangerous scientific exploration are allowed to roam free. The Upside Down dimension "spreads" and "kills" everything in its path, attempting to "infect" reality. By sifting back and forth between the two worlds, *Stranger Things* explores the relationship between these two versions of home: the darker side of the United States in the 1980s, with its lived realities of toxic masculinity and Reagan's military-industrial complex, and its nostalgic Spielbergian counterpart.

Stranger Things takes us back to the 1980s but employs conditions to its nostalgic project, transforming the nature of its representation of childhood. First, the show glorifies 1980s adolescence and its association with "wish fulfillment" and "freedom" (Levy in McIntyre 221; Duffer in McIntyre 22) but the 1980s 'nuclear' family is disrupted and reforged, as Eleven, the boys, and by extension the audience, are invited to find home in their twenty-first-century-inspired surrogate family. Second, *Stranger Things* references 1980s popular culture through the characterization of the kids' friendship group, The Party, but uses its audience's intense intertextual engagement to reflect and critique the problematic ideologies of these narratives. While acknowledging the traditions and values of its 1980s source texts, *Stranger Things* employs a "chronological transfer" of values, making its nostalgia more "user friendly" (Clavin and Kuryloski; Kalinina, 10). Through a specific deployment of intertextual, conditional nostalgia, *Stranger Things* situates its protagonists and audience in the same cultural space, ensuring that we feel at home in the past and in the present.

At Home with Freaks and Outcasts: *Stranger Things* and the Surrogate Family

Intrinsic to the feeling of nostalgia evoked in *Stranger Things* is the emphasis on childhood and its exploration of the family. Indeed, Ryan Twomey suggests that the series exudes warmth and a yearning for childhood (43). Although he insinuates that *Stranger Things* employs its 1980s aesthetic not to pass commentary on the decade or contemporary society, I argue that the show's implementation of nostalgia does just this. *Stranger Things* takes us back to 1980s childhood, but it does so with a critical eye on the nuclear family structure and offers its protagonists a palatable, inclusive, twenty-first-century alternative.

In 1983, the setting of the first season of *Stranger Things*, Reagan garnered significant support from the American middle classes as he raised concerns regarding the erosion of traditional family values (Butler). His social policies specifically linked femininity with the domestic sphere and masculinity with athleticism, "an unemotional disposition and aggressive tendencies" (Jeffords 34). The nuclear family was the structure through which these values would take hold, stressing the continuity between parents and their children. In *Stranger Things*, the Wheeler family embodies the nuclear family structure. They have a Reagan-Bush '84 sign in their front garden and are shown to have significantly benefited from the Reagan administration (evidenced by the commodities in their family home). However, the show does not seek to reconstruct the nuclear family; rather, it highlights its inherent flaws and gives contemporary values to its children, Mike and Nancy (Natalia Dyer). Ted and Karen Wheeler (Joe Chrest and Cara Buono) are shown to be in an unhappy marriage. Ted is the emotionally detached breadwinner, and Karen acts as the devoted housewife, making dinner every night for the family and watching over the children. Karen attempts to connect with Mike and Nancy, but is often unsuccessful and spends most of her time drinking and on the phone with friends. Her lack of emotional and sexual gratification in her marriage is evidenced when she is shown reading an erotic novel in the bath and openly flirting with teenager Billy (Dacre Montgomery).

However, both Wheeler children break away from the constraints of the nuclear family, physically and emotionally. While Ted Wheeler is stoic, patriotic, and conservative, Mike is sensitive, passionate, and rebellious. For example, in season 2, episode 2, Ted confirms his patriotism to government agents with a salute, whereas Mike defies the agents' requests for information on Eleven, prioritizing his bond with her over any loyalty to the state. He is also shown to be incredibly emotional on reuniting with her and remains understanding of her feelings of isolation, showing *Stranger Things*' endorsement of sensitivity as a masculine strength (Mollet, "Demogorgons"; Li). The show's narrative also dictates that Nancy follow a different path from her mother. This is most apparent in a scene where Nancy declares her distaste for her mother's life choices, shooting a can and uttering "Screw that!" (season 1, episode 5). While Nancy "chooses" secure jock Steve Harrington (Joe Keery) at the end of season 1, her discomfort in the predictability of the relationship is quite clear. Notably at the beginning of season 2, Steve says he is considering staying in Hawkins and not going off to college, seeking out a job, "benefits and all that other adult stuff" (episode 1), and it is after this declaration that Nancy begins to pull away from him. She seeks out an alternative, liberating twenty-first-century path for herself. She calls their facade of happiness "bullshit" when she gets drunk on Halloween (season 2, episode 2), and prioritizes emotional fulfillment over material security in her eventual romantic union with sensitive Jonathan Byers (Charlie Heaton). Mike and Nancy also physically abandon the Wheeler family home, to the extent that Ted comments that his "children don't live [there] anymore" (season 2, episode 5). The continuity between parents and children is broken, history is rewritten, and twenty-first-century conditions are added to *Stranger Things*' exploration of the 1980s family unit.

However, the show does not simply critique the nuclear family. It surveys its characters from its twenty-first-century vantage point, places value on belonging and emotional inclusivity, and offers an alternative: the surrogate family. The surrogate family is notably a simple extension of the Byers family but is made up of the boys' ensemble of friends, siblings, and adoptive parents: the 'home' the protagonists choose for themselves. This is further evidenced by the central narrative's sympathy with the Byers family, who, unlike the Wheelers, show genuine familial affection.

Although Mike cries in front of his parents after losing Eleven, they do not understand why he is so upset (season 1, episode 8), which provides a stark contrast to his impassioned breakdown with Hopper in season 2 final episode. The children's emotional connection to the surrogate family is also evidenced by the comfort Eleven derives from Joyce's (Winona Ryder) motherly affection when she seeks out Will in the Upside Down (season 1, episode 7) and the parodied 'father–son' relationship between Dustin and Steve, in which Steve advises Dustin on girls (season 2, episodes 6 and 9). While many of their individual families are deficient, the tweens and teens of *Stranger Things* find fulfillment in their family of friends and 'adoptive' parents. The show doesn't attempt to salvage the broken nuclear family but simply reconstructs the family in contemporary terms, where "family is not something bound by blood but rather is found through acceptance of the individual" (Franklin 178). *Stranger Things* thus distances itself from the traditional home of the 1980s. Much like Eleven, we are invited to find home in our twenty-first-century, inclusive surrogate family unit of friends.

Reconstructing Childhood: Transforming and Critiquing the Kids' Ensemble

From its very first scenes, *Stranger Things* immediately references the 1980s childhood ensemble films to which it pays homage. From the boys' game of Dungeons & Dragons, to the familiarity of their bike rides home and the dynamic synth music that accompanies their adventures, the show embodies the narratives of films such as *E.T. The Extra-Terrestrial* (1982), *The Goonies* (1985), and *Stand by Me* (1986). While Ryan Lizardi has argued that "a past defined by surface media texts is commodified and uncritical" (18), in its nostalgic references to these films, *Stranger Things* repairs the potential traps of its narrative through self-aware reflections on the problematic nature of many of its source texts. In doing so, it applies twenty-first-century values to its 1980s childhood, underscoring the conditional nature of its nostalgia. Michael Pickering and Emily Keightley underline that nostalgia is often conceived as "seeking to attain the unattainable, to satisfy the unsatisfiable" (920). However, in *Stranger Things*' simultaneous channeling of the familiar aesthetic and freedom of Spielberg's childhood alongside inclusionary twenty-first-century considerations of adolescence, contingent nostalgia enables the reconciliation of the two periods, creating an atemporal home for its audience.

Donald Trump was elected on the back of an exclusionary wave of nostalgia, a central component of which was the perceived contemporary assault on white hypermasculine privilege. However, none of the boys in *Stranger Things* aspire to be hypermasculinized 1980s heroes such as John Rambo and the Terminator. They are "othered" in the narrative as the target of knife-toting bullies (season 1, episode 6). They are also labeled as freaks and nerds because of their love for science, technology, and vast knowledge of 1980s popular culture. They even exhibit a hyperawareness of the otherness of that culture, shown specifically when Lucas confronts Mike's assumption of white privilege when he dresses as Venkman from *Ghostbusters* on Halloween (season 2, episode 2).

In terms of gender, the antifeminist messages inherent in the contemporary sociopolitical climate and the Harvey Weinstein scandal led to numerous high-profile women's protests and the #MeToo movement, articulating widespread disgust with toxic masculinity. This is acknowledged in the *Stranger Things* narrative, which, according to Kathleen Hudson, speaks to "a contemporary moment." The 1980s source texts from which *Stranger Things* takes its inspiration are notable in their marginalization of women. For example, there are no women in *Stand by Me*, and Andy (Kerri Green) in *The Goonies* simply functions as a love interest for Brand (Josh Brolin), and tween crush for Sean Astin's Mikey. In *Stranger Things*, the boys' homosocial friendship group is transformed significantly with the appearance of Eleven and Max (Sadie Sink). These girls function as love interests for Mike and Lucas, respectively, but I would argue that their characterizations are far more nuanced than their 1980s predecessors.

Eleven is not only the object of Mike's affection, she is also the superhero of *Stranger Things*. Her telekinetic powers allow her to save the entire ensemble from certain death on numerous occasions throughout the show (season 1, episodes 6 and 8; season 2, episodes 8 and 9). Emily McEvan has argued that the severity of her bleeding (particularly in displays of considerable strength) shows *Stranger Things*' engagement with gothic horror stereotypes of the monstrosity of female rage and anger. Gackstetter Nichols has also expressed similar concern over Eleven's gendered identity, stating that Eleven is "made" socially acceptable through various makeovers. This is particularly apparent when the boys dress her in an ultrafeminine blonde wig and pink dress so she "blends in" at school (season 1, episode 4). However, the show's pop culture–savvy audiences are invited to make comparisons with Elliott, Mike, and Gertie's transformation of E.T., and thus her appearance is an object of humor, rather than the imposition of a heteronormative gender role.

It is true that the Snow Ball sequence at the end of season 2 sees Eleven playing her part in the heterosexual fantasy of 1980s high school narratives by adorning a pretty blue dress and dancing with Mike. However, *Stranger Things* attaches conditions to their union, ensuring that viewers feel 'at home' with her narrative journey. First, Mike is shown to be deeply sensitive toward Eleven's feelings. This is made particularly evident in the Snow Ball scene where Eleven shares she does not know how to dance and he articulates that he doesn't know how to dance either (season 2, episode 9). Thus, Mike's characterization as a sensitive, emotional male underlines him as a worthy partner for Eleven. Second, the narrative shows Eleven actively seeking out Mike throughout season 2, visiting him in her mind: he is her choice of home.

Furthermore, Eleven is not simply a love interest or a "monstrous" female. I would argue the show continually insists that she is "not the monster" (season 1, episode 6) but a victim of Reagan's dangerous industrial complex. She is, however, not defined by her victimhood. She goes on a significant independent feminist journey in season 2. She seeks revenge against the male scientists who kept her prisoner throughout her childhood and who performed electroshock on her mother (season 2, episode 7). Her anger is also transformed into the source of her strength in her final confrontation with the Mind Flayer monster (season 2, episode 9). This shows a twenty-first-century acknowledgment of the inherent strength of female rage and, most important, underscores its justification. She is thus the subject of her own narrative, not simply the object of Mike's affection. This allows us to feel at ease with the wish fulfillment of the 1980s prom narrative (Bernstein) as *Stranger Things* shapes this dated scenario with the ideology of an acceptable contemporary heterosexual romance and facilitates a significant independent character arc for Eleven.

Similar concerns also shape the narrative's handling of Max Mayfield. Max's very arrival into Hawkins immediately challenges the boys' dated, 1980s assumption of appropriate gender roles. She beats Dustin's high score on the arcade game Dig Dug, forcing the boys to rethink their mantra that "girls don't play video games" (season 2, episode 1). Fascinated by such an original creature, the boys pursue Max for a number of days, but their behavior does not go unchecked. She notices the boys' attention immediately and leaves them a note, calling them "creepy" and labeling them stalkers. She also confronts their presumption that she would want to be their friend, an exchange that leaves Lucas and Dustin looking foolish but aligns Max's character with the critique of the show's modern audience. Furthermore, she challenges the boys on what she perceives to be the exclusionary gendered nature of their friendship group, thus questioning not only the homosocial tradition of childhood ensemble films from the 1980s but reshaping the nature of *Stranger Things*' nostalgia as she does so. Much like Eleven, Max is also a significant tour de force against toxic masculinity. Her stepbrother, Billy, is shown to be abusive and violent toward her, and yet at the end of season 2, she violently stands up to him, using his own words against him ("Say you understand! Say it! *Say it!*"). Max does conform to her heteronormative gender role at the close of season 2 by dancing with Lucas, but she is shown to be a tomboy throughout season 2 and does not change her appearance significantly for the Snow Ball dance. Furthermore, her stubborn confrontation of the boys throughout the narrative and her challenge of Billy allows audiences to feel at ease with her character's narrative journey.

The series critiques its 1980s source texts and their ideological expectations, thus adding modern conditions to allow for their rehearsal in the show. This contingent nostalgia allows us to feel at home with these narratives through their critique and reconstruction. *Stranger Things* uses this intertextual awareness to align the show's subaltern tween protagonists with its audience, creating an atemporal home for the fans of the show, in the past and the present.

Turning Nostalgia Upside Down?

Through its overall critique of exclusionary conservative values, *Stranger Things* distances the show's protagonists from the politics of the Reagan era (echoed in the present by those of Donald Trump). The forces of toxic masculinity and neoconservatism are associated with the show's human antagonists and the horrifying monsters the show's tweens, teens, and adults must face, notably in and around an alternative version of Hawkins, the Upside Down dimension. However, this is a place that the show's protagonists are encouraged to escape from and return to the safety of home. But as Eleven's contemplations remind us, home in *Stranger Things* is a complex construct. It is not a specific location, but somewhere she is among friends: accepted, included, and safe. Home is where the kids choose to go, not where they have to go. Gina McIntyre reflects that "*Stranger Things* [has] become a cultural touchstone that [reaches] beyond any single demographic" (149) as through the show's platform, disparate audiences of all ages relate to the show's characters, identifying with the inclusive otherness at the heart of the show's surrogate family of outcasts.

Trump's 2016 election to the US presidency reminds us that nostalgia has been used "to create negative identities through identifying the significant other" (Kalinina 9), justifying policies against marginalized groups. Yet an important part of the *Stranger Things* narrative is for the surrogate family to find a safe space away from these kinds of bad men, where they can belong. This ensemble and its inclusivity thus becomes a "trans-historical reconstruction of the lost home" (Boym xviii): an idealized version of the United States. This is nicely demonstrated by how Hopper welcomes Eleven home into the fold of the surrogate family at the end of season 2, the US flag clearly visible on his arm. This home rejects the nuclear family of Reaganism and the escalation in ultraconservatism in the Trump era and promises a better, more inclusive future for its children.

By acknowledging the pain of the past and using its media-literate audience to critique the questionable ideologies of its source texts, *Stranger Things* uses the past as a site for the critical evaluation of the present. As Janelle Wilson has highlighted, nostalgia and nostalgic texts reveal "what we value" (26), and *Stranger Things* makes its nostalgia contingent on a liberal twenty-first-century value system for its protagonists. It forms a new inclusive surrogate family home for its audience. *Stranger Things* thus underscores that although we cannot return to the past, much like Eleven, we can certainly go home to our friends.

Works Cited

Baker, Dyomi. "Terms of Excess: Binge-Viewing as Epic Viewing." *The Age of Netflix: Critical Essays on Streaming Media, Digital Delivery and Instant Access*. Ed. Cory Barker and Myc Wiatrowski. Jefferson, NC: McFarland, 2017. 31–54.

Bergman, Andrew. *We're in the Money: Depression America and Its Films*. Chicago: I. R. Dee, 1992.
Bernstein, Jonathan. *Pretty in Pink: The Golden Age of Teenage Movies*. New York: St. Martin's Griffin, 1997.
Boym, Svetlana. *The Future of Nostalgia*. New York: Basic Books, 2001.
Butler, Rose. "The Eaten-for-Breakfast Club: Teenage Nightmares in *Stranger Things*." *Uncovering Stranger Things: Essays on Eighties Nostalgia, Cynicism and Innocence in the Series*. Ed. Kevin J. Wetmore. Jefferson, NC: McFarland, 2018. 72–83.
Clavin, Keith, and Lauren J. Kuryloski. "Queering the Clock: Narrative Time and Genderfluidity in Stranger Things." *Refractory: Journal of Entertainment Media* 31 (2019). https://refractory-journal.com/queering-the-clock-narrative-time-and-genderfluidity-in-stranger-things/.
Davis, Fred. *Yearning for Yesterday: A Sociology of Nostalgia*. New York: Free Press, 1979.
Dunleavy, Tricia. *Complex Serial Drama and Multi-Platform Television*. London: Routledge. 2018.
Franklin, Anthony David. "Half Lives of the Nuclear Family: Representations of the Mid-Century American Family in *Stranger Things*." *Uncovering Stranger Things: Essays on Eighties Nostalgia, Cynicism and Innocence in the Series*. Ed. Kevin J. Wetmore. Jefferson, NC: McFarland, 2018. 174–82.
Gackstetter Nichols, Elizabeth. "Weirdo Barbie and Punk-Rock Daddy's Girl: Ambiguity, Gendered Identity and Appearance of Eleven in *Stranger Things*." *Refractory: Journal of Entertainment Media* 31 (2019). https://refractory-journal.com/vol-31-2019/.
Goddu, Teresa A. *Gothic America: Narrative, History and Nation*. New York: Columbia University Press. 1997.
Grainge, Paul. *Monochrome Memories: Nostalgia and Style in Retro America*. Santa Barbara, CA: Praeger, 2002.
Grandinetti, Justin. "From Prime-Time to Anytime: Streaming Video, Temporality and the Future of Communal Television." *The Age of Netflix: Critical Essays on Streaming Media, Digital Delivery and Instant Access*. Ed. Cory Barker and Myc Wiatrowski. Jefferson, NC: McFarland, 2017. 11–30.
Hamilton, Kathy, Sarah Edwards, Faye Hammill, Beverly Wagner, and Juliette Wilson. "Nostalgia in the Twenty-First Century." *Consumption Markets and Culture* 17.2 (2013): 101–4.
Higson, Andrew. "Nostalgia Is Not What It Used to Be: Heritage Films, Nostalgia Websites and Contemporary Consumers." *Consumption Markets and Culture* 17.2 (2013): 120–42.
Hofer, Johannes. "Dissertation medica de nostalgia." University of Switzerland, 1688. Trans. Carolyn Kiser Anspach. *Bulletin of the History of Medicine* no. 2 (1934).
Hudson, Kathleen. "'Something from Your Life, Something that Angers You . . .': Female Rage and Redemption in Netflix's *Stranger Things* (2016–2017)."

Refractory: Journal of Entertainment Media 31 (2019). https://refractory-journal.com/something-from-your-life-something-that-angers-you-female-rage-and-redemption-in-netflixs-stranger-things-2016-2017/.

Jameson, Frederic. *Postmodernism, or, The Cultural Logic of Late Capitalism*. London: Verso, 1993.

Jeffords, Susan. *Hard Bodies: Hollywood Masculinity in the Reagan Era*. New Brunswick, NJ: Rutgers University Press, 1994.

Kalinina, Ekatarina. "What Do We Talk about When We Talk about Media and Nostalgia?" *Medien und Zeit* 31.4 (2016): 6–15.

Li, Amy S. "Reconstructing the '80s Man: Nostalgic Masculinities in Stranger Things." *Refractory: Journal of Entertainment Media* 31 (2019). https://refractory-journal.com/reconstructing-the-80s-man-nostalgic-masculinities-in-stranger-things/.

Lizardi, Ryan. *Mediated Nostalgia: Individual Memory and Contemporary Mass Media*. Lanham, MD: Lexington Books. 2015.

Mangan, Lucy. "Stranger Things Review: A Shot of '80s Nostalgia Right to Your Heart." *Guardian*, July 15, 2016. https://www.theguardian.com/tv-and-radio/2016/jul/15/stranger-things-review-a-shot-of-80s-nostalgia-right-to-your-heart-winona-ryder/.

McEvan, Emily. "The Monstrous Sacred: The Intrusion of Otherness into Stranger Things." *Refractory: Journal of Entertainment Media* 31 (2019). https://refractory-journal.com/the-monstrous-sacred-the-intrusion-of-otherness-into-stranger-things/.

McIntyre, Gina. *Stranger Things: Worlds Turned Upside Down*. London: Century, 2018.

Mollet, Tracey. "Demogorgons, Death Stars and Difference: Masculinity and Geek Culture in *Stranger Things*." *Refractory: Journal of Entertainment Media* 31 (2019). https://refractory-journal.com/demogorgons-death-stars-and-difference-masculinity-and-geek-culture-in-stranger-things/.

Mollet, Tracey. "Looking through the Upside Down: Hyper-Postmodernism and Trans-Mediality in the Duffer Brothers' *Stranger Things*." *Journal of Popular Television* 7.1 (2019): 57–77.

Niemeyer, Katharina, and Daniela Wentz. "'Nostalgia Is Not What It Used to Be': Serial Nostalgia and Nostalgia Television Series." *Media and Nostalgia: Yearning for the Past, Present and Future*. Ed. Katharina Niemeyer. Basingstoke: Palgrave Macmillan, 2014. 129–38.

Otterson, Joe. "Stranger Things Season 2 Premiere Draws More Than 15 Million Viewers in 3 Days." *Variety*, November 2, 2017. https://variety.com/2017/tv/news/stranger-things-season-2-ratings-nielsen-1202605585/.

Pickering, Michael, and Emily Keightley. "The Modalities of Nostalgia." *Current Sociology* 54.6 (2006): 919–41.

Power, Ed. "Stranger Things Season 2, Episode 7: The Lost Sister, Recap: The Worst Episode Ever?" *Telegraph*, October 29, 2019. https://www.

telegraph.co.uk/on-demand/0/stranger-things-season-2-episode-7-lost-sister-recap-worst-episode/.

Smith, Kimberly K. "Mere Nostalgia: Notes on a Progressive Paratheory." *Rhetoric and Public Affairs* 3.4 (2000): 505–27.

Sollosi, Mary. "First Look: *Stranger Things* at Universal Studios Halloween Horror Nights." *Entertainment Weekly*, September 5, 2018. https://ew.com/tv/2018/09/05/stranger-things-universal-studios-halloween-horror-nights-first-look/.

Spigel, L. "Postfeminist Nostalgia for a Prefeminist Future." *Scree* 54.2 (2013): 270–78.

Twomey, Ryan. "Competing Nostalgia and Popular Culture: *Mad Men* and *Stranger Things*." *Uncovering Stranger Things: Essays on Eighties Nostalgia, Cynicism and Innocence in the Series*. Ed. Kevin J. Wetmore. Jefferson, NC: McFarland, 2018. 39–48.

Vanderbilt, Tom. "The Nostalgia Gap." *Baffler* 5 (1993): 152–57.

Weinstock, Jeffrey. "Introduction." *The Cambridge Companion to the American Gothic*. Ed. Jeffrey Andrew Weinstock. Cambridge: Cambridge University Press, 2017. 1–12.

Wetmore, Kevin J. "Introduction: Stranger Things in a Strange Land or, I Love the '80s?" *Uncovering Stranger Things: Essays on Eighties Nostalgia, Cynicism and Innocence in the Series*. Ed. Kevin J. Wetmore. Jefferson, NC: McFarland, 2018. 1–7.

Wilson, Janelle L. *Nostalgia: Sanctuary of Meaning*. Lewisburg, PA: Bucknell University Press, 2005.

Part 3

The Politics of the Past

9

A Confrontation with History

Re-Viewing the Horror Film Sources of *Get Out*

VERA DIKA

> The idea of *Get Out* being a horror film is crazy because the only thing scary about it is that it is the truth.
>
> —Kishawn Jack, student, New Jersey City University

THE EPIGRAPH IS FROM Kishawn Jack, an African American media arts student at New Jersey City University. I offer it here because of the clarity and conviction of Kishawn's statement, and because Kishawn posits a tension between a fiction film and an experiential truth of race relations. In this chapter, I argue that *Get Out* employs fiction, in this case horror film conventions, for the purpose of foregrounding social realities.

Jordan Peele, the writer and director of *Get Out*, has often claimed that his intention was to make a film that both black and white audiences could appreciate but perhaps experience differently. I draw from Kishawn's initial reactions to *Get Out* and from my experience as a white woman academic to explore potential areas of dialogue between the two. This method will begin an inquiry into the film, addressing the social and cultural material it presents, as well as analyzing how *Get Out* renders critical historical points in textual and cinematic terms. My purpose is to show that *Get Out* uses elements from myriad earlier horror films and other social and cultural sources to interrogate the past and, in doing so, comment on the present.

But first I must say a few words about the word *nostalgia*. I have always found the term to be rather problematic. In my 2003 book, *Recycled Culture in Contemporary Art and Film: The Uses of Nostalgia*, I take Fredric Jameson's position that the "nostalgia" that appears in cultural productions since the early 1970s is not the same as an earlier longing to return to a lost plenitude. Rather, it is a recycling of past cultural artifacts. The "nostalgia film" returns, not necessarily to take us to a lost past, but to a past movie (Carroll). It creates a shifting superimposition of past and present film references and their historical implications. In the clash that results, the past is used to speak the present. Of course, some texts are more critical than others. I argue that Peele's film *Get Out* makes a distinctive use of past horror film references, in combination with references to African American social experience, for the purpose of confronting history.

Cultural Readings: Differing Perspectives

In November 2018, Kishawn Jack gave a class presentation on *Get Out* and the horror film and what he saw as today's reality. He began by citing the dates of the slavery of black people in America as spanning from 1619 to the present. Claiming that *Get Out* was an allegory on slavery, Jack offered his personal responses. For example, he commented that the ghetto photographs displayed in the apartment belonging to Chris (Daniel Kaluuya), the film's main black character, looked like "he was into poverty," while the posh apartment itself "doesn't look like my apartment." (Kishawn lives in Jersey City, New Jersey). Going on to discuss the scene in which Chris is interrogated by the police officer, Kishawn remarked, "When I am stopped by a cop, either I am going to get a ticket, or I am going to die." And when Kishawn saw Chris and his white girlfriend, Rose (Allison Williams), drive up to her country home, complete with black gardener and black maid, he knew immediately that the film was about slavery. "The image looks the same as slavery. The jobs the black characters are performing are the same as slaves. The pay scale and the job titles may have changed, but the jobs are the same."

I will provide a few more of Kishawn's comments because they are useful to the larger discussion, especially the way *Get Out* openly references earlier cinematic works and outside historical sources. The question of extratextual referencing is pivotal to the discussion. For example, Kishawn saw a similarity between Rose's white family and the dysfunctional and dangerous families of past horror films, such as in *Texas Chainsaw Massacre* (1974) and *Psycho* (1960). He also noted that Chris "picks cotton" from the chair (referring to the work in cotton fields that slaves were forced to do) and then stuffs this into his ears so he won't hear the sounds of the tinkling of the tea cup by which he is being hypnotized. Kishawn painfully observed that the tinkling of the silver spoon in the china cup is at once a symbol for wealth and privilege, and the means by which slaves were historically summoned by their masters. He then related the events to today: "In a world run by white people, it is becoming extremely hard for blacks to survive."

These harsh but true words referring to our past and the present society are tragic to hear spoken by a twenty-two-year-old black man in America today. My own initial viewing of *Get Out* was distanced by comparison and centered more on the cinematic properties of the film, especially my responses to the opening sequences. I present a selection of my reactions to support my later description of how horror conventions are manipulated to reveal a social truth and create experience in the viewer.

The allusions to slavery certainly became clear to me as *Get Out* progressed, but in the early scenes, I took an attitude of assumed knowingness based on my personal academic history. In 1986 I had completed my doctoral dissertation, titled "Games of Terror: *Halloween, Friday the 13th*, and the Films of the Stalker Cycle," and in 1991, the manuscript was published as a book. Over the years, I have published essays on the horror film, taught university courses on the genre, and seen many of the remakes, sequels, and prequels so characteristic of the form. Not surprisingly, I have a set of assumptions I bring to new works, and my first viewing of *Get Out* was no exception. I was very sensitive to the cinematic references the film offered. I found myself thinking things like, "Oh, I get it, this is going to be a Stalker film knock-off with a black male protagonist." Or, "OK, I recognize the *Halloween*-style references in the suburban neighborhood opening sequence—it's been done before."

And when we came to Rose's country house, "It's an 'old dark house' movie, like James Whale's classic in 1932, and like so many others to follow, complete with a crazy family." Here, I, like Kishawn, thought of *Texas Chainsaw Massacre* and *Psycho*, but my associations also drifted to such films as *Rocky Horror Picture Show* (1975), and even *Guess Who's Coming to Dinner* (1967).

Then I started to feel a little uncomfortable first in the sequence with Chris and Rose in Chris's apartment. I conveniently had a genre category for this, too. I attributed my sense of disturbance to what I saw as bad acting, as well as bad writing, and the low-budget horror film tendency toward bad casting. So many horror films could be described in these ways. For me, Chris and Rose didn't seem right together. There was something fake about the situation. Compared with other leading interracial couples in the movies, Chris seemed too black, too real, to Rose's too brittle, almost anorexic whiteness. What's more, Allison Williams's acting as Rose was so obviously acting. All of her lines were delivered in the same high-pitched tone and improbable accent. Throughout the sequence, I thought I had control over the image, that I was safely on the outside, at a comfortable distance.

As I continued to watch, however, I slowly realized that within the fiction, Rose *is* acting, and there is no love between these two people, at least not on Rose's part. Rose is a fake. Yet as I subsequently learned while sitting in a Manhattan restaurant, the accent Williams used in her role as Rose is indeed quite accurate. The hollow tone coming from high in the nasal passages and clipped condescending speech are often heard in New York City these days, and Williams delivers a spot-on caricature of privileged New York whiteness. I understood that, yes, Williams's performance is dead at its emotional core, and yes, it is a fault of the acting, only now the acting is part of Rose's character. Rose is putting on an act to seduce her victim.

Any type of agency or control I initially thought I had over the image in *Get Out* was further destabilized as the film progressed and then came to a terrifying halt during the hypnosis sequence. I must say that I am not always subject to this type of horror effect, perhaps because of the analytical position I take toward the cinematic material. But in *Get Out*, like so many other members of the audience, I became frightened by being taken down into the Sunken Place, the place downward into the center of the image, with no way out (see figure 9.1).

The film's brilliant hypnosis sequence has been much lauded in the press and evidenced in viewers' online comments. My question now is,

Figure 9.1. Chris (Daniel Kaluuya) falls into the Sunken Place: *Get Out* (Jordan Peele, 2017). Digital frame enlargement.

how was this effect cinematically constructed in *Get Out*, and how was it, along with the additional strategies of the film, especially the intense referencing of past film sources, used to produce such a potent metaphor for past and current racial conditions in America?

The Game of References: Theoretical Models

The use of extratextual references in film has been widely theorized in postmodern culture, initially by Noel Carroll in "The Future of Allusion: Hollywood in the Seventies (and Beyond)" and by Fredric Jameson in "Postmodernism and Consumer Society." Carroll, for example, saw the tendency to quote earlier films or to employ allusion to be a distinctive feature of a significant number of 1970s Hollywood films. Film historical knowledge understandably varied among audience members, so Carroll noted a two-tiered structure, one separating those who were in-the-know regarding cinematic sources from the more naïve viewers (56). Carroll claimed that the latter understood the film at a surface level, while the savvier members could appreciate the allusion as a "wink" from the director. Jameson took a broader view of the phenomenon. He claimed that the tendency to use earlier material in new work, a method he called pastiche, or blank parody, was not limited to film but evident in a wide range of cultural productions and was even a distinguishing characteristic of postmodernism itself. I claim that *Get Out* encourages a play of references, not as pastiche or nostalgia but as a strategy that opposes the past to the present, and so fosters a dialogue. Moreover, it does so with an audience whose ability to be "in the know" regarding past cinematic sources has only increased over the years.

What becomes apparent about the contemporary popular reception of *Get Out* is that in some ways it is a kind of "game," a call and response similar to what I had originally cited in *Games of Terror*. It is well known that the Stalker Films in the late 1970s and early 1980s often elicited energetic shouts from the audience, warning the characters of oncoming assaults, for example, based on the audience's knowledge of past horror conventions. The gaming feature first noted in the 1970s is evidenced in *Get Out*, only now the popular response is voiced on the internet, blogs, and social media, further fueling the referencing process but also engaging different forms of dialogue and meaning.

A considerable number of internet sites, for example, offer lists of the films seen as being referenced by *Get Out*. Often mentioned are the works we have already cited, as well as *Rosemary's Baby* (1968), *The Stepford Wives* (1975), and *The Shining* (1980). Most interestingly, there is also a YouTube video with Peele himself, titled "*Get Out* Reddit Fan Theories." Peele appears in the video and addresses popular responses to his film. In an affable and nonchalant manner, he reads references and meanings offered by viewers, noting the ones he had intended, the ones he had not intended, and the ones that are not acceptable. Peele's comments are a testament to the intensity and speed of the referential process, as well as the ability of the author to talk back to his viewers, engaging the cultural, social, and racial themes of this film. Peele even says, "I honestly never thought people would pick up on this stuff so fast."

As a point of entry, we can consider the history of the horror film, one long theorized as using variations on horror conventions to dredge to the surface "all that a society attempts to suppress or oppress," as Robin Wood describes it. Wood writes: "Central to the effect and fascination of horror films is the fulfillment of our nightmare wishes to smash the norms that oppress us and which our moral conditioning teaches us to revere" (72). But how does the high-pitched referencing of past films in *Get Out* result in this critical effect? According to postmodern theory, the opposite would seem to be the case. In his discussion of postmodernism, Jameson originally posited that the insistent use of pastiche in contemporary culture actually displaces real history. According to Jameson, the return of older cultural productions in new works closes us to the past, offering only aesthetic styles on a depthless surface. I argue, on the other hand, that *Get Out* puts us in a kind of dialogue with history because of our changed present social and cultural relationship to past material.

For a renewed perspective, I again turn to the comment of one of my students, Jabriea Montague, in 2018. On her first viewing of Alfred Hitchcock's iconic film *Psycho*, Jabriea commented that she found the 1960 film to be "cliché." From her historical perspective, especially because of the myriad *Psycho*-inspired Stalker Films from the 1970s to the present that she has seen in her young life, the original film now appears already seen and, more, as referencing the present. At first glance, Jabriea's comment supports Jameson's claim of a loss of a sense of history. But in Peele's film, the look back is more critical, creating a kind of deferred action, an "afterwardsness" (Breuer and Freud; Freud), resulting in a belated understanding of the past. If we now look back from the perspective of *Get Out*, especially because of the oppositions created by Peele's film, we can reassess the past cultural products it references as well as engaging African American history.

I first address how *Get Out* affects *Guess Who's Coming to Dinner*, for example, allowing us to reexamine the power relations that were always there but now experienced differently. *Get Out* reconfigures past horror film conventions retroactively to expose suppressed meanings and feelings in both past and present films. In addition to *Guess Who's Coming to Dinner*, I discuss *Eyes Without a Face* (1960), *Psycho*, and *Ringu* (1998), noting how standard horror motifs such as the old dark house, the loss of identity, and the film image as a screen, can be reexplored in racial terms. To give some examples, *Guess Who's Coming to Dinner*, a romantic drama rather than a horror film, is retroactively revealed in its racial "monstrosity"; the loss of identity, a mainstay of mad doctor/scientist movies, is reexplored as African American historical trauma through re-viewing *Eyes Without a Face*; and the look of the camera, as a mask that conceals as well as reveals in *Psycho* and *Ringu*, is reactivated in *Get Out*, allowing audiences to experience a sense of entrapment, viscerally, psychologically, and historically.

Re-viewing Horror Film Motifs: The Old Dark House and the White Patriarchal Family

> For filmmakers as well as for audiences, full awareness stops at the level of the plot, action, and character, in which the most dangerous and subversive implications can disguise themselves and escape detection.
>
> —Wood (70)

One of the most prominent early motifs in the horror film is that of the old dark house, a residence often located in a rural environment, accompanied by a story about young people who travel into the night and by chance stop for shelter. Here they meet the inmates of the dwelling and find the people there not as welcoming or benign as one might expect. The plot can be seen in the 1932 film *The Old Dark House* by James Whale cited earlier. The group of young people in Whale's film encounter the elderly, infirm, and insane inhabitants of the house who threaten them and against which the health and fecundity of the younger characters is juxtaposed. Any hope of a homey environment, of the *heimlich* as Freud has noted, becomes its opposite: threatening, un-homey, or *unheimlich*, causing feelings of dread or the uncanny. The dangerous inhabitants in variations of the old dark house can be seen in many films—in *Dracula* (1931), for example, in *Rocky Horror Picture Show*, *Psycho*, *Texas Chainsaw Massacre*, and in *Get Out*. And also, as I will argue, in *Guess Who's Coming to Dinner*.

But there are differences. The binaries between guests and inhabitants carry differing meanings in these films. The meanings include alive/dead in *Dracula*, conventional/unconventional in *Rocky Horror Picture Show*, and sane/insane in *Psycho* and *Texas Chainsaw Massacre*. In all of these, the first term of the binary embodies the more naïve characters, that is, those who enter into the second term—the unsafe space. Alternately, in *Get Out* and *Guess Who's Coming to Dinner*, the binary is created by the racial confrontation of black/white and so creates an important social connotation. In these films, the black man is in the more vulnerable first term and enters the second term—the dangerous space of the white man. Whiteness is the monster.

There are also other important differences in the structure of these films. Although *Get Out* is generally accepted as a horror film, and *Guess Who's Coming to Dinner* as a romantic drama, they share plot elements that feature the initial meeting of the socially mismatched in-laws of a young couple in love. Examples of such films are *The In-Laws* (1979), *The Birdcage* (1996), and *Meet the Fockers* (2004). But there are differences here, too. In all of the above, we have white family dramas where the primary conflict is between the two sets of mismatched in-laws. In *Guess Who's Coming to Dinner* and *Get Out*, on the other hand, the primary conflict is between the black man and his white girlfriend's parents. And while in *Guess Who's Coming to Dinner*, the arrival of the black man into the home initially seems to threaten the existence of the white family and its white privilege, quite the opposite is true. In both *Guess Who's Coming to Dinner* and *Get Out*, the black man is taken to the house, "captured" in a sense, lured by a white woman. There is a threat to the male character here, one not present in the other mismatched in-laws films. In *Get Out*, the reference to the violent abduction of black people for slavery and subjugation is closer to its representational surface. In *Guess Who's Coming to Dinner*, this meaning is insistently suppressed, for the fiction of *Guess Who's Coming to Dinner* is that the film is a love story.

Guess Who's Coming to Dinner

> Otherness represents that which bourgeois ideology cannot recognize or accept but must deal with in one of two ways: either by rejecting it, and if possible, annihilating it, or by rendering it safe and assimilating it.
>
> —Wood (66)

Stanley Kramer's *Guess Who's Coming to Dinner* begins with the contradictions we have been discussing. The film opens with a wide shot, a vibrant color image of an international flight coming into San Francisco airport, accompanied by the lyrics to an upbeat 1960s love song, "The Glory of Love." At the outset, the film attempts to position itself in a long tradition of such works as *Romeo and Juliet*, stories about two young people who love each other above and beyond the disputes of their quarreling families. The ultimate goal in *Guess Who's Coming to Dinner* is to progressively reduce the racial conflict in the courtship and marriage plot it presents. By appropriating plot elements taken from *Guess Who's Coming to Dinner*, *Get Out* allows us to look back from our current historical perspective and reconsider the earlier film, revealing how much of the racism it claims to counter is actually embedded within it. The manifest content of *Guess Who's Coming to Dinner* does not openly engage in a discussion of slavery, but the latent content, especially its formal and structural properties, reveals a continuation of the ethos of slavery and subjugation on a Hollywood and societal level. As we shall see, *Get Out* offers a present-day challenge to this ongoing cultural conflict.

Guess Who's Coming to Dinner begins with a cab ride in which the young couple's kiss is seen in the rearview mirror. As the first interracial kiss in film history, John Prentice, played by Sidney Poitier, is presented as already compromised. After the kiss, Prentice, not once but repeatedly rubs the kiss off his mouth with a handkerchief, perhaps meant to indicate his sense of disturbance, while the girl, Joanna, played by Katharine Houghton (Katharine Hepburn's niece) does not have to adjust herself. The threatened first term in the binary black/white is established, as is the privilege inherent in the social position of whiteness in the second. This will be built on in the remainder of the film, in narrative terms, as well as in the formal and spatial structure of the film.

The couple continue their journey to Joanna's home to meet her parents and finally arrive at a palatial white town home that recalls both a plantation mansion and the White House. Here, too, as in *Get Out*, we are soon introduced to the black maid, Tillie. Tillie will be the voice of strident racial objections in the film, publicly opposing the presence of a black man as a guest in the house and the proposed marriage. As the young couple enter the central room of the home, Joanna encourages Prentice to marvel at the sumptuous upper-class environment, with the subtext being that he has not lived in places like this before. Prentice stands in the living room, viewing the overstuffed furniture and overabundance of high-priced art on the wall, and then makes a gesture as if to see around corners into the other rooms.

Prentice seems to be impressed, but we and the camera rarely see what he sees in his exploration of the room; moreover, we do not explore the three-dimensionality of the house or its grounds. Instead, we are confined to the invisible editing style of the Classical Hollywood narrative, one that here defines only a few constructed sets, each made to resemble the rooms of a house. Even when Prentice is repeatedly invited to come out to the terrace to enjoy the view of San Francisco Bay, this is obviously a set, and the view is a painted backdrop. The important result of this mise-en-scène and editing structure is that it creates a flat, two-dimensional visual field, one strongly coded as a Hollywood film and one that emphasizes a style of filmmaking from a past Studio Era. As the film progresses, the power of white male society embodied in this Hollywood system further encases the visual field, figuratively and literally, as well as the black male within it.

When Joanna's parents arrive at the home, for example, the Studio Era effect is accentuated, because her parents are played by none other than Spencer Tracy and Katharine Hepburn. Now all bets are off. Any hope that Sidney Poitier is the star of this film, or even the central character, is overwhelmed by the sheer super-power of this legendary Hollywood couple. For it must be noted that by 1967, the history of Tracy and Hepburn in American film was already legendary, and the two stars were remembered as the dynamic couple in such films as *State of the Union* (1948) and *Adam's Rib* (1949), as was Tracy's position as the patriarchal father to a young Elizabeth Taylor in *Father of the Bride* (1950). Moreover, the real-life passionate love affair between Tracy and Hepburn was known, and very importantly, was reaching its end in 1967. Tracy's illness during the filming of *Guess Who's Coming to Dinner* was publicized, as was his eventual death seventeen days after the shooting of the film was complete.

On the other hand, much was also made in the press regarding the unbelievability of Sidney Poitier's character of John Prentice in *Guess Who's Coming to Dinner*. Many commentators found Prentice to be too contrived a representation of a black man. Observers in the black and white communities questioned why Prentice had to be rendered, not only as a thirty-seven-year-old renowned medical doctor but also a Yale University professor, a widely published author, and an assistant director at the World Health Organization, to make its point in this film about interracial marriage. And although some bitterly criticized Poitier for having taken such a role (see Mason), little is written about the top-heavy pairing of Poitier with the two Hollywood legends, ones that throughout the film occupy a position of white dominance, not to mention most of the screen time. In *Guess Who's Coming to Dinner*, John Prentice has come to Matt and Christina Drayton's home to ask for Matt's blessing to marry his daughter. Prentice consistently defers to Matt as the white patriarch worthy of utmost respect, and in the process, he displays an uncomfortable level of anger and verbal abuse against his own father, Mr. Prentice (who tellingly is not given a first name in the film or in the credits), for voicing similar concerns against the marriage. Clearly, it is only the position of the white power that matters.

In *Guess Who's Coming to Dinner*, the young couple go for the love, but like any fairy tale, this leaves many questions unanswered. First to note is that after their marriage, John and Joanna will live in Africa, where Prentice does most of his work. By not allowing the interracial couple and their offspring to stay in America, the limitations society will impose on them are not only revealed but also upheld by the film. *Get Out*, on the other hand, as we shall see, challenges the treachery of reigning social structures of subjugation, confinement, and rejection and the white threat to the black community based on these strictures.

The tension between *Guess Who's Coming to Dinner* and *Get Out* causes a ricochet effect. By this I mean it allows meanings to bounce off each other, revealing what had been submerged in the earlier film while foregrounding each film's cinematic strategies. In *Guess Who's Coming to Dinner* the social order cannot accept otherness and so rejects it by literally ejecting it, reestablishing white male power. When comparing *Guess Who's Coming to Dinner* with *Get Out*, we can see the latter's attempt to subvert white male power by telling a different story about family relations and in a different way. *Get Out* ends with a free black man who fights and defeats the villains—a black man who is still at large, and so, a lingering threat to white male supremacy.

To Lose the Self

The narrative surface of *Get Out* is highly referential, encouraging associative readings generated by material such as types of locations, lines of dialogue, characters, and music, while the deeper structures offer supporting insights. I will give examples of the surface referencing from the beginning of *Get Out*, leading to an important discussion of the plot structure from Peele's film, especially as it engages with the horror film *Eyes Without a Face* by Georges Franju. Through confrontations and meanings generated by the process of comparing the films, looking back at *Eyes Without a Face* will help us understand the historical strivings of *Get Out* as well.

Get Out opens abruptly, before offering a title sequence. We watch a young black man walking down a white suburban street, speaking on his cell phone, and then quietly to himself, indicating that he feels unsafe. This begins the black/white binary we discussed, that is, the presentation of a black man threatened in a white space. The binary is supported by a number of extratextual references. In *Get Out*, Peele supplies not only the visual image of a *Halloween*-like suburb but also a *Halloween*-style camera movement to embody it. The camera disconcertingly swirls around the black character, making us uneasy, as we wonder who is off screen, who is the author of this camera movement, creating an apt metaphor for the ubiquitous threat to black lives. Suddenly, we see a *Halloween*-like stalking vehicle, a car, approaching the black male. A hooded figure emerges from the car, seizes the black man, anesthetizes him, throws him in the trunk, and drives away. The music over this sequence, emitting from the car radio, can best be described as "white music with an old time feel." A quick internet search reveals the recording to be a 1939 British song. In this way, whiteness and old age is associated with the oppressors, two qualities that prove deadly to the young black men in the film. The meaning is further supported by the song, which is titled "Run, Rabbit, Run," and contains the following lyrics:

> Run rabbit—run rabbit—Run! Run! Run!
> Don't give the farmer his fun! Fun! Fun!

The title sequence of *Get Out* is then presented and features a rapid traveling shot that moves laterally across a wooded landscape. Encouraged by the play of references begun in the opening of the film, this image may recall the moving camera shots through the woods in *The Blair Witch Project* (1999) (Guerro), or the point-of-view shots of slaves escaping on foot in *Mandingo* (1975). And while the musical score that accompanies this shot is a low and mournful sound that can be experienced by general audiences on the level of feeling, it can also be recognized by others for what it is: a slave song (Guerro). In the composite of these references, there is a growing sense of an off-screen menace. From *The Blair Witch Project*, for example, we remember the presence of the murdering witch who lurks in the space off camera, and in *Mandingo* there is the imminent danger of the trackers who hunt the runaway slaves. The threat to life in these films is positioned as existing in the space beyond the screen, chasing, insidious, but in *Mandingo* it is a specific black racial identity being endangered.

I will supply another surface film reference to underscore the physical threat introduced by these methods, as well as the threat to identity. It has often been noted, for example, that *Get Out* references *Rosemary's Baby* because of the elderly white people who abduct young bodies for their fecundity, using them to ensure their own ability to survive across generations. In *Rosemary's Baby*, this life force is put to the service of the Devil. In *Get Out*, young black men have their bodies stolen to pleasure white postmenopausal wives. This condition impedes future generations and symbolizes another way of killing off black men. But in *Get Out*, this method is also implemented for the purpose of prolonging white consciousness by transplanting white brains into black bodies.

The feeling of a profound threat, even of the fear of extinction, is further embodied in the plot structure of *Get Out*, which bears an interesting relationship to *Eyes Without a Face*. The reference to *Eyes Without a Face* foregrounds themes of the loss of identity, as we have noted, as well as the struggle for survival, themes that have often been presented in horror films featuring a mad doctor/scientist as a central character but are put to differing effect here. *Get Out* brings to the surface the racial content of this threat to human existence, and in the process symbolizes historical trauma. For the major portion of this chapter, I have conducted a thematic analysis of the works. I now analyze the deep structural elements of the narrative.

Eyes Without a Face tells the story of an original crime committed by a father against his daughter, and subsequently, the continuation of that crime against a series of young women. The daughter has lost her face, her identity, in an accident caused by the father. The father, a medical doctor, attempts to reconstruct his daughter's face through transplant surgery. Across multiple attempts, the father fails but tries again. The daughter sees his crime: the abduction of a series of young women and the destruction of their identity. The daughter has the father killed. The daughter disappears wearing a mask, a symbol of her lost self.

The following is a pared-down version of the plot functions, reducing the symbolic surface of the actants to their more basic elements and so revealing the deeper structure of the story:

1. The villain has committed a crime.
2. The victim has lost her identity because of the crime.
3. An accomplice hunts down the new victims.
4. The villain removes the identity of the new victims.
5. The villain attempts to graft the new identity onto the victim.
6. The villain fails.
7. The victim sees the crime.
8. The victim kills the villain.
9. The victim removes the villain's identity.
10. The victim is not free.

The relationship of *Eyes Without a Face* to historical trauma has been discussed by Adam Lowenstein in "History Without a Face: Surrealism, Modernity, and the Holocaust in the Cinema of Georges Franju." Lowenstein notes how Franju's work references the Holocaust and other historical traumas, such as colonization and the Algerian war and French culpability. Important in this analogy is the resulting loss of identity at the hands of a white Christian power against those who have been deemed as racially or ethnically other. The patriarchal father in *Eyes Without a Face* symbolizes that power—the power to subjugate by the violent destruction of the national and ethnic identity of the oppressed.

The Plot of *Get Out*

As noted, *Get Out* begins with the abduction of a black man, symbolically representing a past crime of slavery by means of a present time event. The title sequence further supports the theme of threat to body and mind. The contemporary action begins by introducing Chris, who is initially seen alone in his upscale apartment. As Kishawn Jack pointed out, a reference to poverty is made by the photographs of black ghetto life displayed on the apartment walls. On a manifest level, these artfully composed images, identify Chris as an accomplished professional photographer. But we should consider Kishawn's other observation as well. Why would a black man have pictures of black ghetto life on his wall? What is Chris's relationship to that reality?

The rest of *Get Out* works to supply answers to the questions raised by the ghetto images. Our attention is specifically directed to the history of the crimes against black people that continue to be committed. The relegation of entire lifetimes and generations to conditions of poverty is exemplified by the photograph of a pregnant black woman, her distended belly dominating the foreground of the image, set against the projects visible in the background. This and the other photographs in the scene evoke lives of personal denigration, of the loss of identity and culture. Chris, and by extension, Peele, are showing us representations of black lives, Chris by the pictures displayed on the apartment wall, and Peele across the whole of the film, referring to the history of subjugation, only now symbolized in the structure of a horror film. The purpose of this representation in *Get Out* is to make the societal and historical issues visible to a large public and encourage discussion.

Get Out tells the story of Chris, a black man who is taken by his white girlfriend to visit her parents for the weekend. Chris and Rose are an interracial couple, but the parents accept them together and accept Chris. Chris meets other members of the family and the family friends who come to visit. He becomes suspicious when he sees the family and friends conducting an auction. When Chris is hypnotized, he discovers that the family is abducting black men to take their brains and their identities by substituting white brains into black bodies. Chris fights the villains. He defeats the villains. At the end, he is still free.

I list the plot sequence of *Get Out*, filling in a little more about its symbolic surface, to compare it with the plot structure from *Eyes Without a Face*.

1. Past event: A crime of slavery has been committed against black people.

2. Present event: The legacy of the crime continues across the twentieth and twenty-first centuries.

3. The accomplice takes the black protagonist to meet the white villains.

4. The white villains introduce the back protagonist to the old white community.

5. The black protagonist sees the serial abductions of young black bodies.

6. The black protagonist is next.

7. The black protagonist sees the placing of a white brain into a black body, with only a sliver of black identity remaining.

8. The black protagonist fights the white villains.

9. The black protagonist defeats the white villains.

10. The black protagonist is still free.

This plot sequence bears a striking resemblance to that of *Eyes Without a Face*, especially to the loss of identity presented in Franju's story. In *Get Out* and *Eyes Without a Face*, the loss of bodily parts and bodily power is used to symbolize an extreme attack on identity. The horror film has previously used this trope of loss in many ways. A few examples from film history will help us understand how the new dramatization in *Get Out*, a movie about black history, has used these meanings.

In *Frankenstein* (1931) by James Whale, for example, it is made clear that the creature, or what society has deemed the "monster," became so because of his lack of acceptance in the social order, a condition forced on him by the white male doctor. Dr. Frankenstein has constructed a man from dead human material but altered his identity by mistakenly implanting a criminal brain. All the creature was in a previous life or hoped to be in the future was removed from him. For our analysis, the type of operation conducted in *Get Out* and its resultant loss of identity are especially important. The placement of an exterior brain into a host body is the image that Peele has recalled from *Frankenstein*. But here too there are differences. The doctor in *Get Out* is specifically placing the brains of white people into black bodies, adding new levels of symbolic meaning.

The Skin I Live In (2011) by Pedro Almodóvar also presents us with an extreme loss of identity relevant to our discussion. Here, a mad doctor takes revenge on the violator of his young daughter by castrating him, turning Vicente into Vera. To forcibly destroy one's sense of self is a profoundly devastating loss. In these stories, the loss has been symbolized by the loss of body parts but also by the replacement of those parts with a new identity. As the ultimate subjugation, this has often been the tactic of the colonizer, that is, to enter the host country and take over the bodies and the minds of the people. In *Frankenstein*, the self has been replaced as self-hating monster, in *The Skin I Live In*, it is the unwanted change of man into a woman, and in both, the acts of subjugation are administered at the hands of a white male doctor. In *Get Out* it is, the removal of black identity that is replaced by a white identity.

This insight too comes from a student of mine, Anthony Davila, who made the following comment after watching *Get Out*. He simply stated, "They steal your culture, and replace it with white culture." For Anthony, the removal of the black brain was a metaphor for that ongoing cultural conflict. I took his statement for what it is, a profoundly devastating insight into the process of subjugation: to be colonized from within, to be forced to see the world as a white man, but to be a black man. This loss of culture, this loss of self in *Get Out*, goes far beyond the narrow confines of a horror film. Or as Kishawn Jack says, "The idea of

Get Out being a horror film is crazy because the only thing scary about it is that it is the truth."

No Space beyond the Screen

There has been much discussion in the media regarding the Sunken Place in *Get Out*, understood by the general public as that place within the fiction of Peele's film referring to experience of slavery and, by extension, to the African American experience of dispossession in American society. I will describe the cinematic strategies Peele used to evoke this visceral response from the audience. I must make clear that I am not claiming *Get Out* re-creates the feeling of slavery itself (this is too profound a historical trauma to reproduce in one cinematic trope) but rather, that the film makes metaphors on the feeling of entrapment referring to this historical event and does so, chillingly, in the well-known hypnosis scene. I claim that *Get Out* employs effective cinematic means, yet ones that have been used by previous horror films. In keeping with the general strategy of the film, however, Peele does not copy the earlier films; he advances their logic to a new meaning and purpose.

I will again start with my own experience of past horror films to describe this felt response. *Psycho* and *Ringu* are two films that frightened me, eliciting a strong bodily reaction, and they did so especially by their use of space in relationship to the characters on screen but also in anticipation of the off screen. I begin with a discussion of *Psycho*.

The first time I saw *Psycho* I was fourteen years old, but I can still remember the terror, the psychic dread, of one sequence. This is the scene where Lila Crane (Vera Miles), Marion Crane's sister, decides to examine Norman Bates's (Anthony Perkins) old dark house on her own. Lila is looking for Norman's mother, Mrs. Bates, and we, the audience, know full well that Norman's mother is not a feeble old woman but a vicious killer. We have witnessed two murders, brutal physical attacks, on Marion Crane (Janet Leigh) and the private detective, Milton Arbogast (Martin Balsam). We have also heard stories that raised our fear of Mother's mental instability and her evil. The fear mounts as Lila approaches the house. The space of the Bates house, as well as the whole of the motel compound, has been dynamized by Mother's presence. She is off-camera, seemingly omnipresent, and her intrusion into the screen space is immanent.

At this point, it is important to interject observations from film theory that will be useful to our analysis. Andre Bazin has noted the distinctive characters of the film screen as it differs from the frame in painting (164–69). In painting, the frame creates a boundary beyond which no space exists. The frame of a painting directs our attention only to the interior of the picture plane. In film, the opposite is true. What we see on a film screen is a mask, one that at once blocks off the rest of the world yet implies the reality beyond its edges. The out-of-field, as Gilles Deleuze called it, is always imminent. That is, the film screen masks the reality that can reveal itself at any moment. In *Psycho*, Alfred Hitchcock uses this cinematic dynamic to create suspense and the fear of sudden physical attack in the viewer.

In *Psycho*, the tension builds as Lila moves into the house and up the stairs and reaches its apex. She enters Mother's bedroom, a place where the mise-en-scène implies old age and death. This meaning emanates from the outdated furniture, the bronze cast of once-youthful hands, and the impression of a motionless human form on the bedclothes. Lila moves into this space, but the centered framing of her living body underscores an imminent threat from the outside. The room is presented in a sequence of full shots, medium shots, and close-ups, all keeping Lila and what she sees on screen. Suddenly there is a shock cut, punctuated by Lila's sense that someone else is in the room. We jump, seeing now from Lila's point of view. Because the camera's look is joined to our point of view but taken from Lila's position in the room, we see her reflection in the mirror almost as our own. We are in the room. But more, we are Lila, that is, our body is identified with Lila's body, making us more vulnerable than ever. Yet for now, we are safe. The out-of-field has been revealed as an illusion. There is no one else in the room, only Lila.

The film *Ringu* returns to this play of spaces, this tension between the edges and the surface of the screen. What is seen and what is not seen across boundaries is engaged, only now the possible directions of viewable and inhabitable space have been altered. We are not just dealing with a lateral directionality—to the right and left of the film screen—or even vertically, outside to the top or the bottom. Now we are crossing another boundary. Our attention is directed to the surface of the screen itself. The breaking of the fourth wall has often been done on film, most notably in the self-reflexive cinema of Jean-Luc Godard. In the New Wave films, the illusion of a cinematic fiction is broken to reveal the reality of the film medium itself. In *Ringu*, this strategy is extended and intensified to horrific effect—it is reversed, further implicating the viewer, by now allowing the fiction to enter reality.

This effect is aided by the narrative elements of *Ringu*, ones that include an encroaching ghost as well as other insinuating strategies. The goal is to bring the film into the reality of the viewer by cojoining the narrative and the visual elements. Included in the fiction, for example, is the image of a home viewing device and the film character's action of inserting the VHS tape into the player. Here the space in the center of the frame is engaged, creating a tension linking the inside of the screen, across the surface of the screen, into the space of the viewer. To complete the effect, the ghost within the fiction is pictured as crossing that divide, emerging from the center of the televised screen and now entering the space, implicating the reality of the viewer. This is quite effective. Typically, the surface of the film/video screen protects the viewer. That which is being viewed is securely screened off from the reality opposing it. In *Ringu*, that divide is broken, using the center of the image as the portal by which the ghost can enter the viewer's space.

The Sunken Place: Entrapment

> Those who think they see ghosts are those who do not want to see the night.
>
> —Maurice Blanchot (163)

By comparison *Get Out* uses another set of strategies to make its point felt. In Peele's film, we are now taken metaphorically down by going deep into the center of the image. Peele accomplishes this by again using various conditions of the film screen only now in a new way.

The scene in which the revelation of the Sunken Place occurs begins with a sequence of shots across the door frames separating the rooms of a house, creating a frame-within-a-frame composition. Chris is walking in the house when he encounters Rose's mother, Missy (Catherine Keener), a psychoanalyst who has a home office. Through a series of shot/countershot exchanges, Missy offers Chris the possibility of curing his smoking addiction through hypnosis. She encourages him to enter her office (a kind of abduction). As he takes a seat across from Missy, the casual conversation about quitting smoking suddenly turns to the topic of Chris's dead mother. A point of focus is created, for Chris and for us, returning to "mother," a universal primal memory.

This conversation and its sudden turn to Chris's personal trauma puts us into a sensory heightened position, one where the accompanying sound of Missy stirring the china tea cup with a silver spoon becomes more audible. Popular notions of the techniques of hypnotism include the understanding that the procedure is enhanced by creating a point of focus for the person being hypnotized. This dynamic is re-created in the sequence primarily through the type of shot exchanges. We are placed in the viewing position of Chris, seeing from his point of view, in a shot/countershot pattern that alternates between a close-up of Chris's face that is progressively placed centrally in the frame and that of Missy in the same screen position. These two shots' set-ups are joined by the alternating shots of Chris's additional point of view of the tea cup and spoon. The tinkling sound obsessively continues across these three-shot variations. We hear what Chris hears, and we see what he sees, with the trajectory of the close-ups following at rapid succession. We are literally pulled into the screen's center. The outside of the screen, that is, to the right, to the left, to the top, or to the bottom, becomes increasingly off-limits to us.

I felt a terrible tension here, especially the fear of myself being hypnotized, the fear of no escape, and the fear of being psychologically and physically trapped. And then, as the sound of tinkling continues, Missy finally says to Chris, "Now sink into the floor." The experience has a visceral effect on the members of the audience, regardless of ethnic or racial background. And we go down—sinking, as Chris does—metaphorically and visually into the center of the screen. We are given a cinematic experience of entrapment for political purposes.

In the shot that follows, Chris is seen falling vertically across the surface of the screen, his body pictured against the black void. This type of shot has been used before in film history, in *Murder, My Sweet* (1944) for example, when the character falls vertically downward against a black background to imply a dream state; or in *2001: A Space Odyssey* (1968) when the astronaut is disconnected from the space capsule, floating in a breathless void. But in both scenes, a space outside the screen is narratively featured as still existing, connected to the waking state that frames the dream in *Murder, My Sweet* and the spaceship in the reverse field in *2001*. In *Get Out* the left, right, up, and down axes have been narratively disconnected, now by the screen image of Missy in this space. We are metaphorically and experientially in a void, locked into the confines of the picture frame, blocked off and falling, defined as such by the dominating floating screen with a close-up of Missy's face. Overseeing, dominating, it is an emblem of a coextensive real space, a real world, a place of whiteness, a faraway place where Chris is not allowed. Instead, Chris is confined to a nonplace from which he cannot escape. Peele has thus given us an experiential and dramatic use of film form to confront the condition of historical trauma for black people in America.

Conclusion

In *Get Out*, a social and cultural truth has been expressed by the process of referencing past film material and recombining those elements to speak a new text. *Get Out* often references conventions of past horror films and reorders them, causing us to look to our past and to our present. The looking back is not for the purpose of nostalgia, or as a play of references for the fun allusion, or for the conceit of appropriation; rather, the references are metaphorically used to direct attention to race relations, to the threat posed to blacks by white society. This is a message received by many. *Get Out* is a broad-based cultural product, one that makes a considerable communication with its audience, but it is also a work of formal innovation. Although the horror film has been used to address social and racial conditions before, with *Night of the Living Dead* (1968) as an important example, *Get Out* accomplishes its goal in novel ways and to brilliant effect. Racial conditions are seen through the fictional construction of *Get Out*, while also encouraging us to acknowledge those realties embedded in the source material.

A complex web of meaning ensues. By looking back to *Guess Who's Coming to Dinner*, for example, we see an example of the hegemony of Classical Hollywood style and, by extension, of white capitalist ideology and its structures of subjugation. In *Eyes Without a Face*, we see the metaphors of depersonalization, a potent statement on historical trauma, now recombined in *Get Out*. By experiencing the Sunken Place, we are offered a felt metaphor of the entrapment of a marginalized group and the fear of extinction. And, through the plot functions and the action of the protagonist, we engage in his struggle to fight back.

Works Cited

Bazin, Andre. "Painting and Cinema." *What Is Cinema?* Trans. Hugh Gray. Berkeley: University of California Press, 1971.

Blanchot, Maurice. *The Space of Literature*. Lincoln: University of Nebraska Press, 1982.
Breuer, Josef, and Sigmund Freud. *Studies in Hysteria*. Trans. and ed. James Strachey. *The Standard Edition of the Complete Psychological Works of Sigmund Freud*, vol. 2. London: Hogarth Press, 1955.
Carroll, Noel. "The Future of Allusion: Hollywood in the Seventies (and Beyond)." *October* 20 (Spring 1982): 51–81.
Deleuze, Gilles. *Cinema 1; The Movement Image*. Trans. Hugh Tomlinson and Robert Galeta. Minneapolis: University of Minnesota Press, 1986.
Dika, Vera. *Games of Terror: Halloween, Friday the 13th, and the Films of the Stalker Cycle*. Teaneck, NJ: Fairleigh Dickinson University Press, 1991.
Dika, Vera. *Recycled Culture in Contemporary Art and Film: The Uses of Nostalgia*. Cambridge: Cambridge University Press, 2003.
Freud, Sigmund. "The Uncanny." *The Standard Edition of the Complete Psychological Works of Sigmund Freud*, vol. 17. London: Hogarth Press, 1964. 217–56.
Guerreo, Ed. "*Get Out*! Guess Who's Coming to Dinner Now: The Black Body and Scientific Materialism." Columbia Film Seminar, April 5, 2018. Columbia University Seminar on Cinema and Interdisciplinary Interpretation no. 539.
Jameson, Fredric. "Postmodernism and Consumer Society." *The Anti-Aesthetic*. Ed. Hal Foster. Port Townsend, WA: Bay Press, 1983. 111–25.
Lowenstein, Adam. "History without a Face: Surrealism, Modernity, and the Holocaust in the Cinema of Georges Franju." *Shocking Representations: Historical Trauma, National Cinema, and the Modern Horror Film*. New York: Columbia University Press, 2005. 17–53.
Mason, Clifford. "Why Does White America Love Sidney Poitier So?" *New York Times*, September 10, 1967.
Peele, Jordan, "Jordan Peele Breaks Down 'Get Out' Fan Theories from Reddit." Vanity Fair, YouTube, December 2017. https://www.youtube.com/watch?v=hBvcngHRTFg.
Wood, Robin. "The American Nightmare: Horror in the 70s." *Hollywood from Vietnam to Reagan . . . and Beyond*. New York: Columbia University Press, 2003. 63–84.

10

"Why Can't We Go Backwards, for Once?"

Nostalgia, Utopia, and Science Fiction in Steven Spielberg's *Ready Player One*

MATTHEW LEGGATT

Imagining the future is a kind of nostalgia.
—John Green, *Looking for Alaska* (54)

IN THE 2018 MOVIE *Ready Player One*, adapted from Ernest Cline's 2011 best-selling novel of the same name, the inhabitants of 2045 America occupy a scantly detailed world of chronic poverty, overcrowding, energy shortages, and climate disasters. As a result, people spend much of their time jacked in to a simulated multiworld environment known as the OASIS (Ontologically Anthropocentric Sensory Immersive Simulation, to give its full, jargonistic title). The OASIS, the brainchild of the duo James Halliday (played by Mark Rylance) and Ogden Morrow (Simon Pegg), allows users to create alternate identities through fully customizable avatars and explore a seemingly limitless set of "off-world" locales. As we are told in the opening of the movie, the OASIS is "a place where the limits of reality are your own imagination. You can do anything, go anywhere, like the vacation planet, surf a fifty-foot monster wave in Hawaii, you can ski down the pyramids, and climb Mount Everest . . . with Batman." To put it simply, in its initial conception, the film styles the OASIS as a utopian space, free from the cares of ordinary living beyond the occasional need for a bathroom break or the necessities of nourishment and sleep. Indeed, John Opie wrote that "each time we fire up the computer, we whisk ourselves into cyberspace to inhabit a seductive alternative existence" (6) and when expressed in this way, cyberspace becomes the ideal place for utopian dreaming; a construct capable of resolving the paradox at the heart of the term, which combines the Greek eu-topos (good place) and ou-topos (no place). But as *Ready Player One* progresses, the spectator comes to trust less and less in this cyber-utopia that seems, at least in part, to have caused the gradual decline of society at large. By the end of the movie, the OASIS is depicted as little more than an escapist fantasy.

In its ending, *Ready Player One* ultimately seems to advocate a return to the "real" world that has been neglected. Whereas Spielberg might want us to associate this real world with the world of his own movies, his fantastical cinematic spaces are no more real than the cyberspace he seems to want us to leave behind. In fact, unlike cyberspace, which is intrinsically liberating, Spielberg's movie—like much Hollywood fare—is decidedly conservative, dictating the terms on which the viewer can engage in its utopia of play. Alfie Brown—author of *The Playstation Dreamworld* (2017)—suggests that despite the fact that "the video game world has great potential to represent progressive agendas," the politics displayed by *Ready Player One*'s "supposedly revolutionary team of libertarians" is "decidedly right-wing" (9). As a result, Brown argues that "Spielberg's movie neglects [its progressive] potential," instead "show[ing] gaming simply in its worst light" (9). The failure of the movie, despite the utopian potential evident in its central technological premise, I argue, stems from Spielberg's abandonment of the codes of science fiction and the movie's surrender to a willful nostalgia which is in itself perfectly Spielbergian. Today, we might see *Ready Player One* as a fitting, if deeply pessimistic, emblem of the crisis of imagination we face.

Nostalgia: It Was Acceptable in the '80s

Kevin Wetmore suggests that "since the millennium and 9/11, American culture has called a 'do over' and run straight back to the '80s" (2). Indeed, *Ready Player One* is just one of many recent entertainment products from *Stranger Things* (2016—) and *The Americans* (2013–2018), to movies like *Guardians of the Galaxy* (2014) and *Atomic Blonde* (2017) to generate nostalgia for the period. Spielberg's movie begins with the death of James Halliday; as spectators, we are shown a video, broadcast around the world, bequeathing Halliday's vast fortune and control of the OASIS to the winner of a system-wide contest to find a particular Easter egg hidden by the inventor somewhere inside his virtual world. Halliday appears in the video to explain that this contest will require an intimate knowledge of the introvert's mind, and in this sense his death initiates the revival of 1980s culture within the confines of the OASIS. Consequently, in the years that follow, many egg hunters—or "gunters" as they become known—spend their lives obsessively familiarizing themselves with the pop culture of that decade and of Halliday's youth.

Asked in interview what it is about the 1980s that Spielberg finds particularly attractive, the director responded,

> It was a great decade for me. So much happened in my life in the '80s. In the '80s I met my wife, Kate. In the '80s, my first child was born. In the '80s I formed Amblin Entertainment. In the '80s I made *Raiders of the Lost Ark* and *E.T.* I mean, the '80s was a boom town decade for me and it was a relatively quiet decade politically. We had a robust economy under Ronald Reagan, things were pretty chill. Not everything was chill in the world or in our country but overall it is not a decade we think of as the kind of stress we're all experiencing geopolitically today. (Nannar)

In Spielberg's overtly personal recollection of the 1980s, then, we glimpse the depoliticization that often accompanies nostalgia. The present may, like the personal, always be political, but by comparison our furtive glances backward are often stripped of such a dimension. One might note that many of the policies and much of the rhetoric on which our present 'stress' is founded were, in fact, made in Ronald Reagan's America: even Donald Trump's calling card—"Make America Great Again"—is a repeat of Reagan's successful election campaign slogan of 1980. Spielberg's failure to recognize this, however, shouldn't be too surprising given that, as Peter Biskind highlights, he was always an establishment figure even if this isn't how he had wanted to be perceived early in his career. Spielberg recalled of his attempts to break into Francis Ford Coppola's group in the late 1960s, "I was an outsider, I was the establishment, I was being raised and nurtured at Universal Studios, a very conservative company, and in his eyes, and also in George's [Lucas] eyes, I was working inside the system" (cited in Biskind 258). The 1980s that Spielberg remembers is not defined by the AIDS crisis and the Reagan administration's callous response. Nor is it remembered for the recession of 1981 and 1982 (sparked by the oil crises of 1973 and 1979). For Spielberg, rather, the 1980s are defined by personal relationships, movies he made, and a booming economy (it's pretty easy to think of the economy as booming when you have suddenly become one of the richest men on the planet).

In fairness, Spielberg's rather selective memory might still be more inclusive than author (and screenwriter for the movie) Ernest Cline's. Philip Nel attacks the novel for its dearth of cultural references to non-white artists during a decade that saw Michael Jackson as its best-selling musician, arguing that the book offers "nostalgia for a very particular, apolitical, very white culture" (iii). By contrast, Michael Jackson does find his way into Spielberg's more eclectic version: at one point when trying on outfits for his date with Art3mis (Olivia Cooke), Parzival (Tye Sheridan) considers Jackson's iconic red jacket from the music video to "Thriller" (1982). The director also opts not only to include key 1980s references throughout, as with the selection of Van Halen's 1984 hit "Jump" to strike the opening chords of the movie's soundtrack—described in subtitles for those hard of hearing and who are perhaps too young to recognize the song as "1980s rock music"—but also to assault the viewer's senses with a dazzling array of pop culture references from beyond. This was, at least partly, a practical measure as much as it was an effort to broaden the movie's audience: one of the most significant challenges facing Spielberg's crew was attaining copyright permissions for the vast collection of references that appear in the movie (Power). As a result, Spielberg relied heavily on properties owned by Warner Bros., *Ready Player One*'s production studio, because these were considerably easier to clear in terms of copyright.

While Josh Rottenberg, writing for the *Los Angeles Times*, saw this as the movie's great strength, claiming that *Ready Player One* "is the most impressive cinematic exercise in pop culture cross-pollination since

'Wreck-It Ralph' and 'The Lego Movie'—if not of all time" (6), Peter Rubin, writing in his review for *Wired*, suggests that Spielberg's movie "conflates recognition with enjoyment" (5). Indeed, one might ask what this level of intertextual saturation achieves. During the final battle sequence, we see iconic video game characters Lara Croft (Tomb Raider, 1996), Cassie Cage (from the Mortal Kombat series), Tracer from Overwatch (2016), Chun-Li from the classic arcade franchise Street Fighter (which began in 1987), and skeletons from the 1992 cult film *Army of Darkness* all in one frame (see figure 10.1). Indeed, as the Iron Giant from Brad Bird's 1999 film of the same name does battle with Mechagodzilla—the Teenage Mutant Ninja Turtles hacking and slashing on the planet's surface below—one wonders whether the movie collapses under the weight of its referential nostalgia.

Rubin argues that *Ready Player One* fails to represent the truly progressive potential offered in the virtual reality utopia promised by the central narrative. "That's not Steven Spielberg's aim," Rubin writes. "He wants you to feel like a kid again." Indeed, to this extent *Ready Player One* takes the spectator back to one of Spielberg's enduring interests: childhood. In this way the movie is, like many of Spielberg's celebrated 1980s movies (most notably *E.T.* [1982] and the Indiana Jones movies [1981, 1984, 1989]), a return to the story of a boy with an absent father (see Le Gall and Taliaferro). Thus the director isn't really interested in the technology as such, or certainly not its utopian potential. Rather, he sees in it a means by which one might be transported to the director's

Figure 10.1. Tomb Raider, Mortal Kombat, Overwatch, Street Fighter, Army of Darkness references, and more in *Ready Player One* (Steven Spielberg, 2018). Digital frame enlargement.

own glorious past. Spielberg may have been too humble to reference his own movies in *Ready Player One* (aside from *Back to the Future* [1985]—on which he was an executive producer—and a nod to *Jurassic Park* [1993] during the race sequence), he was also perhaps too blinkered to realize that the whole film is essentially a homage to his own work.

It is not just Spielberg's nostalgia at stake in *Ready Player One*, however. More important, the movie generates a form of nostalgia for its target audience that needs some unpacking. Halliday's memories have been transformed into digital archives that appear with the announcement of the inventor's death and the beginning of the contest. We are told that these archives used to be teeming with gunters in search of clues, but interest in the hunt has waned after years of inactivity, and Parzival finds the archives virtually deserted. The archives allow Halliday's past to be scoured, returned to, replayed—in short, manipulated by the visitor. "Each entry into Halliday's journals," the curator (voiced by Simon Pegg) informs us, "is meticulously assembled from personal photographs, home video recordings, surveillance and nanny cams all rendered into a three-dimensional virtual experience." Despite the authenticity this would seem to lend the entries, however, the scenes from Halliday's life, which we see play out as Parzival breezes by, appear more like staged re-creations than memories. Their glossy and entirely clean appearance mark them out as twenty-first-century digital images not the grainy home recordings more frequently associated with the 1980s and 1990s (see figure 10.2). This, combined with the age of the moments in question—we see a teenage Halliday working studiously in his bedroom on some tech project, and

Figure 10.2. Parzival (Tye Sheridan) watches an entry in the Halliday Journals in *Ready Player One* (Steven Spielberg, 2018). Digital frame enlargement.

Halliday as a child on the living room floor plugging a game into an early console—suggests that these images have been significantly altered. Although these moments are choreographed like scenes from a play, Parzival responds to them as if they are entirely real. There is no suspicion in his reaction to suggest that these fragments—nostalgic glimpses into Halliday's youth—are anything other than accurate reflections of times gone by. As Parzival asks the curator to focus in on a particular character or go back, rotating or panning the camera's movement in homage to Ridley Scott's *Blade Runner* (1982)—which plays a key role in Cline's novel but for which Spielberg was unable to obtain permission to directly reference in his filmic version—the movie highlights the extent to which these "memories" are, to all intents and purposes, artificial.

In highlighting this artificiality, *Ready Player One* points to the ubiquity of what Alison Landsberg has called "prosthetic memory." For Landsberg, prosthetic memory

> emerges at the interface between a person and a historical narrative about the past, at an experiential site such as a movie theater or museum. In this moment of contact, an experience occurs through which the person sutures himself or herself into a larger history. . . . In the process . . . the person does not simply apprehend a historical narrative but takes on a more personal, deeply felt memory of a past event through which he or she did not live. (2)

Since most gunters, one presumes, are not old enough to have been alive during the 1980s, the OASIS, and more explicitly Halliday's contest, becomes their primary point of contact with the decade. Gunters, in effect, reconceptualize the 1980s through the network of nostalgic texts that are liberally sprinkled throughout the virtual world in which they spend most of their time. In this respect, gunters like Parzival aren't dissimilar from many audience members, perhaps even the primary audience, for Spielberg's movie whose only experience of the 1980s is likely to be through such mediated sources. Indeed, one might question why the movie focuses on the 1980s at all since, while clearly a nostalgic period for Spielberg, the decade cannot possibly be nostalgic in quite the same sense for much of the movie's younger audience.

Landsberg's ideas go further as she insists that rather than just label prosthetic memories as inauthentic, such "memories" should be valued for their power to "shape that person's subjectivity and politics" (2). While I have argued here that the nostalgia on which *Ready Player One* leans offers a depoliticized version of history, particularly of the 1980s, that is not to say that the movie is entirely apolitical. The process of depoliticization is itself political. Landsberg's theories suggest that even though a subject might not have a direct connection to a remembered event, person, or object, the prosthetic memory generated can easily come to inform one's political views. She reads this in a positive sense. For example, such empathetic connections can be made to help teach younger people about the horrors of war or genocide. But when what is being peddled is a decade entirely commercialized and absent of its politics, as in *Ready Player One*, the nostalgia generated hardly seems progressive. As Pam Cook declares of prosthetic memories even as she attempts to redeem them, "such enterprises lay themselves open to charges of lack of authenticity, of substituting a degraded popular version for the 'real' event, and to accusations that by presenting history as dramatic spectacle they obscure our understanding of social, political and cultural forces" (2). These criticisms can certainly be leveled at the production of memory in *Ready Player One* that likewise seems to mirror a wider trend in contemporary popular culture seen in TV shows like *Stranger Things*, *Halt and Catch Fire* (2014–2017), *Deutschland 83* (2015), and *The Americans* where audiences who often have no firsthand experience of a particular period (the 1980s in these examples) are encouraged to consider such times as having—at least in certain cases—a nostalgic simplicity and appeal (think of the child-like Halliday plugging a game cartridge into the machine versus the experience of open-world virtual reality offered by the OASIS, with all its associated dangers both virtual and physical, that Parzival must contend with).

Despite seeing the value of the ideas behind Landsberg's work on prosthetic memory, James Berger identifies the concept as particularly "optimistic" (597) and shows a concern that such "memories" most often take a kind of commodified form. "Products of mass media about the past are not" as Berger argues "'prosthetic' and are not exactly 'memories.' Whether they originate with the testimonies of witnesses or retrieval of other documents or presentation of artifacts or fictional reconstructions, these products are *representations*" (605, emphasis added). As representations, prosthetic memories may promise an access to history that is otherwise unavailable, but it is important to note that they can only ever articulate one interpretation of history. Thus, according to Berger, "memory as Landsberg describes it, as product of corporate capitalist mass media—must be subject to processes of ideology just as are other mass media products" (605).

As a vehicle for prosthetic memory, *Ready Player One* is part of a network of contemporary texts that use nostalgia to encourage the viewer to withdraw from the world—a paradox given the film's final message that the audience needs to stop playing video games and engage with the real world. *Ready Player One* presents yet more evidence that, as Ryan Lizardi argues, "media consumers today are situated facing backwards, driven to obsess upon their "individual" pasts, which they misrecognize through a cultivated dependence on nostalgia" (20). Indeed, the kind of nostalgia generated by Spielberg's movie is particularly for the commercial goods of one's childhood. It is "individual" in its desire to find some product for everyone, hence the messy battle sequences where intellectual property from all kinds of universes collide in an orgy of digital special effects. According to Lizardi, while there is the possibility that an engagement with one's individual history might be "critical, existential, and beneficial" if one "adaptively examined one's own life and culture" (20)—one might think, comparatively of the moment during a near-death experience where one's life is often reported to flash before one's eyes—"instead, the misrecognized ersatz pseudo-individual past cedes the desire to look critically at one's past and present, replacing it with the always mediated mimetic and misrecognized drive to recreate the unattainable media-defined past of one's youth" (20–21). In short, *Ready Player One* offers nostalgia or prosthetic memory not mobilized to actively engage the viewer in a specific history that might enable empathy but designed to draw one back to the beloved, and romanticized, products of one's youth.

Science Fiction, Utopia

If the OASIS is a bastion of nostalgic memory, the technological and utopian solution posited by *Ready Player One* owes little to the traditions of science fiction. Sci-fi has generally been characterized by cognitive estrangement and defamiliarization. The former is a concept that originates with Darko Suvin and is summarized by Patrick Parrinder as the idea that "by imagining strange worlds we come to see our own conditions of life in a new and potentially revolutionary perspective" (4). One might think here of Fritz Lang's fantastical futuristic city-space in *Metropolis* (1927), which is ultimately a cover for the movie's concerns with the plight of the working class. Defamiliarization, on the other hand, involves taking something the viewer is familiar with and making it strange. An example par excellence of this might be seen in *Fantastic Voyage* (1966), which centers on a group of explorers who are shrunk to take a journey through the human body. Instead of following these processes, Spielberg's film meticulously re-creates the familiar and homely environments of the past. From the elaborate showpiece spectacle that is *The Shining* (1980) homage—a five-minute sequence during which Spielberg refashions some of the most iconic moments from Kubrick's classic horror film (see figure 10.3)—to the detail of Halliday's 1980s childhood bedroom, filled with a decade's worth of clutter and references, *Ready Player One* is entirely earnest in its nostalgia.

To make this message even clearer, Spielberg buries the first clue to Halliday's egg hunt in a conversation between Halliday and Morrow that showcases their differences but also neatly epitomizes the message of the movie more broadly:

> MORROW: "Look, invention comes with responsibilities you didn't ask for. All right, if you make something people want or need then it's up to you to set the limits. You have to make some rules."
>
> HALLIDAY: "I don't wanna make any more rules. I'm a dreamer. I build worlds."
>
> MORROW: "We created something beautiful, Jim, but it's changed. Okay, it's really not a game anymore."

Figure 10.3. The Overlook Hotel, the setting for Stanley Kubrick's *The Shining* (1980), as recreated in Steven Spielberg's *Ready Player One* (2018). Digital frame enlargement.

HALLIDAY: "I liked things how they were when they were. When it was a game."

MORROW: "And we're back to where we started. But that's the point, isn't it? Things move forward whether you like it or not." . . .

HALLIDAY: "Why can't we go backwards, for once?"

Halliday's insistence that moving backward might be just as productive as moving forward is exactly why the movie fails to make more of its effective utopian premise. As Cline himself has said of *Ready Player One*: "For me, it was more about exploring the origins of geek culture. I was part of the first generation to have video games, to have computers, to have a VCR. I wanted to pay tribute to that. Nostalgia, I think, is good. Nostalgia is like video games, or music, or movies. It's a form of escapism" (Cline, cited in Brogan). Rather than return to the past, particularly past technologies, to draw inspiration for future developments, then, the purpose of nostalgia in *Ready Player One* is to escape such a future. Of course, *Ready Player One* is not the first blockbuster sci-fi film to imagine using technology to return to the past. Obvious parallels could be drawn with *Back to the Future* (1985)—it's a comparison Spielberg certainly wants the audience to make given that *Ready Player One* contains a number of overt references to Robert Zemeckis's movie from a Rubik's Cube that can turn back time, named the Zemeckis cube, to the time-traveling DeLorean which Parzival drives backward to solve the first riddle in Halliday's quest—but in *Back to the Future* the nostalgia the film instigates is entirely accidental. As a scientist, Emmett (Doc) Brown (Christopher Lloyd) is primarily concerned with the future (hence the playful title of the film). It is only mistaken calculations that take Marty McFly (Michael J. Fox) backward rather than forward in time. As Brown says when explaining the purpose of the flux capacitor, which he hopes to use to travel twenty-five years into the future: "I've always dreamed of seeing the future; looking beyond my years; seeing the progress of mankind."

In fact, Spielberg would rather view *Ready Player One* as an allegory for today's world, a "cautionary tale" as he puts it, suggesting that the OASIS already exists in the form of smartphones, which tend to "make people forget where they are" (Nannar). Thus the film is at least partly intended to warn its audience about the dangers rather than potentials of the incredible technology it showcases. It is perhaps here that the central contradiction of Spielberg's vision lies. And it is particularly Spielberg who is the source of the problem. It is no secret that the director is a purist who made headlines in 2019 for his rejection of the idea that Netflix movies might be nominated for Academy Awards in the future. Whereas the platform is currently in the business of eroding the lines between movies and television, Spielberg is very keen to protect cinema from the onslaught of new media that might challenge its primacy. Indeed, there's a layer of irony here since, as Wetmore highlights, "*Wired Magazine* proclaimed the reason why everyone liked *Stranger Things* [Netflix's flagship product since 2016] is that it was an eight-hour Steven Spielberg movie" (1). Perhaps Spielberg is also familiar with the often noted idea that the video game industry is now significantly larger than the movie business, a misnomer because the statistics often include hardware sales for gaming but discount anything beyond box office receipts for movies. This would explain why *Ready Player One* ends with its protagonists choosing to limit not only their own use of the OASIS but also everyone else's by closing the OASIS for two days a week (an action that does not appear in the source text). When Parzival states at the end of the movie that "people need to spend more time in the real world," one senses that this real world doesn't exclude cinema. For Spielberg, the films he produces are far more 'real' than any video game could ever be—a particularly hypocritical idea given Spielberg's penchant for peddling nostalgia.

In an interview, Spielberg claims to be a big fan of gaming (Nannar), and he even used virtual reality technology to help make *Ready Player One*. During the preproduction phase, every set for the movie was created in virtual reality for the director, who was able to enter these with a headset and direct graphic artists from inside to make live changes, shaping the virtual world as they went (Roettgers). Unfortunately, however, in attempting to broaden the appeal of the movie, the focus on gaming was displaced because Spielberg "wanted to make a movie that didn't require people to have played video games, or have any knowledge of video games, to be able to go on this ride" (Nannar). The role played by insider knowledge is therefore minimized in Spielberg's movie version to promote a more universal product. For Megan Condis, such knowledge is essential to the operation of Cline's novel which, she argues, "serve[s] as a classroom wherein student-readers learn about the origins of gamer-dom, test their knowledge, and prove their geeky credentials by demonstrating their mastery of the texts Cline identifies as foundational to gamer culture" (3). For examples of this, we might consider the extensive and important passages in the novel that Cline dedicates to the first text-based adventure game, Zork (1980), and the phone phreaks (early American "hackers" who throughout the 1960s and 1970s exploited automated switchboard systems to infiltrate America's phone networks). By comparison, and as a result of the restrictive environment in which blockbuster movies are produced, in Spielberg's version there is no coherent "geek canon" for the audience to follow. When we consider the difficulty in obtaining copyright permissions for the various franchises to which the movie refers, the more skeptical members of the audience—like Ed Power, who writes of the movie, "it's geek culture sanitized for non-geeks" (7)—may treat the appearance of these objects as entirely arbitrary: the leftovers from Cline's party. In addition, whereas Cline's cultural references punctuate the narrative, becoming relics for Wade and the reader alike to study in the hopes that they might reveal a clue to aid the heroes by either bombarding spectators with snapshot references or hiding them so that they can only be spotted through screenshots, Spielberg tends to exclude the spectator from taking part in Halliday's quest (at least during the live experience of watching the movie) while also stripping the source text of its utopian aspirations.

This effect is evident in the opening, which contains one of the most spectacular set-pieces of the movie. Among others, King Kong, the T-rex from *Jurassic Park*, Aech's Bigfoot monster truck, Art3mis's bike from *Akira* (1988), and Parzival's *Back to the Future* DeLorean duke it out in this full-throttle scene. To accommodate the spectacle, Spielberg and his writing team axed one of the key motivators for Halliday's quest and with it the utopian intent behind Cline's novel. In the early part of the book, Cline establishes that Wade must go to school on a planet called Ludus—the name of which derives from the Latin meaning both school and game—entirely devoted to free education (Ludus is a planet entirely populated by virtual schools). Indeed, in the novel Cline goes out of his way to sell his vision of free online education as a means to make the OASIS more egalitarian. It is, therefore, an important detail that Halliday places the solution to the first clue on Ludus, as he wants a worthy kid to find it. In Spielberg's movie, however, Ludus becomes merely another Easter egg for fans of the novel—a planet passed over in the opening sequence but given no contextualization, its role in the narrative replaced by a dramatic race scene that give the crew the chance to showcase a few more of those impressive intellectual property acquisitions.

Game playing has traditionally been neglected in utopian fiction and is one of the major driving forces behind the novel's utopianism. As Justin Nordstrom highlights:

while traditional utopias are not completely devoid of games, readers are left with the impression that utopians are nose-to-the-grindstone types. Perfecting society, utopian authors are want to point out, is not a frivolous task. Games, when they are mentioned at all, generally serve to highlight important roles and responsibilities—reinforcing utopians' social hierarchies or moral sensibilities. Utopians might play games, but they don't just play for fun. (241)

A speech given in William Cameron Menzies's *Things to Come* (1936) seems to bear this out: "Do you realize the immense task we shall undertake, when we set ourselves to an active and aggressive peace," enthuses Oswald Cabal (Raymond Massey), "when we direct our energies to tear out the wealth of this planet, and exploit all these giant possibilities of science that have been squandered hitherto on war and senseless competition." Indeed, competition is more generally the domain of dystopian texts. One might think, for example, of the gladiatorial contests of *The Running Man* (1987) or *The Hunger Games* (2012). Condis claims that Cline's *Ready Player One*, on the other hand, is an example of a ludic novel in that it is "not only *about* game playing" it also "*require*[s] game-playing and puzzle-solving of readers" (2). By comparison, Spielberg's movie risks becoming a gratifying yet ultimately empty vessel through which viewers can peek once again at the cherished icons of their childhood as they flash by momentarily on screen: a movie where the only game in which the audience can participate involves competing with one another in identifying each visual cue—a competition that likely takes place only after the film's end in the moments of digestion and reflection as one leaves the theater or inside the virtual walls of film fora. This is also indicated by the many reviews, magazine features, and YouTube videos that surfaced after the film's release all claiming to offer a complete list of the Easter eggs to be discovered in the movie. Rather than participate in the action in Spielberg's movie, one feels entirely a spectator. In this way, the movie shows the limitations of the medium. Movies cannot be games, nor can they do what games do.

Conclusion

In *Ready Player One* the 1980s become cool and exciting. By contrast, the future that is in many ways modeled on the present—the idea that should the evil corporation IOI win the contest, for example, they would sell up to 80 percent of a player's field of vision in the OASIS to advertisers, seemingly a clear poke at companies like Facebook and YouTube, which increasingly rely on advertising revenue—seems not just postapocalyptic but cold and devoid of the creative energies of the 1980s, the period when so much of the technology that the movie celebrates was developed. On another level, however, it would seem entirely appropriate that it is the 1980s to which *Ready Player One* returns; the decade which Mark Fisher noted in 2014 as "the moment when the current crisis of cultural temporality could first be felt" (13–14). Fisher argued in *Ghosts of My Life* that "while 20th-century experimental culture was seized by a recombinatorial delirium, which made it feel as if newness was infinitely available, the 21st century is oppressed by a crushing sense of finitude and exhaustion" (8). When even our science fiction blockbusters look to our most innovative technologies to take us backward into the past rather than to confront and explore new futures, it does start to feel like we have already given up on that future. Spielberg's ending for *Ready Player One* is a fudge: it tells us not to ignore the present and hide in the past even though that's what we have spent the whole movie doing. It suggests that the exciting new virtual reality future it imagines must be held back, to be collapsed into the framing for another classical Hollywood romance.

In an often-quoted aphorism from John Green's *Looking for Alaska*, the author suggests that "imagining the future is a kind of nostalgia" (54). Indeed, to construct our future we must draw on past experience to tell us what might or might not work. It is not nostalgia alone which is the problem. As Anne Friedberg argues, "nostalgia can also take a utopian turn" since it "has the potential to reinvent the past, to contrast its values in a critical combination with the present" (189). Looking to the past for inspiration is not the problem, then, but burying one's head in the past, wanting to return to and even live in that past is a different matter entirely. Thus, although *Ready Player One* explores various utopian ideas and offers the audience progression in terms of its consideration of the place of gaming in tomorrow's utopia, its filtering of the narrative through nostalgia for the 1980s, and its reliance on the creation and maintenance of prosthetic memory undermines its utopian potential. For Christina Lee, "the time-traveler—whether it be the historian or the character in a fictional narrative—commands an unparalleled authority to reimagine, even rewrite, history and vault through the fourth dimension" and to this extent sci-fi texts that involve time travel should be regarded as essentially utopian (2). Marty McFly goes backward and, despite all advice, can't resist changing history. By contrast, the past in *Ready Player One* is always virtual and thus untouchable. It can be dwelled on but never altered, at least not in any sense that can help shape what is to come. It is a film about history masquerading as a film about the future: a fitting analogy for our nostalgic times.

Works Cited

Berger, James. "Which Prosthetic? Mass Media, Narrative, Empathy, and Progressive Politics." *Rethinking History* 11.4 (2007): 597–612. https://doi.org/10.1080/13642520701652152.

Biskind, Peter. *Easy Riders, Raging Bulls: How the Sex-Drugs-and-Rock 'n' Roll Generation Saved Hollywood*. New York: Simon & Schuster. 1998.

Brogan, Jacob. "Imagining the Future Is Dangerous: Sci-fi Writer Ernest Cline Discusses *Ready Player One*, Virtual Reality, and Nostalgia." *Slate*, July 14, 2015. https://slate.com/technology/2015/07/an-interview-with-ernest-cline-author-of-ready-player-one-and-armada.html.

Brown, Alfie. "Steven Spielberg's Film Portrays Video Gamers at Their Worst." *Guardian*, March 30, 2018. https://www.theguardian.com/commentisfree/2018/mar/30/steven-spielberg-video-gamers-ready-player-one-gaming.

Cline, Ernest. *Ready Player One*. London: Arrow Books, 2012.

Condis, Megan. "Playing the Game of Literature: *Ready Player One*, the Ludic Novel, and the 'Geeky' Canon of White Masculinity." *Journal of Modern Literature* 39.2 (2016): 1–19.

Cook, Pam. *Screening the Past: Memory and Nostalgia in Cinema*. New York: Taylor and Francis, 2005.

Fisher, Mark. *Ghosts of My Life: Writings on Depression, Hauntology and Lost Futures*. Winchester: Zero Books, 2014.

Friedberg, Anne. *Window Shopping: Cinema and the Postmodern*. Berkeley: University of California Press, 1994.

Green, John. *Looking for Alaska*. New York: Dutton, 2005.

Landsberg, Alison. *Prosthetic Memory: The Transformation of American Remembrance in the Age of Mass Culture*. New York: Columbia University Press, 2004.

Lee, Christina. "Introduction." *Violating Time: History, Memory, and Nostalgia in Cinema*. Ed. Christina Lee. New York: Continuum, 2008. 1–11.

Le Gall, Michel, and Charles Taliaferro. "The Recovery of Childhood and the Search for the Absent Father." *Steven Spielberg and Philosophy: We're Gonna Need a Bigger Book*. Ed. Dean A. Kowalski. Lexington: University of Kentucky Press, 2011. 38–49.

Lizardi, Ryan. *Mediated Nostalgia: Individual Memory and Contemporary Mass Media*. London: Lexington Books, 2015.

Nannar, Nina. "Steven Spielberg on the Threat of Netflix, Computer Games and New Film Ready Player One." ITV News, YouTube, March 20, 2018. https://www.youtube.com/watch?v=_hTTvO50QTs.

Nel, Philip. "I Love the '80s: Dystopia, Nostalgia, and Ready Player One." Nine Kinds of Pie, October 4, 2013. http://www.philnel.com/2013/10/04/rpo/.

Nordstrom, Justin. "A Pleasant Place for the World to Hide: Exploring Themes of Utopian Play in Ready Player One." *Interdisciplinary Literary Studies* 18.2 (2016): 238–56.

Opie, John. *Virtual America: Sleepwalking through Paradise*. Lincoln: University of Nebraska Press, 2008.

Parrinder, Patrick. *Learning from Other Worlds: Estrangement, Cognition and the Politics of Science Fiction and Utopia*. Liverpool: Liverpool University Press, 2000.

Power, Ed. "Ready Player One: A Guide to the Legal Nightmare of Spielberg's Pop Culture References." *Telegraph*, March 29, 2018. https://www.telegraph.co.uk/films/0/ready-player-one-guide-legal-nightmare-spielbergs-pop-culture/.

Roettgers, Janko. "How Steven Spielberg Used VR Headsets to Shoot 'Ready Player One.'" *Variety*, April 20, 2018. https://variety.com/2018/digital/news/spielberg-ready-player-one-vr-headset-1202771097/.

Rottenberg, Josh. "How the Team Behind 'Ready Player One' Wrangled a Bonanza of Pop Culture References into a Single Film." *Los Angeles Times*, April 1, 2018. https://www.latimes.com/entertainment/movies/la-et-mn-ready-player-one-references-20180401-story.html.

Rubin, Peter. "*Ready Player One* Is a Virtually Empty Good Time." *Wired*, March 29, 2018. https://www.wired.com/story/ready-player-one-review/.

Suvin, Darko. "On the Poetics of the Science Fiction Genre." *College English* 34.3 (1972): 372–82.

Wetmore, Kevin J., Jr. "Introduction." *Uncovering Stranger Things: Essays on Eighties Nostalgia, Cynicism and Innocence in the Series*. Jefferson, NC: McFarland, 2018. 1–7.

11

Replaying Cowboys and Indians

Controlled and Commercial Nostalgia in *Westworld*

CHRISTINA WILKINS

IN RECENT YEARS, NOSTALGIC television has dominated our screens. The desire to return, while not new, has now firmly situated itself in the long-form televisual narrative, demanding a more in-depth consideration of this need to explore the past. The variety of material presented in such series reflects that although nostalgia is ever present, our understanding of it is being altered by the way we understand history via the mediated space. Through its carefully constructed iconography, contemporary nostalgic television asks us to reexamine not an "authentic" past but a mediated one. Often, these series rely on a nostalgia for a past we only know through its images, and HBO's *Westworld* (2016–) is a prime example of this.

In its fusion of the Western and sci-fi genres, *Westworld* relies on the nostalgic iconography of the past as constructed through these genres, using intertextual links to construct a space to think about the future. In doing so, its reliance on genre tropes and images could be said to echo the Jamesonian approach to nostalgia that focuses on the re-creation of "dead styles" (Jameson 286). That does not mean all nostalgic texts are simply re-creations or imitations. Our experience of and interaction with nostalgic texts often resituates the past, as Kaja Silverman posits: "the past is available to us only in a textual form and through the mediation of the present" (cited in DeFalco 35). The mediated past re-creates our understanding of it, altering the details and providing a new story for a contemporary audience. The temporal moment is crucial in adding an aspect of novelty here, something that will be discussed later. The designation of a text as nostalgic is also contingent on how we understand nostalgia in our current moment. As is often detailed in discussions of the topic, nostalgia has its origins in the medical but has shifted toward political, psychological, and geographical conceptions. Recent critical approaches have sought a taxonomy of nostalgia, often dividing it into two: Paul Grainge's assertion of it as mood and mode (*Monochrome Memories*) and Svetlana Boym's restorative and reflective nostalgias, which develops Marc Le Sueur's assertion of nostalgia being either restorative or melancholic.

The attempts to categorize nostalgia reinforce its complexity and myriad uses. Katharina Niemeyer comments on this, arguing that we should consider nostalgia as plural—nostalgias—alongside the idea that the space of media is a place where different nostalgias interact (6). This is the starting point from which to analyze *Westworld*, through an awareness of its mediated space and reliance on the recycled and repeated past image as nostalgic signifier. *Westworld* offers an exploration of nostalgia and its uses in contemporary culture. Particularly, it explores the commercial use of nostalgia as a mode that is Jamesonian. This commercial exploitation of the nostalgic impulse works on the collective and personal levels in its evocation of a mythic American past through the Western setting of the park and its ability to "reveal your deepest self" ("Trompe L'Oeil," season 1, episode 7). Through an exploration of the text, this chapter argues that *Westworld* situates nostalgia as the catalyst for self-actualization and as enabling unification of our past and present selves, thereby positioning nostalgia as a progressive rather than conservative force. However, this is problematized by the role played by time and memory in the text, which disrupts traditional and linear understandings of personal and collective history. By way of engaging this problem, the chapter briefly considers the role of time and memory in the use of nostalgia, exploring our increasingly digital conception of memory and therefore our past.

Putting the West into *Westworld*

As an adaptation of Michael Crichton's 1973 movie, *Westworld* draws on how we have constructed images of our past in the remediation of the original story and the mythic western space at the core of the narratives. Like the original film, the series focuses on the artificial theme park Westworld run by the company Delos—there are other parks such as Rajworld, Shogun world and, in the original film, Medieval world. The core of the Delos universe in both texts is the Westworld park, and this is worth pausing on for a moment. In the context of nostalgia, the imagined past of the American West provides a space to consolidate a particular understanding of American identity, one founded on controlled images and one that is ultimately grounded in myth. The representation of this period comes into cultural consciousness arguably through the genre of the western film, providing the iconography for subsequent re-creations. Michael Coyne's *The Crowded Prairie* is one such critical response asserting the importance of the West in the conceptualizing of American identity. In capturing space and battling for new homelands, the tale of the West is framed by the idea of (re)capturing the original pioneer spirit of the pilgrims and can thus be seen as a return. Furthermore, the cowboy character in these western films offers an archetype in opposition to the "Indians" against which they fight. The binary of us versus them is crucial in texts about national identity as it grapples with what it means to belong to a particular nationality or group.

The western is a genre defined by struggle and suffering, something echoed in the experience of the Westworld park. That the genre itself enables a prolific mediation of a key period of US history allows for recycling and reusing the western-as-imagined in earlier film. The sheer number of texts that touch on the struggles of the frontier and the ideological promises of expansion attest to its importance in the American consciousness. This embedding of the concerns of the frontier and Western expansion within visual culture also complicates the (re)use of its iconography. The signification of the generic iconography becomes not about the period it represents but what the era of the genre's golden age does. Douwe Draaisma argues that people primarily nostalgize a formative period where identity is consolidated in a new environment, or childhood (132). Many of the nostalgic televisual texts refer back to a childhood nostalgia, whereas others examine a formative time in culture. These formative periods are defined by their realization of identities both personal and collective. The western as a collective consolidation of a particular conception of American identity positions it as ideally suited to thinking through nostalgia. In its preoccupation with the image of the West, the genre focuses more on myth than historical accuracy (Cook). In its use of this mythical nostalgic space, the Westworld park reconstructs an experience defined by its image that allows an imitation of the quest of the western film: that of a search for identity. Pam Cook looks specifically at the gendered construction of this, arguing that the western is "a narrative based on a masculine quest for sexual and national identity which marginalises women" (43). We see this particularly in *Westworld*'s privileging of the Man in Black's (Ed Harris) narrative arc over other prominent woman-centered storylines.

Before consideration of the park's visitors, it is useful to expand on the way the park itself is presented. The title sequence for the series lays bare the mechanics of the park, showing the artificial nature of everything we will soon be shown within. This emphasis on artificiality and the mechanical steers us toward understanding the series as sci-fi; a common feature of the genre being laying bare of the truth about humanity through its technological development. In the opening episode, we are introduced to the park from the perspective of the robot "hosts" and given an outline of its workings: narrative loops allow for visitors to take part in a story that has a clear path and easily manageable experience. The hosts replay these loops unknowingly, underscored by the frequent return to the same image to signify its beginning. In the first episode alone, we see the beginning of Dolores's (Evan Rachel Wood) loop four times, each opening with a close-up of her awakening at home (figure 11.1). The visitors to the park are referred to as "newcomers," who come there to "gratify desires" as staff member Bernard Lowe (Jeffrey Wright) notes in the first episode ("The Original"). The nostalgic presentation of the West is supported through the jaunty musical cues, dress, and warm color palette, which is markedly different from the scenes in the Westworld lab. By contrast, these scenes, with their harsh lighting, medical equipment, and stark nudity of the hosts, provide a jarring parallel to the past of the park. The scenes of mayhem in the form of villain Hector and his gang terrorizing Sweetwater would not be out of place in a western film of the 1940s. These are lingered over through slow-motion shots, which give audiences a taste of what park guests are really there for. The park is a place where guests can kill, rape, chase, and fraternize with hosts without consequence, as the motto of the park echoes: "Live Without Limits." As such, the space of the park offers the chance to safely enact violent crimes, situating these as expressions of desire rather than acts of consequence. Like nostalgia, the park allows for an immersion in a secure environment where history can be vicariously (re)experienced, which allows for the fortification of identity through an understanding of the past and its role in the contemporary moment. The Man in Black is the narrative epitome of this, through his claim that "In a sense, I was born here" ("Chestnut," season 1, episode 2). He came to the park when he was younger, and a large part of the *Westworld* narrative is devoted to the journey of his self-actualization.

The importance of the western setting and the fabricated nature of this past is highlighted through the shifts between the park and the Westworld lab. We are shown the creation of hosts, alterations to behavior, in short, the mechanics behind the magic. The artificiality of this nostalgia is strikingly shown through moments such as Dolores being analyzed for deviant behavior—she initially speaks in a Southern drawl, but after a brief retort of "lose the accent" from the tech dealing with her, her voice and manner dramatically change, revealing the reality beneath the mask ("The Original," season 1, episode 1). Nostalgia is shown to be little more than a commercialized product through these nods to the synthetic nature of the park. It is further reinforced by the choice (primarily male) guests are given between white and black hats—a

Figure 11.1. Dolores (Evan Rachel Wood) waking up in *Westworld* episode 1 (Jonathan Nolan, 2016). Digital frame enlargement.

reference to the mode of gameplay in which players can opt to be good or evil. The gamification of the experience is also depicted in the return to the beginning of the loops of the hosts that echo "save points" in a game. The world of the park is framed as game-like and entertaining by the guests who visit it—referring to their time there as "vacation" or a "break from reality," and being offered the chance to take photos on completion of missions such as killing the villain. Similarly, this artifice is shown through narrative details, such as hosts repeating the same lines to different guests. Even seemingly profound statements issued by the hosts are undermined by the characterization of their writer, Lee Sizemore (Simon Quarterman), an abrasive man whose aim for the park is for it to be a "relentless fucking experience" ("Dissonance Theory," season 1, episode 4).

The prioritization of experience for the guests is something highlighted with the routine maintenance of the park being shown in the clean-up of "dead'" hosts and resetting of narrative loops. All of this serves to reinforce the cynicism of the commercialized nostalgia on which the park relies. On the contrary, the experience of the hosts complicates this understanding and conceptualization of memory and time and how they delineate nostalgic experience.

When Are We? Time and Linearity

Along with reinforcing the looping nature of the park, the repetition of particular moments from a host's narrative also allows the audience to spot the difference between timelines and mark the progress of a character's quest to achieve consciousness. At the center of the *Westworld* narrative is a question that recurs in many sci-fi tales: what makes us human? Here it is framed by the acquisition of consciousness, an increasingly pressing question as AI technology develops at a rapid pace. Guests and staff of the park repeatedly assert that the hosts are "not real," and the creators of the park, Dr. Ford (Anthony Hopkins) and Arnold, struggle with the idea of hosts gaining consciousness. The central quest for the host Dolores in season 1 is to find her way to the center of the maze and become fully conscious. In the series, this is presented as a return, as we are frequently shown flashbacks to her in the same locations at different moments. It transpires that Dolores had found her way to the center of the maze and was instrumental in disrupting the park once before. We are given small visual cues to differentiate between times, such as dress, landmarks, and the person she is with. This shifting of time unsettles the linearity of the narrative, echoing the confusion Dolores feels. At one point, unable to work out what is happening, she asks, "When are we?," asserting the idea of time as location ("Trace Decay," season 1, episode 8). Thus, time becomes fragmented, patched together through Dolores's experience of the world around her, presenting a different consideration of narrative forms.

As is the nature of television, the series involves multiple narrative threads and character arcs that interweave. These too switch between times, again nodded to by small details that may go unobserved by some viewers—one of the hosts, Lawrence, features in two different character arcs that are run seemingly in parallel. The conflicting positioning of him geographically and his physical state (heavily injured in one story) guide the audience to the awareness that these stories are occurring at different moments. Our natural tendency on hearing a story is to assume a synchronicity of the temporal moment, to read it as a tale reflecting a message that is bound by certain time limits. While shifting timeframes has been a common feature of postmodern narratives, *Westworld* uses it not to comment on the slipperiness of time but to interrogate the construction of our world and ourselves through linear memory. This shifting between temporal moments is tied to the nostalgic mode. Jameson's conception of nostalgia relies on stylistic conventions that present it as, in Grainge's words, "a consumable style . . . characterised as amnesiac" (*Monochrome Memories* 11). Forgetting and remembering in *Westworld* are made overt through the shifting between timelines, forcing audiences to consider the limits of memory. This shifting also prompts the same question Dolores asks: when are we? In trying to situate or anchor ourselves at a point in the narrative, we are searching for the "now" that will enable us to structure an understanding of the narrative past. This understanding is necessarily mediated by when "now" is, as it provides a temporal space to frame the events of before. As Cook notes: "[the] past is produced by the present, and . . . the result is a hybrid fabrication, a reinterpretation and recombination of primary and secondary materials from the perspective of current concerns and agendas" (3). Again, this is something central to the nostalgic—an awareness of something missing or different in the present that leads to a longing for its reappearance or reinstatement. Yet this idea of nostalgia is that of the nostalgic "mood" in Grainge's terms defined as "longing and loss" rather than mode (*Monochrome Memories* 11). Although both can be seen in *Westworld*, it is primarily the nostalgic mode that is under interrogation here. This can be further elucidated by a consideration of the form of the series: television.

Katharina Niemeyer and Daniela Wentz argue that serial television is inherently nostalgic in its form through its creation of "temporal gaps between episodes and seasons, the void a long-watched series leaves when it finally ends, or the never-arriving closure of an unfinished narrative" (134). The temporal conditions of television make it an apt space to enact and assess understandings of nostalgia. As noted earlier, Niemeyer posits an understanding of nostalgia as plural and media as a space where these nostalgias can interact. *Westworld*'s plural nostalgias are evident in its different elements: the setting of the mythic western space as nostalgic experience functions as mode, a "consumable style" for one, along with the formal qualities of the serialized narrative. Second, the "mood" of nostalgia operates through the characters themselves—not just their feelings of loss and longing but their actions that lead them to continuously return to their designated "home." I now turn to this to examine how the presentation of memory in *Westworld* problematizes its relationship with nostalgia.

Returning Home

Memory and nostalgia are necessarily intertwined; nostalgia functions through a particular construction of and ability to recall memory. Niemeyer's thoughts on time and nostalgia also touch on the importance of memory, arguing that a "non linear social understanding of time and the concept of memory are closely correlated" (3). When we remember, we are—consciously, at least—in a liminal state: neither in the past nor the present. However, although nostalgia is not a form of memory, an immersion in nostalgia is often characterized by a desire to return to a remembered past. This desire links past and present, blurring the experience of time. In the same way, Dolores's continuous shifting of timeframes through her recollections blurs the audience's understanding of linearity. Her quest to return home is underscored by her repeated statement that "There's a path for everyone, and my path leads me back to you." Her search for home is not positioned traditionally as a return to the homestead she repeatedly awakens in, but a return to a sense of unity either through a relationship when she is reunited with host Teddy and guest William, or a unity of self when she returns to the center of the maze, where she finds herself.

Another host, Maeve (Thandie Newton) is similarly struck by reminiscences of the past that push her to seek the truth about her existence.

As her ability to recall the past grows, she begins to question the nature of her reality. With everything running smoothly, the hosts' memories are supposed to be "wiped clean" after the completion of a loop. This controlled forgetting is multipurpose: it allows the experience of the guests to be easily supervised by operating the same narrative loops, and it enables the hosts to interact with the guests without prejudice. Given the often violent behavior of the guests, the hosts' unwiped memory would lead them to either retaliate or attempt to elude those they regard as a threat. Instead, what the hosts are programmed to remember is different and directed toward a particular end. They are given a "cornerstone" memory around which their identity is built—a memory that is frequently returned to, supported by the repeated visual motifs associated with different hosts. Maeve's cornerstone memory is of her child, which the lab techs attempt to change when they move her to another role in the park. This ultimately disrupts her understanding of self, and the intrusion of the memory triggers a nostalgic longing to return to the imagined homeland and imaginary child she saw. As the series moves on, Maeve breaks out of the confines of the park and apparently rebels against her programming. However, we are then shown that this has been the plan all along—her code has been directing this rebellion, despite her belief that she is "writing [her] own fucking story" ("Trace Decay"). While this begins to suggest that she is still under the control of her programming, the final episode of season 1 sees her disregard this directive and return to the park in search of her daughter, exerting her own free will. That the trigger for this progression to true consciousness is a nostalgic drive is interesting given the common perception that nostalgia is conservative.

The idea of progression here is housed in a particular context of technological advancement that is tied to an understanding of the limits of humanity. As with many other sci-fi narratives centered on AI, *Westworld* prompts a consideration of what constitutes human identity. This is achieved through the show's situation of AI in opposition to humanity and the subsequent attempts made by various human characters to justify the exploitation of robots who come to seem as "real," in the audience's mind, as their living counterparts. As Paul Grainge discusses in relation to Ridley Scott's *Blade Runner* (1982)—a movie that shares this agenda— such narratives "demonstrate a more contemporary concern with the unsettled boundaries between reality and simulation in the constitution of remembered identity and experience" (*Memory* 8). With experience becoming progressively more mediated, we move ever closer toward Jameson's idea of the past as a "vast collection of images, a multitudinous photographic simulacrum" (18). The constructed nature of the image and our memory of it is made explicit through the experience of the hosts. Their memories are manipulated images designed to produce a particular response and create a particular identity. Given the frequency of our interactions with the imaginary image through television, film, and other media, our own past becomes a highly mediated and thus imaginary space that is easily altered. This is compounded by the increasing presence of the doctored or fabricated image or video, further destabilizing digital memory. This instability of memory is something already present in our culture, as argued by Andreas Huyssen: "the very structure of memory is strongly contingent upon the social formation that produces it" (cited in Grainge, *Monochrome Memories* 5). Memory shifts under the weight of our remembering, with each remembrance altering the past until it becomes a simulated set of images. This simulated past is bound to the way we remember, our attempt to recall the origins of our memories through the present in nostalgic moods. As Linda Hutcheon argues, "there is no directly and accessible past 'real' for us today" (cited in Sprengler 87). Our desire to grasp memory as something verifiable, tangible, is enacted through our engagement with the nostalgic text or image. Yet in the act of trying to grasp it, we reduce it further to an unstable image.

Imagined Futures

That the hosts trust their memory and continue to return to it nostalgically to help construct their identities reinforces the idea in *Westworld* that we consult a mediated past in order to move forward. In a 1961 essay on the importance of nostalgia, Arthur P. Dudden encourages us to "face the future by facing the past" (530). While essays like Dudden's testify to the continued existence of more positive valuations of nostalgia's place in culture, the dominance of Jameson's conceptions of the term—nostalgia as an empty attempt to seek history "through our own pop images" (25)—suggests another direction altogether. Rather than thinking of memory (and history) as an archive, as Niemeyer asserts, we have moved into the digital era. We talk of bytes and clouds, with memory ever present in our pockets and on our desktops. With the digitization of memory comes the illusion that we can control our remembering, more accurately recall and store moments of our pasts. Yet as *Westworld* clearly shows, the past is still corruptible, and a reliance on digital memory leaves us at the mercy of corporations who hold the power to manipulate both collective and personal memory.

Although the digitization of memory alters our understanding of our capacity for remembered experience, it is still defined by how we categorize memory itself. What we choose to remember and memorialize as a society affects what we become nostalgic for. In constructing our history through images, we mold a particular perception of a period or space. The western film, to use our current example, has provided a host of spaces, conventions, and characters through which we come to make sense of that period. As Scott Simmon notes in *The Invention of the Western Film*, "The A western claims, dishonestly, to bring us the facts of history, while the B western more readily admits its nostalgia" (181). Both strands of the genre present images of the West to be consumed as memory, whether nostalgic or historical. Undermining a particular view of a remembered image is met with hostility, as we see again with this example. The 1991 Smithsonian exhibition "The West as America" recast the experiences of the claiming of the West in a more cynical light, highlighting the suffering underpinning it. There were outcries from the public and critics about the perceived "leftist" or "inaccurate" portrayal of the frontier (Gulliford 77). As we explored briefly earlier, the West provides an understanding of a mythic American identity, a kind of anchor to a crucial point in the past.

Yet this anchor is unstable, reliant on upholding a particular understanding of an image or period that has been proliferated through our mediated spaces. Like *Westworld*, what we make our objects of nostalgia has moved from the geographic space of home to the image that represents it. The slipperiness of this image is underlined in the series by the illustration of its manipulation and commercialization. On attempting to leave the park, Maeve encounters the welcome area for guests, where she sees the memory she has been reexperiencing of her child projected on the wall in front of her as an advertisement (figure 11.2). The marketing of the park relies on a sense of coming home, returning to one's true self, all defined by a particular image of what this entails. Here it encompasses family and the open space of the West. The immersion in the nostalgic image is what is afforded by the space of the park itself—which functions as what Huyssen calls a "usable past" as opposed to "disposable data" (431). This is complicated by the series's status as adaptation; it takes the narrative of the *Westworld* film as precursor and uses it to offer a multilayered approach to the nostalgic image. Although

Figure 11.2. Maeve (Thandie Newton) encountering the Westworld reception in *Westworld* episode 10 (Jonathan Nolan, 2016). Digital frame englargement.

there are no direct references to the 1973 film (aside from the title), it takes the same world of the park and re-creates an updated version that develops the narrative past of *Westworld*. In doing this, the series draws on a repository of images and visual memories of what constitutes the technology of the future.

Westworld moves on from these past understandings of our imagined futures and offers progression. Building on the somewhat sympathetic approaches to AI in *Blade Runner* (1982), *I, Robot* (2004), and *Ex Machina* (2014), it gives us an insight into the experience of these machines through glimpses of their past. While Roy Batty in *Blade Runner* may have begun to evoke this by recounting his memories as he lay dying, these were verbal tales. In *Westworld*, we are given visual access to the image, which becomes the nostalgic currency. That these images are in some cases implanted triggers an anxiety about memory. As Grainge notes, the "desire for memory as stable, reassuring and constant [. . .] is] plagued by the fear of its instability" (*Memory* 5). The experience of the hosts is not too dissimilar from our own; the nonlinear recollection of past moments, the confusion about the veracity of the image, and the use of a nostalgia around which we construct our sense of identity are all elements of the postmodern condition. Although amplified through its digital form, the disrupted past and the change in nostalgic object from geographic space to desired image highlights the fragmentary nature of our experience. In talking of nostalgia, Bryan D. Price argues that "in Benjamin's estimation it was an ambivalent gaze that fell upon the past as a dispersion of fragments that could never attain their original unity" (107). This desire for unity is sought after by both the hosts and the guests—a unity that brings self-actualization. In the hosts' nostalgic experience, they can piece together their pasts to understand the world around them and gain full consciousness. This enables them to break out of the controlled remembering the park imposes on them; escape from, as Dolores says, feeling "trapped in a memory from a life long ago" ("Trace Decay"). The immersion in the nostalgic image for the hosts allows them to break their loop and move forward. For the guests, nostalgic reminiscence is presented as a way to trace their development, a kind of map to understanding oneself. In both cases, it is key to note that the act of remembering is not nostalgic, but the nostalgia emerges with how those memories are depicted and positioned as desired. The act of nostalgic immersion could arguably be seen as revelatory, giving us an understanding of what functions as formative for us, following on from Draaisma's point about what it is we nostalgize. As Ron Eyerman argues: "Memory provides . . . a cognitive map" and is therefore "central to individual and collective identity" (305). We see this with the dual timelines of the Man in Black. He seeks a way to the center of the maze, which is presented in parallel with his earlier experience of the park. This allows for an audience understanding of how his past has created the self he attempts to find. The moving through the geographic space of the park visually represents his moving through the map of his memory to direct himself toward his center, a place where all points meet and unite.

Nostalgia is complex; while it allows for self-actualization here, its fabricated nature underscores our fragile relationship with both time and memory. Our memories are reconstructions of the past, not reality itself, yet we see them as real. The *Westworld* park, as site of memory, feels "more real than the real world," as the Man in Black states ("The Bicameral Mind," season 1, episode 10). Yet the treatment of the hosts with their digital memories leads us to question how we will understand memory and our nostalgic recollections as traditional understandings of memory are altered. The commercialization of collective pasts is used as a framework for understanding the personal past and its role in constructing our present selves. Although nostalgia is aligned with progress, allowing hosts to break out of their loops and for guests to encounter their true selves, *Westworld* is ultimately inherently critical of attempts to commercially deploy nostalgia and control memories both personal and collective.

Works Cited

Boym, Svetlana. *The Future of Nostalgia*. New York: Basic Books, 2001.
Cook, Pam. *Screening the Past: Memory and Nostalgia in Cinema*. Oxford: Routledge, 2005.
Coyne, Michael. *The Crowded Prairie: American National Identity in the Hollywood Western*. London: I. B. Tauris, 1997.
DeFalco, Amelia. "A Double Edged Longing: Nostalgia, Melodrama and Todd Haynes' *Far from Heaven*." *Iowa Journal of Cultural Studies* 5 (2004): 26–39.
Draaisma, Douwe. *The Nostalgia Factory*. New Haven, CT: Yale University Press, 2013.
Dudden, Arthur. P. "Nostalgia and the American." *Journal of the History of Ideas* 22.4 (1961): 515–30.
Eyerman, Ron. "The Past in the Present: Culture and the Transmission of Memory." *The Collective Memory Reader*. Ed. Jeffrey K. Olick and Vered Vinitzky-Seroussi. Oxford: Oxford University Press, 2011. 304–7.
Grainge, Paul. *Memory and Popular Film*. Manchester: Manchester University Press, 2003.
Grainge, Paul. *Monochrome Memories: Nostalgia and Style in Retro America*. Westport, CT: Praeger, 2002.
Gulliford, Andrew. "Visitors Respond: Selections from 'The West as America' Comment Books." *Montana: The Magazine of Western History* 42.3 (1992): 77–80.
Huyssen, Andreas. "Present Pasts: Media, Politics, Amnesia." *The Collective Memory Reader*. Ed. Jeffrey K. Olick and Vered Vinitzky-Seroussi. Oxford: Oxford University Press, 2011. 430–36.
Jameson, Fredric. *Postmodernism or The Cultural Logic of Late Capitalism*. London: Verso, 1991.
Le Sueur, Marc. "Theory Number Five: Anatomy of Nostalgia Films." *Journal of Popular Film* 6.2 (1977): 187–97.
Niemeyer, Katharina. "Introduction." *Media and Nostalgia*. Ed. Katharina Niemeyer. Basingstoke: Palgrave Macmillan, 2014. 1–23.
Niemeyer, Katharina, and Daniela Wentz. "Nostalgia Is Not What It Used to Be: Serial Nostalgia and the Nostalgic Television Series." *Media and Nostalgia*. Ed. Katharina Niemeyer. Basingstoke: Palgrave Macmillan, 2014. 129–38.
Price, Bryan D. "Material Memory: The Politics of Nostalgia on the Eve of MAGA." *American Studies* 57.1 (2018): 103–15.
Simmon, Scott. *The Invention of the Western Film: A Cultural History of the Genre's First Half Century*. Cambridge: Cambridge University Press, 2003.
Sprengler, Christine. *Screening Nostalgia: Populuxe Props and Technicolor Aesthetics in Contemporary American Film*. New York: Berghahn Books, 2009.

12

Contradictory Reminiscences

Post-9/11 Cold War Nostalgia, *The Americans*, and *Deutschland 83/86*

IAN PETERS

SINCE THE SEPTEMBER 11, 2001, terrorist attacks, popular media has revived the archetypal Cold War narrative that the "enemy" can be anyone—including your neighbor. Remakes of classic TV shows and films from the Cold War populate the media landscape and were some of the first post-9/11 texts to reengage in this rhetoric. For example, shows like *Battlestar Galactica* (2004–2009) and *Gerry Anderson's New Captain Scarlet* (2005)—both reimaginings of important shows from the 1960s and 1970s aired within five years of the attacks—dealt with these concepts in a sci-fi atmosphere where parallels between the War on Terror and the Red Scare were central to the narrative. In recent years, we have seen an increasing number of original programs and films, in the United States and abroad, that instead seek to re-create the Cold War themes in a realistic depiction that often frames the discourse within a nostalgic celebration of that era's popular culture. This is an approach that is common in narratives that examine the later years of the Cold War, where 1980s consumerism, music, and popular media transformed the consumptive landscape while the superpowers continued their feud on the global stage. While films like the critically acclaimed *Bridge of Spies* (2015) revisit an early period of the conflict, shows like AMC's *The Americans* (2013–2018), and the first two seasons in RTL/Sundance's *Deutschland* trilogy—*Deutschland 83* (2015) and *Deutschland 86* (2018)—instead focus on the Cold War's final years in the 1980s, its main events, and the pop cultural world that emerged simultaneously. In the end, the resulting programs are less a celebration of history and more a reminder that the past and the present are eerily similar. They are essentially a nostalgia of contradiction.

As discussed by Emmanuelle Fantin, nostalgia is frequently linked to material pastness (95). Paraphrasing Vladimir Jankélévitch, who argues that "nostalgia is triggered by the regret of a subjective event, place or time," Fantin proposes that exposure to our ordinary, daily material world is enough to "evoke an entire epoch" (95). Encountering everyday material objects such as the furniture, clothing, cars, and artifacts of popular culture, according to Fantin, "[maintains] a link to the lost past that continually perpetuates its relevance" (95). Furthermore, she proposes that the past is also sometimes used in an antinostalgic capacity. In her discussion of the Citroën DS advertising campaign, Fantin highlights how the company used famous, long-dead celebrities like Marilyn Monroe and John Lennon—celebrities who are frequently the focus of nostalgia themselves—to discuss how nostalgia is a trap that keeps society from advancing (96). This contradiction identifies what Fantin calls an expression of nostalgia "through the filter of what we could call 'baroque aesthetics'" (96). In this case, the "baroque aesthetic" highlights "antithesis" as a thematic and semiotic tool to emphasize strangeness and contradiction.

Whereas most nostalgia-oriented programming tends to be a celebration of an idealized past, *The Americans* and *Deutschland 83/86* offer a different sort of nostalgia in the post-9/11 world—one that, like Fantin's baroque aesthetic, celebrates nostalgic popular culture while simultaneously reminding us that the past wasn't as pleasant as our memories frequently imply. Furthermore, these programs challenge the Cold War narrative in ways that programs produced during that era did not, thereby reflecting the ambiguity of contemporary post-9/11 existence and the social, political, and cultural debates that emerged as a result of those events. In the end, the resulting programs are a hybrid of nostalgia and antinostalgia that both celebrates the past and criticizes the present for failing to learn from it. Simultaneously, this blend of pro- and antinostalgia challenges the benefits of nostalgic thought and reminds us how troubled the past really was.

Building on existing scholarship in media and Cold War studies, this chapter identifies this special blend of pro- and antinostalgia as "post-9/11 Cold War nostalgia." This trend revisits one of the most terrifying moments of our recent past, at first as a way of coping with the global War on Terror and later as a means of examining recent developments in an increasingly hostile global political landscape. We live in a time where our sense of national identity has come under increasing pressure, where organizations like ISIS belong to no nation, often resulting in an unfortunate tendency toward racial and cultural profiling in ways that didn't occur during the Cold War (i.e., on bodies of color). The "enemy" has become harder to locate geographically, and "threats" appear to proliferate.

The Cold War was a moment where civilization was brought to the brink of destruction and we lived to tell the tale. However, in the past several years (since the election of Donald Trump to the office of the US presidency in 2016), the function of this nostalgia and how it resonates has changed dramatically. In addition to the investigations into Russian involvement in the US electoral process, the Bulletin of Atomic Scientists' "Doomsday Clock"—a symbol that represents the scientific possibility of humanity destroying itself—advanced to "2 minutes to midnight" on January 25, 2018. On this clock, midnight represents the total annihilation of humankind. As Sewell Chan points out in his *New York Times* article, this is the closest the clock has come to midnight since 1953 during the Cold War. A year later, the clock remained at the same position, indicating that the tensions remained. In a *Washington Post* article by Lindsey Bever and Abby Ohlheiser from January 24, 2019, they quote Bulletin President Rachel Bronson as stating that the unpredictability and volatility of the 2019 political landscape has put civilization at "a state as worrisome as the most dangerous times of the Cold War." According to Bronson, one of the major contributing factors to this dire assessment of humanity's future is that "U.S.-Russian relations are near an all-time low" (Bever and Ohlheiser). The parallels between the past and the present in contemporary political discourse are striking.

Michael Kackman argues in *Citizen Spy: Television, Espionage, and Cold War Culture* that "the political Cold War has long since passed, though its successors are forming; the cultural struggle over boundaries, limits, and responsibilities of citizenship are ongoing" (xiii). This is truer now than ever before, although the Cold War seems like it isn't quite so long ago anymore. Arguably, these narratives in the pre-Trump post-9/11 era provided a comparatively hopeful reminder that civilization would survive and (hopefully) also not repeat its past mistakes. This was further accomplished by shows like *The Americans* and *Deutschland 83* through the humanization of former enemies, which reminded us that we are all people with similar hopes, dreams, and fears, while simultaneously reminding us that no side is inherently free from guilt over its actions during times of conflict. However, since the 2016 election, these historical narratives took on a more contemporary relevance. What began as a reminder that, as *The Americans* creator Joe Weisberg stated, "'Hey look, these people who we think of as enemies are just like us'" (quoted in Sandberg) transformed into a reminder of how the past, present, and future are inherently linked through cycles of political and sociocultural repetition.

Several US reviewers (see Brennan; Valentine; Poniewozik) have noted thematic similarities between *The Americans* and *Deutschland*, not only due to their chosen era but also because of their focus on the infiltration of the West by Eastern bloc agents. These texts present us with a unique parallel that has not yet been fully explored: how a global superpower and major Cold War player (United States) and a country previously divided between capitalist and communist rule (Germany) use this era to reflect their distinct visions of the Cold War and simultaneously comment on the present. Both shows attempt to humanize the other side of the conflict in ways that are not only synonymous with their political history, but also their cultural history. However, this humanization was not always positively received in their respective domestic markets. While *The Americans* was a critical and commercial success in the United States, *Deutschland 83* failed to capture a similar response in its native Germany—probably due to its focus on making the audience "engage with the socialist regime's worldview" and the show's overly simplistic approach to a distinctly complex point in Germany's history that is still felt today (Oltermann). Consequently, the historical perceptions of nostalgia, along with their contemporary functions, are culturally specific.

For the purposes of this chapter, I examine *The Americans*, *Deutschland 83*, and *Deutschland 86* in three specific contexts: (1) as contemporary texts that illustrate the modern trend of Cold War nostalgia, (2) as the antithesis of the programming from the eras that they embody in each nation's distinct sociopolitical-industrial landscapes, and (3) as reflections of contemporary US and German society. Cold War nostalgia as seen in these popular texts approaches the conflict from a more balanced perspective than the popular media of the historic era. However, this balance is coded differently in each national context, and is influenced by each nation's distinct past and present.

Beginning with an analysis of *The Americans* in US media culture and a discussion of *Deutschland 83* and *86* and their place in contemporary unified German media, this brief overview hopes to highlight how each nation copes with their present sociopolitical identity by drawing comparisons to the past. These texts, when viewed in the context of contemporary society looking toward the past, argue that we managed to survive an era where two global superpowers stood on the brink of mutual annihilation. Many young adults who make up the audience of these programs were children when they lived through this era, and consequently the threats that were going on around them were likely never fully realized. This is particularly true of the US audience, whereas viewers who grew up in a divided Germany would have a different view—one that, as previously stated, resulted in a less positive reception of *Deutschland 83*. Popular culture references therefore serve distinct functions in these shows: as providing familiar context to shape key political events (in *The Americans*) and as a reminder of the restrictions and differences a population faced during an era of national division (in *Deutschland 83/86*).

This study and the shows that it focuses on began prior to the 2016 election and Trump's subsequent presidency. Consequently, many of these concepts transformed over the life of these shows. What began as fulfilling one set of sociohistorical functions ended up resonating completely differently after 2016. Given the relevance that these concepts presently play in the global politics of the late 2010s—particularly in the United States—this chapter ends with a discussion of how events from the 2016 presidential election, the subsequent investigations, and the presence of Cold War rhetoric in the media have transformed these concepts from what was arguably a more abstract glimpse into 1980s history into a concrete reminder that the sociopolitical issues of the past can always return to the present if we aren't careful.

The Americans

The Americans premiered on FX in 2013 and was created by former CIA officer Joe Weisberg. Completing its 6-season run in 2018, the series explored the Cold War from the perspective of the dominant figures during the conflict (the United States and the Soviet Union), while simultaneously commenting on Soviet austerity and US consumerism. Starring Keri Russell and Matthew Rhys as Elizabeth and Philip Jennings (two Soviet sleeper agents living in the United States with their two-American born children), the premise of *The Americans* was inspired by Weisberg's time working at the CIA and the 2010 arrest of ten Russian agents working undercover as part of the Illegals Program. This incident, which resulted in widespread international news coverage, seemed like something out of a classic Cold War narrative. The agents, who had been living in the United States, and several of whom had children here, were deeply ingrained in American life. Of the "illegals" involved in this bust, Anna Chapman, then a twenty-eight-year old woman, came to the forefront in most media coverage. Due to her youth and good looks, Chapman was referred to several times as a "real-life Bond girl," (Weaver; Esposti) and, in one case, a "reported 28-year-old secret agent/ Maxim model look-alike who specialized in sultry-eyed, pouty-lipped, come-hither stares" (Hesse). Interestingly, Chapman later did model for Russia's edition of *Maxim* magazine, appearing on the cover and in a photographic spread in October 2010 (Grove). To further compound this lurid, sexual fascination with Chapman, nude photographs purportedly taken by her British former husband were leaked online shortly following her arrest (Sherida). The focus on Chapman's sexualization rather than on her status as an accused enemy agent hearkens back to the espionage entertainment of the Cold War where, as Michael Kackman points out, an entire special issue of *Esquire* magazine in 1966—"Spies, Science, and Sex"—was devoted to the rise in spy-related entertainment (xvii). More broadly, this entire story was covered as a Cold War–era spy narrative come to life in the early twenty-first century, when hostilities between the United States and Russia were no longer thought plausible by many. In other words, the past had resurfaced in the present but was seen as more of a fascination than a threat. Although espionage is a serious concern, other issues, such as the War on Terror, tended to seem more "real" to modern audiences.

Media coverage of this incident highlighted three overarching themes surrounding contemporary Cold War intrigue: (1) an ingrained family life as cover, (2) reinforcement that spies are involved in the kinds of sex acts frequently romanticized in popular entertainment, and (3) the reemergence of dubious espionage-related activities between the two major Cold War–era opposing powers. Weisberg used all three of these themes in *The Americans*, choosing to set his series toward the end of the Cold War in the early 1980s, where the Jennings operate behind the scenes during such historical events as John Hinckley Jr.'s attempted assassination of President Ronald Reagan, the Soviet-Afghan War, Reagan's "evil empire" speech, and the death of Soviet leader Leonid Brezhnev. In between dealing with various typical family crises, the Jennings used sex as a weapon, lies as weapons, and weapons as weapons as they strove for "world peace" (as they called it multiple times) in the service of their country, the Soviet Union. Time and time again, civilization skirts the edge of its own destruction, as paranoia reigns on both sides.

Central to *The Americans* is the show's ability to make the world of espionage, intrigue, and potentially apocalyptic disaster identifiable. A key way the show accomplishes this is by exploring the Cold War as a family drama. We see these events through the points of view of the Jennings and their American children, their CIA agent neighbor Stan Beeman and his co-workers, the Soviet embassy, and various supporting characters in the United States and the Soviet Union. Each group forms unique social units (such as families or office cohorts), where the individuals respond differently to various "real world" historical conflicts that are then seen in the context of their everyday lives. These families fall victim to moments of familial melodrama, where typical milestones like puberty, first love, wanting to be popular, and other angsty themes plague the children. We also see the effect that infidelity, divorce, and other relationship issues have on children. Each moment is sandwiched in between key political moments as well as references to popular culture in the era, such as the impact that the introduction of the home computer had on domestic life, what music/movies/TV was popular, and the importance of shopping malls in 1980s American society. All of this adds a human element that moves beyond the issues as historic sociopolitical fact, and instead enters the realm of sociocultural context. The result is that the audience gains insight into how each side views the conflict officially and unofficially. When historically parallel events resurface, such as war in Afghanistan or the fear that enemies live among us, the audience can see how people responded to these events in the past as a means of reflecting on what their reappearance means in the present. Both the CIA and the KGB are depicted as complex, flawed organizations that commit acts of mercy, compassion, and brutal savagery. Neither side can truly claim the moral high ground in the conflict, as universal paranoia runs rampant, forcing the viewer to realize that "good" and "evil" are not as one-sided as most media portrayed in the era.

The concept of good versus evil is wrapped up in notions of nationalism, nationality, and cultural identity. In this regard, *The Americans* follows a trend that Kackman identified as existing during the Cold War. According to Kackman, "the cultural Cold War's underlying questions about national identity and citizenship" were reflected in the popular entertainment and news stories of the era (ix). In popular entertainment at the time, this was not an ambiguous concept. During a war of ideology, ambiguity weakens the tactical approach—particularly when mass communication technology's reach into American homes was on the front lines of the conflict. Alan Nadel argues that television's emergence as a "social and cultural phenomenon" in the United States is linked, in technology and substance, to Cold War culture (146–47). During this era—specifically through to the end of the 1950s—television rapidly became a major link between the American populace and the war through news reports, entertainment, and as a window into the major players in that conflict. Nadel states that "television's role as the apparatus of reality merged with its role as a technology of the surveillance state" (147). During this era, as Nadel argues, television united reality and fantasy together in a flow of content that presented viewers with a singular vision of the world "without contradiction" (146).

Nadel also draws parallels between Cold War television propaganda and brainwashing techniques, where both methods "used technology to invert and confuse, without detection, the relationship between inside and outside, producing a psychological (and, perhaps, characterological or even spiritual) manipulation" (147). Although the comparison results in an overly emphasized reduction of the American public's agency as an active audience, Nadel's observation that the content on American TV screens during this era was overwhelmingly united in its anticommunist message is an important one. His focus on the 1950s, at the height of McCarthyism, does present us with a set of social/technological/cultural and political contexts that are not as applicable even ten years later in the 1960s, when shows like *Star Trek*, *Mission Impossible*, and *The Man from U.N.C.L.E.* questioned the ideological dominance through generic masking and "fool" the censors. However, by the 1980s, American television was still largely discussing the Cold War through a lens of American hawkishness, with a shift at this point to mirror Reagan's White House. This isn't to say that US audiences automatically took to this dominant Cold War rhetoric in every instance. However, 1980s shows like *The A-Team*, *G.I. Joe: A Real American Hero*, and *Airwolf*—that did little to challenge Reagan-era hawkishness—dominated various demographic markets. In comparison, shows that regularly questioned such actions, like *M.A.S.H.*, were rare in the TV landscape following that show's conclusion in 1983.

As a technology, TV was a window to the world. Nadel points out, "television technology evoked an uncanny power of the real, which to a large degree drew upon a faith in visual representation" (152). This unity of message emerged as a result of the political and industrial climate of the era, which influenced what could and could not be shown on broadcast television. This message subsequently shaped people's perceptions of the conflict, although not as universally as Nadel seems to argue for previously stated reasons. After the contemporary US media landscape was expanded and regulatory restrictions were changed, it was able to overtly feature content that was more ideologically complex. Nostalgic reminiscences of this era consequently deliver a harsher, more complex glimpse into the past that both celebrates that past and challenges it. Revisiting the Cold War from both sides in shows like *The Americans* allow modern programming to question our national, fictionalized past while simultaneously commenting on our actions in the present.

The Deutschland Saga: *Deutschland 83* and *Deutschland 86*

Deutschland 83 (*D83*) and *Deutschland 86* (*D86*) examine Germany's Cold War history as a means of commenting on the present. Although Germany has thankfully not experienced a 9/11-scale terrorist attack, the country has unfortunately been the victim of numerous terrorist incidents during the Cold War and the War on Terror. *Deutschland 86*, in fact, deals with one of the most famous of these, the La Belle discotheque bombing at the hands of Libyan terrorists, which resulted in the deaths of 2 US servicemen, a Turkish civilian, and injuries to 229 others. More recently, and in the years following *Deutschland 83*'s premiere in June 2015, Germany has experienced a rush of terrorist attacks at the hands of Islamic extremists and home-grown right-wing extremist groups. This, coupled with postunification national identity conflicts, resulted in a series that critically examines Germany's past while alluding to issues of the present (Oltermann).

D83 and *D86*, which are the first two seasons of a three-season arc (*Deutschland 89* premiered in September 2020), are the products of the US/German writing team Anna and Joerg Winger. Airing in the United States on Sundance as the first German-language TV show to appear in its entirety on US television, the first eighteen episodes making up seasons 1 and 2 examine the Cold War from the point of view of a country that had literally been split in two. Before its reunification in 1990, Germany was the geographical and ideological embodiment of the Cold War, where communism and capitalism faced off over the border that divided the nation and particularly its capital, Berlin. *D83* explores how East and West Germany were caught in the middle of two opposing giants engaged in the ultimate nuclear staring contest, and how these conditions formed the counterculture/antiwar movements that emerged as a result. Starring Jonas Nay as East German soldier Martin Rauch, *D83* follows Rauch as he goes undercover in West Germany as Lt. Moritz Stamm, attaché to West German General Wolfgang Edel (Ulrich Noethen) during the deployment of the US-led Pershing II nuclear weapon system. The presence of these missiles put East and West Germany in the crosshairs of potential nuclear war. Balancing the narrative between East and West German perspectives through an ensemble cast, *D83* explores this conflict not through the eyes of Washington or Moscow but through the eyes of the German people and a young soldier stuck in between his love of home, family, and country and his love of freedom.

As is the case in *The Americans*, *Deutschland 83* and *86* juxtapose key political events with a nostalgic walk down pop-culture memory lane. As Gabriel Tate states in an article in *The Guardian*, titled "*Deutschland 83*: 'A lot of people were happy in East Germany,"* 1980s German "music was unusual in unifying the youth cultures of East and West at the time the era's Euro hits make an undeniably apt accompaniment." This is reflected at various points throughout the series, such as Nena's hit song "99 Luftballons" appearing several times early in the series. This song, which was universally popular on both sides of the Berlin Wall, helps bridge the transition from East to West in *D83*'s first episode as it illustrates a link between German communist and capitalist youth. As Matthew Leggatt points out in *Cultural and Political Nostalgia in the Age of Terror*, this West German song's presence on both sides "serves to highlight an underlying Western cultural dominance" in the East during this era (133). The importance of music and the ways we consume it continues throughout the two seasons, with Martin encountering his first Walkman and the music of Duran Duran while undercover in the West in season 1, episode 3 ("Atlantic Lion"). This was a transformative moment for the character, whose unbridled joy at this new sound and the innovative way of consuming it illustrated the stark difference between East and West.

Leggatt argues that Martin's encounters with Western music and 1980s popular culture in *D83* essentially minimizes the hardships of the era at the expense of embracing nostalgia. As Leggatt states, "by telling the story through 1980s music, *Deutschland 83* recreates the 'feeling' of the 1980s as glamorous without complicating this sensation with any acknowledgments of the hardships of the period that are, instead, papered over through the cultural excitement of Martin's stay in the West" (133). At the same time, that pop culture frequently examined the tensions that existed at the time. For example, the theme song—a section from Peter

Schilling's "Major Tom (Coming Home)" from his 1982 album *Error in the System*—is indicative of how the Cold War was reflected in popular music of the era and mirrors *D83*'s and *D86*'s overarching concept of possible nuclear war. As Tate discusses, Schilling's hit is "a song that casts [David] Bowie's Space Oddity character into the chill of a nuclear winter"—a future that Martin is desperately trying to prevent, even at the cost of betraying his own people. In instances like these, nostalgia and antinostalgia merge in a contemporary exploration of Cold War–era tension.

Music and other examples of popular culture, while ever present in these shows, are never truly presented as a nostalgic celebration of the era but are there to provide added context and help the audience relate to the events more easily. Unlike in *The Americans*, where popular culture is never seen as a threat to the show's characters, *D83* and *D86* remind us that under communist rule, consuming unauthorized cultural products like music or books could result in imprisonment if one was caught by the authorities. In *D83*, Martin's mother is arrested for her involvement in an underground library of banned books (which included George Orwell's *1984*), and pirate radio broadcasts from the West play a key role in *D86*. Exploring these cultural artifacts and how people consumed them remind us of the restrictions that existed alongside the political events of this era. While still consumed today, the context surrounding many of these songs, books, and other artifacts is more easily forgotten in contemporary society.

In another similarity to *The Americans*, *D83* and *86* rely on the family dynamic theme to help the historical drama resonate with modern audiences. When Martin is selected by his Stasi-officer aunt in *D83* to go undercover in the West, he leaves behind his mother, who is promised a kidney transplant by the government in exchange for her son's service, and his fiancée, who may or may not be carrying his baby. After infiltrating the West, Martin, now disguised as Moritz Stamm, finds himself amid a family feud between his cover's boss, General Edel, and his rebellious twentysomething children. Family conflict is at the heart of *D83*, as well as *D86*, and Martin is faced with a choice between the freedom he so actively seeks and returning home to his family and a son he has never known. The struggle between duty to the state, duty to the family, and duty to oneself mirrors the struggle to reunite East and West Germany following the fall of the Berlin Wall—a division that remains today between former citizens of each side due to lingering stereotypes. The series addresses many of those stereotypes while also serving as a means of exploring censorship, terrorism, bigotry, intolerance, and the paranoia that is always present in "us and them" narratives. The continuing rawness that remains in a society where neighbor turned against neighbor is, as Oltermann stated, one of the main reasons that this show has failed to catch on as popular entertainment in its home country.

All these themes are crucial to understanding contemporary Germany's media in relation to its past systems in the East and West. Similar media conditions existed on the Eastern bloc side of the ideological divide during the Cold War, albeit with a focus on reinforcing communist ideology, a fight against anticommunist imagery, and a war against socioeconomic class and its cultural trappings. However, in the context of East and West Germany, this ideology becomes uniquely problematic when it comes to national identity construction and the media's role in this process. Claudia Dittmar states that East German TV "encompassed more than just 'television,'" it was also the locus of a war of the airwaves between East and West (2). Because of the proximity of these nations, television and radio broadcasts from both sides could be accessed by the other, with underground media consumption playing a major role in the ideological warfare between East and West Germany.

As was the case in the West, content changed over time as shifts occurred in both German governments and their media regulation, which affected its domestic media. East German television in the late 1960s was developing its content to potentially influence West German audiences through communist ideology, but Dittmar writes that by the end of the decade their focus had shifted toward domestic audiences through "a strategy of distancing itself from the other German state" (3). Quoting Heinz Adameck, the head of East German state television in the early 1970s, Dittmar highlights how East German television shifted during this era to meet the needs of its citizens to reduce their desire to watch illicit West German programming. Underground "eavesdropping" on West German broadcasts was so common that, as Dorothee Wierling argues, there was pressure put on East German students and apprentices to "pledge in a written declaration to give up" such practices (161). Dittmar quotes Adameck as stating that East German TV needed "to create primarily a socialist television program that is so attractive and so effective that fewer citizens will wish to satisfy their needs of entertainment and information with the help of West-TV" (3). Dittmar states that this was accomplished by offering a second TV channel and strengthening television's purpose as an instrument of East German propaganda through the content that it offered (3).

D83 and *D86*, like *The Americans*, are the antitheses of this ideological division between East and West. Instead, they combine elements of each nation's propagandistic leanings in a narrative that challenges both. While the shows do at times lean more toward the West in their depiction of East German officials—particularly the Stasi—they are not overtly positive in their portrayal of the West or its agents. For example, toward the end of *D83*, we see characters living in East Germany imprisoned for distributing banned literature like the increasingly relevant *1984*, while we simultaneously see the West as primarily a puppet of the United Nations (and the United States in particular). Just as East and West Germany's broadcast histories struggled in opposition of their neighboring nation's ideological focus, *Deutschland 83* and *86* reflect unified Germany's struggle to find its ideological identity in the present.

Conclusion

In 2019, the world again appears to be at a crossroads where the ultimate destruction of civilization at the hands of paranoid governments seems a distinct possibility. Since 9/11, fear and paranoia seem to have increased rather than decreased. Recently, the US government has also repeatedly used Cold War imagery in its official (and unofficial) rhetoric, with terms like "McCarthyism" being mentioned regularly in an out of their historical context. Furthermore, since the arrest of Chapman and her compatriots in 2010, additional Russian undercover agents, such as gun rights activist, graduate student, and spy Maria Butina, and internet trolls accused of interfering in the 2016 presidential election through their online activities, have been exposed in the United States (see Polantz; Barrett, Horwitz, and Helderman). With these frequent references and situations reentering public and political discourse on a regular basis, Cold War nostalgia allows audiences to cope with the present by revisiting the past. Simultaneously, these shows remind us how little has changed in the past several decades and that, if we are not careful, society will slip back into its old ways like no time has passed.

In the case of tensions between the United States and Russia, Cold War paranoias are apparently as real as they once were—particularly with continuing threats on both sides to boost nuclear arms production (Kramer). Comparisons to the Cold War continued to appear in the political rhetoric surrounding United States–Russia relations following the aggressive militaristic campaigns overseen by Vladimir Putin in Georgia, Crimea, and the Ukraine. As Leggatt writes, "the war of words itself has been central to this, culminating in Russian Prime Minister Dimitri Medvedev's statement at the Munich Security Conference in

2016 that, 'we are rapidly rolling into a period of a new Cold War'" (134). In the same interview, Medvedev goes on to question if we are living in "2016 or 1962" (Leggatt 134). Leggatt points out that "considering the prime minister was not born until 1965, the comment seems particularly resonant of a nostalgia stretching beyond personal memory" (134). In statements like the ones made by Medvedev, where Cold War–era blustering continues into the present day, nostalgia and antinostalgia collide in terrifying clarity.

In Germany, time does little to dull the pain of the past, and the victims of the Cold War continue to be plagued by their memories. However, nostalgia and antinostalgia continue to interact in contemporary German society as well. Almost as soon as the Berlin Wall fell, a certain subsection of German society known as Ostalgie have embraced a nostalgic longing for East German cultural goods. These goods include East German foods, fashion, music, and a variety of other products—many of which are available at a variety of specialty stores (Zeitchik). Quoting Christine Keßler, Aline Sierp argues that Ostalgie's "meaning ranges from 'the denotation of a geographic and political origin to the rejection or affirmation of specific identities grounded in the "other" Germany'" (47–48). According to Sierp, the reasons for this primarily stem from questions of identity and feelings of alienation that emerged following the collapse of East Germany and the German reunification (50). After this occurred, Sierp argues that certain "symbols of everyday life suddenly started to acquire a certain 'remembrance value' and were thus marketed in this way" (48). Those objects took on additional symbolic meaning as they functioned as signs of "resistance to Western-style consumerism and a [globally] competitive environment" and as "a response to the stigmatisation and demonisation by a West that concentrated only on the negative aspects of the communist regime without paying enough attention to citizens' everyday experiences" (Sierp 51, 57). However, this nostalgia for East German life at the erasure of its dictatorial elements is not embraced by everyone who lived through that era. The domestic German response to *Deutschland 83* is indicative of this. Shows like *D83* and *D86* highlight that although elements of the East Germany social space, at least in the public's imagination, have regained a certain positive cultural symbolism in the years following the country's collapse, humanizing the Stasi and its members does not fall under that purview.

While history is unfortunately repeating itself on the global stage, our media industries allow us to explore this turn of events in ways that reflect the messiness of historical ideological conflict. This is accomplished in post-9/11 Cold War nostalgia by merging nostalgia with antinostalgia in ways that remind us how problematic the past was. Good and evil tend not to be universally unambiguous concepts in the real world, where their definition is instead up for debate depending on a person's point of view. Shows like *The Americans*, *Deutschland 83*, and *Deutschland 86* remind us of this as we struggle to survive the bleakness of the present.

Works Cited

Barrett, Devlin, Sari Horwitz, and Rosalind S. Helderman. "Russian Troll Farm, 13 Suspects Indicted in 2016 Election Interference." *Washington Post*, February 16, 2018. https://www.washingtonpost.com/world/national-security/russian-troll-farm-13-suspects-indicted-for-interference-in-us-election/2018/02/16/2504de5e-1342-11e8-9570-29c9830535e5_story.html.

Bever, Lindsey, and Abby Olheiser. "The Doomsday Clock Is Stuck at 2 Minutes to 'Midnight,' the Symbolic Hour of the Apocalypse." *Washington Post*, January 24, 2019. https://www.washingtonpost.com/science/2019/01/24/doomsday-clock-is-stuck-minutes-midnight-symbolic-hour-apocalypse/.

Brennan, Matt. "'Deutschland 83,' 'The Americans,' and the End of TV Drama." *IndieWire*, June 23, 2015. https://www.indiewire.com/2015/06/deutschland-83-the-americans-and-the-end-of-an-era-in-tv-drama-trailer-186944/.

Chan, Sewell. "Doomsday Clock Is Set at 2 Minutes to Midnight, Closest since 1950s." *New York Times*, January 25, 2018. https://www.nytimes.com/2018/01/25/world/americas/doomsday-clock-nuclear-scientists.html.

Dittmar, Claudia. "Television and Politics in the Former East Germany." *CLCWeb: Comparative Literature and Culture* 7.4 (2005). https://doi.org/10.7771/1481-4374.1279.

Esposti, Emanuelle Degli. "Anna Chapman: CV of a 'Real-Life Bond Girl." *Telegraph*, April 5, 2011. https://www.telegraph.co.uk/news/worldnews/europe/russia/8429609/Anna-Chapman-CV-of-a-real-life-Bond-girl.html.

Fantin, Emmanuelle. "Anti-Nostalgia in Citroën's Advertising Campaign." *Media and Nostalgia: Yearning for the Past, Present, and Future*. Ed. Katharina Niemeyer. Basingstoke: Palgrave Macmillan, 2014. 95–104.

Grove, Thomas. "Russia's 'Sexy Spy' in Provocative Photo Shoot." Reuters, October 19, 2010. https://www.reuters.com/article/us-annachapman-photo/russias-sexy-spy-in-provocative-photoshoot-idUSTRE69I3LW20101019.

Hesse, Monica. "Alleged Russian Agent Anna Chapman Could Have Warmed Up any Cold War Night." *Washington Post*, July 1, 2010. http://www.washingtonpost.com/wp-dyn/content/article/2010/06/30/AR2010063005074.html.

Kackman, Michael. *Citizen Spy: Television, Espionage, and Cold War Culture*. Minneapolis: University of Minnesota Press, 2005.

Kramer, Andrew E. "Russia Follows U.S. Out of Landmark Nuclear Weapons Treaty." *New York Times*, March 4, 2019. https://www.nytimes.com/2019/03/04/world/europe/russia-inf-treaty.html.

Leggatt, Matthew. *Cultural and Political Nostalgia in the Age of Terror*. New York: Routledge, 2018.

Nadel, Alan. "Television: Cold War Television and the Technology of Brainwashing." *American Cold War Culture*. Ed. Douglas Field. Edinburgh: Edinburgh University Press, 2005. 146–63.

Oltermann, Philip. "*Deutschland 83* Has Wowed the World—Pity the Germans Don't Like It." *Guardian*, February 17, 2016. https://www.theguardian.com/commentisfree/2016/feb/17/deutschland-83-wowed-world-germans-dont-like-it.

Polantz, Katelyn. "Alleged Russian Spy Maria Butina Pleads Guilty to Engaging in Conspiracy against US." *CNN*, December 13, 2018. https://www.cnn.com/2018/12/13/politics/maria-butina-guilty-plea/index.html.

Poniewozik, James. "Review: In *Deutschland 83*, East Meets West Germany." *Time*, June 16, 2015. http://time.com/3920575/review-deutschland-83-sundance/.

Poniewozik, James. "Review: 'Deutschland 86,' an East-West Thriller Looks South." *New York Times*, October 28, 2018. https://www.nytimes.com/2018/10/24/arts/television/review-deutschland-86.html.

Sandberg, Bryan Elise. "'*The Americans*' Showrunners on Donald Trump, Current U.S.-Russia Relations." *Hollywood Reporter*, January 12, 2017. https://www.hollywoodreporter.com/live-feed/americans-showrunners-donald-trump-current-us-russian-relations-963929.

Sierp, Aline. "Nostalgia for Times Past: On the Uses and Abuses of the Ostalgie Phenomenon in East Germany." *Contemporary European Studies* 4.2 (2009): 47–60.

Sherida, Michael. "Anna Chapman, Sexy Russian Spy, Nude in January Issue of Playboy." *New York Daily News*, December 21, 2010. https://www.nydailynews.com/news/world/anna-chapman-sexy-russian-spy-nude-january-issue-playboy-article-1.473567.

Tate, Gabriel. "*Deutschland 83*: 'A Lot of People Were Happy in East Germany.'" *Guardian*, January 3, 2016. https://www.theguardian.com/tv-and-radio/2016/jan/03/channel-4-cold-war-drama-deutschland-83.

Valentine, Genevieve. "*Deutschland 83* Takes its Spycraft Straight Up, with a Twist." *AV Club*, June 17, 2015. https://tv.avclub.com/deutschland-83-takes-its-spycraft-straight-up-with-a-t-1798184095.

Weaver, Matthew. "Anna Chapman, the Russian Spy Loved by the Media." *Guardian*, June 30, 2010. https://www.theguardian.com/world/blog/2010/jun/30/anna-chapman-russian-spy-ring.

Wierling, Dorothee. "Youth as Internal Enemy: Conflicts in the Education Dictatorship of the 1960s." *Socialist Modern: East German Everyday Culture and Politics*. Ed. Katherine Pence and Paul Betts. Ann Arbor: University of Michigan Press, 2008. 157–82.

Zeitchik, Steven. "German Ostalgie: Fondly Recalling the Bad Old Days." *New York Times*, October 7, 2003. https://www.nytimes.com/2003/10/07/opinion/IHT-german-ostalgie-fondly-recalling-the-bad-old-days.html.

Part 4

Not My Nostalgia

13

Remembering It Well

Nostalgia, Cinema, Fracture

MURRAY POMERANCE

Starving for guaranteed prophecy.
—George Steiner

1

ENSCONCED COMFORTABLY IN Vincente Minnelli's *Gigi* (1958) is a gentle paean to nostalgia. Two old chums, Madame Alvarez (Hermione Gingold) and Honoré Lachaille (Maurice Chevalier) sing together the somewhat peculiar Alan Jay Lerner-Frederick Loewe number, "I Remember It Well," which begins like this:

HE: We met at nine.

SHE: We met at eight.

HE: I was on time.

SHE: No, you were late.

HE: Ah yes, I remember it well.

And so it continues, for many piquingly uncomfortable screen minutes. (The Broadway play opened November 13, 1973, with Maria Kamilova and Alfred Drake in these two roles.) In the background, there is a splendid sunset.

Perhaps we have the impression that Madame remembers better than Monsieur, because, *bien sûr*, what is he but a man happy to be happy and she but a woman diligent to be diligent. Could this song be a little nod to a more general, pathetic hopelessness of male intellect in contemporary culture and a thoroughly diffused, superior female intelligence: every second line is a correction of the one before it, and Gingold and Chevalier broadly caricature gender types. Surely, whatever else the song is, we hear in it a mini-lecture on the way any fond regard for the past is cultured and warped, restricted, contested, dependent on the vagary of personal memory and thus up for grabs.

The idea of remembering well is fraught from the outset. As in remembrance, we have no measuring rod outside the remembering itself, no fully objective past, the act of committing memory is a flotation on the waters of some always receding tide. The idea of capturing, of having the past again therefore has charm in itself, and when we listen to Honoré and Madame gently arguing about what happened a long time ago, we tend to appreciate each of them claiming to validate a personal recollection as true. That is the colloquial meaning of "I remember it well": "well" means, "without error." The argumentative modality of the song also neatly raises the force of political, hegemonic power to establish dominance among competitive claimants to an authentic version of an event. Every individual touts memories, after all, but only some of these memories become official, gain public celebration, go into the record, become history.

Memory is often punctual. We call up a scenic moment by way of certain key points of reference that stand out and endure, but not in a wholesale re-vision that brings back, arranged in proper perspective, every detail of the place and the happening. The little metal teapot on the table, perhaps, spilling tea unless you know the secret of holding back the lid when you pour. But not the saucer beneath the teapot, not the face of the server who delivered it to the table, not the color of the tiles on the floor. Memory is a storeroom filled with points, fragmented, disparate, seeking but never finding the unity of the past (which was then a limited unity of the present).

Nor is the claim "I remember," as a grammatical proposition, more than a contraction and easeful abbreviation of something more complicated and problematic, something we do not usually take the liberty to say: that one can never be sure, that memory is frail—even recent memory—in the face of the onslaught of perceptions and calculations that we must survive in the everyday. One means to claim instead, "I would like to think I remember." The so-named "memory" is a proposition, not an assertion. It isn't possible to escape the disturbing admonition that time changes all things, that events are brushed aside, turned on themselves, substituted one for another. It wasn't that Bast came to lunch with the Schlegel sisters, he came to tea. Or it wasn't tea, it was lunch. And the brother was also there, brooding; or joking. At the end of his very splendid (and very moving) film *Remember* (2015), Atom Egoyan makes a close shot of Christopher Plummer suddenly opening his eyes wide and saying, shocked, "I remember!" What it is that he remembers, the subject of the film, the cause of the long and painful journey we have undertaken with him, is something proportionately gigantic, emotionally drowning, totally horrifying, and unbearably present once again, but also of the instant. Through the film Plummer's character Zev has been suffering extreme fragmentation of memory because of dementia. He weaves in and out of temporal placement in his consciousness, experiencing a state of confusion the narrative adopts for the viewer's inhabitation. He is here, but he doesn't know, through a sense of memory, what here is—until that concluding moment, when he knows too well. But this dementia, to some degree, is the human condition.

There is a conventional trope in artistic fictions dealing with memory and its retrieval, and that is the direct figuration of a long passage of time, designed into the narrative in explicit terms: an adult coming to terms with her youth, a technician trying to bring back a formula lost decades ago, a young autistic surgeon recalling the traumas of his childhood, and so on. The remembered "experience," if we can call it that, occurred dozens and dozens of pages back on the calendar, months before, years before, decades before. In a wonderful little emotional twist at the end of Joseph Losey's *The Go-Between* (1971, based on a novel by L. P. Hartley) we learn, astonishingly, that a memory now being played out originated in another century. Yet action is fleeting and experience rich, our awareness riddled by pellets of emotion to such a degree that even in a brief passage of clock time a considerable chain of associations might pass by and hide in the clouds of the past. To remember might be a short-term affair, yet still problematic. The sense of déjà-vu addresses exactly the feeling of a long-lost experience that is not verifiably from a past far, far away. We can feel a memory as relating to a distant past: the distance is part of the feeling. We may persist in feeling a memory as fixating on a very distant reality as long as nothing interrupts to displace that feeling, to cause us to doubt it. Jeannot Szwarc's very moving film *Somewhere in Time* (1980) gives an unforgettable rendering of this problem of interrupting a hitherto integrated feeling of the "past."

As we listen to "I Remember It Well," do we presume that each participant to the duet is making a claim to memory, or making a claim about the desire for memory? Is the recollection a complete one? Even moments after this song is finished, can we call up a complete recollection of it? Might these two not be calling up differential pasts or calling up what they wish had happened? Pinioning our thought to a calendar, might we not ask, "How long ago was this, anyway? In your youth, many, many decades ago? Or yesterday?" It is not by mere circumstance that in trying out our nostalgias we call the past "yesterday": all our troubles seem so far away, but are they?

To focus more acutely on the pleasure this ditty is intended to bring audiences: viewers are directed implicitly (by the singers' postures and facial gestures, their tones of vocalization and pausing, the grace of the accompanying violins, that fading sunset) to recognize that this aging man has lost more vitality and agility than this aging woman, because no matter what claim he makes she offers a direct "fix." She is the fixer, so wise, apparently, that hearing her memories, line by line, we tacitly assent to their accuracy. Although philosophically there is reason for both believing and doubting both singers, although the song is about uncertainty and time, about nostalgia and fracture, we do not hear it that way inside the frame of *Gigi*. The moment Madame offers correction we defer—and note ourselves deferring—to hers as the sounder memory, the keener sensibility. Hers is not just a hypothesis about what happened, it is, finally, an announcement. Madame is not just offering an alternative reading of the past, another angle; she is telling it like it is, which is to say, as it was. Honoré is inflating his memories with the hot air of speculation and self-regard, weaving a gilded history.

In calling up memory of the past this way, especially with an intimate friend (as Honoré definitely considers Madame Alvarez), does one not hope for its resurrection? Resurrection in this case may be far short of bringing back the past, or having the past come alive again in practicality. The past may revivify only—but thoroughly—as consideration, as reflection. When we see something we take it in, perhaps, and hold it. Later on, we look at it again, Wordsworth's emotion recollected in tranquility. Looking at it again, we "bring it back to life," as long as it stands fully illuminated before our gaze, as long as we see today as we saw before, or at least, because time always alters vision, as long as we think we see today as we saw before. Nostalgia is in the maintenance of feeling through memory, the preservation of insight.

2

While in conventional thinking about representation, characters always seem to call up and invoke emotional commitment to some distant past, blossoms on the cherry trees a legion springtimes ago, there is nothing inherent to the issue of nostalgic memory that requires considerable time. Time moves at different rates for different lives. What constitutes "a long time ago" might vary depending on how much one accomplishes and remembers accomplishing in the interim. Any memory is susceptible to erosion, and thus in need of preservation, even a recent memory. One can wish to preserve a reaction to a work of art to which one was exposed only recently, since once an event moves into history it is gone, gone, and fully gone, and other experiences move in to take its place.

Nor is it necessary that one's firmly grasped memories should relate only to pleasurable things. Pain, too, fades and can be reflected on. Dismay, no less than elevation, can be recollected, and one's recollection of it subjected, like Honoré Lachaille's, to correction or query. With nostalgia comes second sight.

At a movie theater on Main Street in Buffalo, New York (the name has sailed from my harbor), very early in 1968, which is to say, within only weeks of its December 22, 1967 release and while eager whispers about it were bruiting about town, I sat to watch Mike Nichols's *The Graduate*, in the capacity of being a recent graduate, too, and, like Ben Braddock in some ways, out in but thoroughly confused by the world. I was twenty, the same age as he, and like Benjamin I had just received my diploma (in my case from the University of Michigan; he was schooled somewhere in the East). I was enrolled in a graduate program, a pathway of sorts leading I could not tell where. Watching the emotional roller coaster of Benjamin's life, as it seemed to me in the dark theater—because, as I now believe, it was making me think of the roller coaster of my own—I felt a chillingly deep sense of recognition and a dull sense of strangeness, because he was so very like, but at the same time so very unlike, the person I understood myself to be. I was surely not having a sexual affair with an older woman, as he plainly was; nor had the dream of so improbable a situation even filtered into me in the depths of night. I was not cavorting in a real Californian space; indeed, California was all myth and image to me, the bulk of it sketched and filled in with the crayons of my imagination. I did understand something about the condition of floating in the limbo of time, so brilliantly conceived in the film by Buck Henry's script and realized by Nichols with Dustin Hoffman. I did understand Benjamin's nervousness, his very powerful yearning, the sense of intelligence unresponded to. I also understood, the way he did, how parents systematically fail to comprehend. At any rate, the film succeeded in sweeping me away, and for a long time I could not get it off my mind. Part of what sealed it was probably the music of Simon and Garfunkel, whose *Parsley, Sage, Rosemary and Time* I had acquired as a junior in Ann Arbor—about a year before—and listened to every day until I knew every chord change by memory and every lyric lived on my tongue: the music took me back.

But now, humming the same songs, I was at the State University of New York at Buffalo to study with Edgar Z. Friedenberg, author of *The Vanishing Adolescent* and *Coming of Age in America* and one of the leading thinkers about youth and society in the English-speaking world. (I am looking back . . .) Frequently this genteel and hospitable man invited me to his home, where I learned about Swedish fish cakes, how to write a successful metaphor, and much else. Something happened there shortly after I saw the Nichols film, something that disturbed my still coherent memory of it. On the polished little side table beside my professor's great leather reading chair, I found on display the current (March 28, 1968) issue of *New York Review of Books*, in the pages of which lay "Calling Dr. Spock!," his review of *The Graduate*. Needless to say, I pounced.

And there he was, "remembering well." Yet was the author of the piece the man I knew, the man at whose table I was reading it? Or had he morphed into another figure altogether, who hid somewhere nearby: a figure who could see easily, so very articulately, and seem critical, unreservedly critical, of a film that had touched me to the core. Not only critical but surgical. This is how his piece began, and we must remember as we read it that in 1968 there were no videocassettes or DVDs, that he was writing from a memory of the film, which he had watched in the way that I had, projected brightly on a screen in a dark theater (and likely even the same screen in the same theater):

> Twice, in Mike Nichols's motion picture, *The Graduate*, its young and fashionably heroic central character, Benjamin, is shown driving to Berkeley across the familiar, still magnificent Bay Bridge. As most readers will know by now Benjamin, who has just graduated from an Eastern college, lives in one of the more expensive neighborhoods of the Los Angeles area; and the transition to Northern California is treated in the film as it were a passage from a region of unalloyed cruelty and egocentric sham to one of ambiguous but decisively human beauty. Northern California is shown as more real even though not always nice—a little like Paris in old René Clair movies. Accordingly, Benjamin soars toward Berkeley on the upper deck of the bridge in his graduation present: a little red sports car, gay and promising against the superb blue sky and the distant skyline.
>
> Unfortunately for Mr. Nichols's purposes each deck of the Bay Bridge is one-way; and, in fact, traffic to Berkeley travels on the prosaic lower deck from which no picturesque view is possible. They don't close the Bay Bridge to facilitate such Southern Californian activities as movie-making. The distant, alluring skyline Benjamin is driving toward proves, on scrutiny, to be not that of the East Bay but the industrial skyline of San Francisco south of the bridge—the familiar landmarks like Telegraph Hill and Alcatraz that might have given the trick away are all north of it and out of sight. Benjamin, of course, is presented throughout the movie as a disoriented youth with confused goals, and it would be quite in character for him to try to drive to Berkeley on the top deck; after the initial shock I thought this was going to turn out to be the point and prepared myself for a Keystone-type

chase. But no, this is just a bit of artistic license for the sake of the scenery. Benjamin has no trouble on the bridge; it is about the only place in the whole film where he knows how to handle himself. He gets to Berkeley both times, though he has trouble enough *there*.

In a more obviously conventional picture this little gimmick would not be worth mentioning, and would in any case be well within the director's rights as a way of establishing place, mood, and atmosphere. But from the very beginning *The Graduate* is cutely literal and pseudo-documentary.

So it went, with image after image disassembled and acidified so as to reveal the underpinning charlatanry (my word) involved in depicting this particular graduate in this particular way. To reiterate—because my penchant for this nostalgia demands it—I had at that point never been to California, and Friedenberg, to give him his due, had been professor at University of California, Davis and knew the San Francisco area very well. His analysis was impeccable—all his writing was impeccable, that was one of the reasons I wanted to study with him—and he wrote with a keen aesthetic sensitivity (he had introduced me to Bizet's Symphony in C!). Yet he wrote—something I did not state to myself as unequivocally as perhaps I should have, because, as I remember it now, fifty years later, I was so stunned by the displacement of my point of view from my teacher's that I did not notice—without the commitment to art that had long been mine. He appreciated art, but he was not an artist. He was a brave analytical sociologist, a sharp-minded observer of social class issues, and from his review one could not fail to be enlightened about these. But as I proceeded to read, I did feel the film, my film, slipping away from me, the charge of the colored vision weakening in the excruciating critical light. My California, which is to say the California of my waking dreams, was gone into the waters beneath the Bay Bridge, now replaced by something distressingly factual, socially engineered, hard-core real. That they divide the traffic on that bridge. And that Southern California activities such as movie-making are negotiated into the convenient crevices of an already functioning and, to some, very familiar social order with which, a Canadian living in New York, I was unfamiliar. *The Graduate*, my *Graduate*, the *Graduate* I was nostalgic for only weeks after seeing it, the one that called up my education and my own self, was a put-up, a fantasy pretending to be real.

3

I am sure that for some protracted time I fell into a swoon, out of which came the kind of analysis my teacher demonstrated so articulately. I surely began to wonder, regarding one film after another, how, if at all, it had remained true to some authentic vision of the world or else had veered into the "poetic license" to which Friedenberg gives assent but clearly does not really celebrate. It wasn't until long afterward that, gazing back nostalgically to my college days, I began to realize that "poetic license" is actually more important to me than documentary realism, whatever on Earth that could claim to be. The poet is alive too, after all, and has his methods. The poet must claim (in his text) to see the world in a particular (and not journalistic, not scientific) way to move his readers toward the enrichment of a sighting, themselves.

I grew into the knowledge that *The Graduate* was not a film—had never been conceived as a film—about the way things were in 1967–68, that it was no record presuming to official status but instead a poetic invocation: for me, in reflection, a way of bringing back how I felt in those days. It captured and reflected—it could always enduringly capture and reflect—the way the world seemed to me then, however inaccurately, indeed, the scene of my feeling and the character types who inspired feeling in me. Character types, not actual persons. The thing was in some way operatic, exaggerated for effect, but the effect was far more than a stretching or augmentation for dramatic emphasis, it was a condition in itself. It was both technical and emotional, an achievement of experts in the name of a vision that could affect the viewer. As a way of expressing a view, this is certainly a manipulative, symphonic method, and perhaps in some cases even a dishonest one, because it contains efflorescence that saturates color, intensifies melody, and heightens the moment. Even the skeptical Friedenberg had noted the "superb" blue sky and its contrast with the little red car. I had to accept that Bizet's Symphony in C was, indeed, the great composition my teacher had said it was, and that it was structurally as sound as every great metaphor should be, but also that it was not the music I really loved. It did not quite get off the ground. Perhaps my teacher and I had different attitudes or made different assumptions about the central importance of the ground. At any rate, I wanted to fly.

The nostalgic memory I was rekindling, ungrounded, soaring, as I watched the film was about love and connection, not just the recognition of terms and conditions. Thinking back to my feeling while I watched, as I framed it in light of Friedenberg's vision, was a way of being nostalgic about a nostalgia, in effect, about what I remembered and another man's different way of remembering. Friedenberg's became a nostalgia within my nostalgia. And here I found in myself traces of Honoré Lachaille singing that silly song, listening to his dear old friend with patience and adoration and sweetness but honestly never, for a second, believing that his own memory of things was any but the true one. Had I trusted myself more at the time—in the way that Honoré trusts himself as he sings—I might have come to the conclusion, even while reading my teacher's words, "Delicious, but this is not *my* film." I might have "argued" for my feeling, as Madame Alvarez does for hers. The song wasn't finally about correction and dominance, after all, it was about the nature of deep friendship in the face of disagreement. It was about life. But when I was twenty, as I could not have said then but can say looking back fondly now, I didn't know what life was yet, except that it felt like desire and the frustration of desire, attempts and the incompleteness of attempts. It seems today that I must have feared feeling that things could go wrong at every turn. That feeling was not the thing to be trusted.

Now it seems somewhat sensible to think that if Dustin Hoffman (or his stunt double) is driving the wrong way on the Bay Bridge, Benjamin Braddock is going precisely where he needs to go. Benjamin Braddock is driving in fictional space, not urban topography. He is aching for Elaine, driving to Elaine, Elaine wherever she may be, "whenever he may find her" (to cite Simon and Garfunkel). To see it more "realistically," one would have to admit the presence of the camera (which, of course, Friedenberg almost instantaneously does), that device we may claim to know about but that is perforce invisible, unimaginable, utterly nonexistent for us when we watch films. Just as, in his desperate moment on the bridge, Elaine is invisible, unimaginable, utterly nonexistent for him.

4

It is not difficult to misconceive the nostalgic impulse as a drive toward the realization of some utopian conceit, posed against the insuperable obstacle of practical events and their outcomes. In such a construction, one wishes to reestablish the environment or moment of childhood freedom, but is incontrovertibly blocked by the fact of time passing, of erosion; or the brutality of the will of Others, thus conflict; or the simple alteration of desire, thus fresh invention. We yearn for the past, but the past is gone, replaced—replaceable—by nothing less than a hollow simulacrum, some superficies of which have a "sufficient" resemblance. If, as such an argument would claim we cannot ever be anywhere or anytime other than where and when we are, then nostalgia's yearning, as I sketch it here, is but a waste of time, a false magnetic pull on the instruments of navigation.

Are we looking closely enough at nostalgia if we think of it this way?

Fond memory may not be an aspiration to another life, it may be an affirmation of the life we have, and that life includes images, not just things. If, separated from its subject, the image may still have its own life, its curious illumination, its organization of color and form, its dispensation of space, its magnifications and subtractions, it may also constitute an event in itself, far more than a reflection of events. (A picture may be more than a picture-of.) Indeed, the nostalgic urge might direct us to reenvision an image first seen long ago but preserved, somehow, in a store to which only the nostalgic urge gives us access. Nostalgia may be nothing other than our way of accessing a past fantasy, in whole or in part, the fantasy by its nature being alive in itself, in the strange way that fantasies having once come alive remain alive. Reinvocation is thus a blossoming of life. By reinvoking lost fantasy we do become young again. To the degree that their stimulus is helpful in bringing about such a recall, we can be grateful for the continuing presence of artifacts that act as spurs to memory: a bar of music heard on the radio, a photograph reproduced in a book, a film scene drawn from a DVD. If, for example, I think back to Charles Walters's *Lili*, a film I saw when it came out in 1953 (I was seven), I do not need to wish to be a child again to recapture what was and remains magical about it, especially the mauve and the spring green and Carrot Top's borscht-red hair. Then, I had invested myself without reservation, entered the screen world perhaps never to return to the everyday, and I can do that again because it is the same screen world, and today is a similar enough everyday (the world outside the theater remains incomprehensible, conflicted, surging). I may become again what I became on first experience—the person willing to abandon everything for the vision.

Is this too romantic a view of nostalgia as it actually functions for us in our complicated world? In giving ourselves to art, do we lose our lives? But great art does compel us, lure us, riddle us, animate us; the riddling animation is real. When one has nostalgia for what is truly great, one travels willingly wherever one must and gives oneself up to whatever degree to accomplish the taste. A profound expression cannot be grasped partially.

Friedenberg did not regard *The Graduate* as a supreme work of art. As for myself, I think I was callow enough then to submit myself to the charms of anything sufficiently stirring. Looking back now, I can see how the film has its limits, yet how I was able to be seduced (as Benjamin, my age-mate, was seduced, too). But I am profoundly grateful for that seduction and for all the seductions that formed my youth. Today I would much prefer to stand in front of a Rubens painting than watch Nichols's film again. But that doesn't change my simple esteem for the simple esteem I had when I had just graduated from college. The film is one of the cherished tokens I guard. Like sun-dappled snow, which never fails to bring me back a very long way, to winters long forgotten and, more poignantly, to depictions in paint-by-number kits I was allowed to use only when, sick for days on end, I could stay home from school. Paint by number, with sleds and pine trees and little houses and birds on branches, canasta on the bedcover with my grandmother, Hardy Boys books.

My teacher was more than twenty-five years older than I was, and although I knew this as a fact, I didn't (I now surmise) fully grasp that he had been born to another generation. We never discussed this fault in the geography of our experience: I don't remember, at any rate, telling him how his review had affected me, so I have no reason for thinking he ever knew.

5

Because nostalgia is a fundamental aesthetic issue and problem, at least for me a phenomenon of colors and textures, tones and harmonies, compositions and decor, more in every way than an affair of logical progressions and characterological outcomes, my ability to go back in time—my time travel—is facilitated to the extent that these aesthetic features can be reconstituted in present-day experience. It is for emotion, not logic, that I seek in the past, in experiences dissolved by time. My nostalgic impulse is utterly ruined when the aesthetic forms are wrong.

So it comes about that certain contemporary appeals to the nostalgic impulse, some commercialized *nostalgies*, all of them attempts to "invoke," or "reinvoke" earlier decades today deemed socially significant, lack the capacity to absorb me, much as *The Graduate* had lacked the capacity to absorb Friedenberg. For one example, *Mad Men* (2005–2014) is not about the 1950s I know. It is too snippy, too slick, too confident of itself. The colors are wrong, the fabrics too fresh, the tones of voice and the distances people set between themselves as they interact: all miscalculated. The anxious desperation and the blind hope of a time when Eisenhower was president and spoke in muddled riddles: none of it is conveyed. The use of intelligence is far too glib and too smart, too twenty-first-century, too fast-talky. In that decade, one was not swarmed over by opinionated speakers, articulate philosophers of the everyday, one was not living in an Aaron Sorkin–style script packed with machine-gunned speech. The material world dominated in its silence. (*Suburbicon* [2017] works far more powerfully.) But one should never forget Erving Goffman's implicit dictum in *Frame Analysis*, that the outermost "rim" of the frame is the one that ultimately dictates: in the case of "retrospective" shows, the fact that they are present-day productions aimed to catch the attention of a current, very possibly uninformed audience (whose deep pleasure I respect). So we get "the 1950s" as presented to the consciousness of consumers in 2018, not the spirit of the time as it might be recognized or remembered by someone who grew up through it. Some of the color and tonality of Todd Haynes's *Carol* (2015) was very evocative, and some of the lighting appropriately on the warm side, but both the slouchy Cate Blanchett (born 1969) and the waiflike Rooney Mara (born 1985), brilliant enough in contemporary terms, failed to catch the expressive gestures of the era they were "reproducing," gestures based finally on not quite knowing, through a sharply exteriorized consciousness, what was going on. By 2015 everybody had a far too confident sense of the culture.

In Netflix's *The Crown* (2016–) we find an opulent re-creation of space and color of the late 1940s and 1950s, pure Colefax and Fowler, but it is hard to deny that many of the actors are just too svelte, too hip in their physiques and postures. Casting Matt Smith as Philip is a smart audience grabber because he was adored on *Dr. Who*. But when he came on the scene in real time, that is, presented himself as image to the observing multitudes, Philip was in fact taking a bold step out of nowhere: he was a complete unknown who exploded on the scene. He radiated magically, not through the agency of broadcast. Contemporary looks back, these "nostalgic reflections," I critique here only because they openly pose as voyages in time, and in doing so they negate my own fragile, possibly inaccurate but nonetheless cherished visions. There is a relationship between *The Crown* as portrait of Elizabeth's early life and conventional period epics, such as *Ben-Hur* (1959) or *The Silver Chalice* (1954), which reach so far back in their derivations that no living viewer can use memory for measurement, so far back that they merely conjecture as to the shape, flavor, and quality of ancient experience and do not invoke what I call "nostalgia" at all. Of the Roman era, the days of Christ, we have a received vision, a received "memory," but no actual memory at all. And the public memory of the 1950s is also now largely received.

On occasion, indeed, the current "re-presentation" of the past can be recognized as pointing to something it does not claim to point to. Two episodes of *The Crown* involve the hungry Princess Margaret (Vanessa Kirby) in her early dalliance with Anthony Armstrong-Jones (Matthew Goode). As he photographs her in his studio, we begin to see redepictions of Assheton Gorton's design of the photographer's studio in Michelangelo Antonioni's *Blow-Up* (1966). In the second episode, the David Hemmings-Veruschka shooting/fucking scene is replicated with alarming fidelity. It is a true fact that the photographer's locale used in *Blow-Up* was authentic to the sorts of spaces fashionable London photographers (like Armstrong-Jones) were using in the 1950s and 1960s, yet there is an unmistakable chain of references to the Antonioni film, not to working London photography of the time. The scenes are constructed very artfully, with profound aesthetic taste (darker than what Antonioni achieved on screen) and invite us to enter and lose ourselves in the action. Here my nostalgic impulse is blocked by a second nostalgic impulse, which, to my mind greater, steps in almost naturally to obstruct it: my memory of the aesthetic taste of *Blow-Up*, an important film for me, and thus my tendency to travel not to Peter Morgan's TV construction today and what it references of Armstrong-Jones's life but to Antonioni's nameless photographer and his adventures.

6

George Steiner suggests that over and above anyone's idiosyncratic desires for return, there is a nostalgia for the absolute, "directly provoked by the decline of Western man and society, of the ancient and magnificent architecture of religious certitude. . . . we hunger for myths, for total explanation: we are starving for guaranteed prophecy" (5–6). Thus, not the particular memories of an individual, not whether we met at nine or at eight, or whether we were on time or were late, but what happened to humankind, how our great ship foundered in the stormy waters and turned in the gale, how Memory itself shifted through Historical Circumstance. It is plain, I think, that prophecy can be guaranteed—can seem to us guaranteed—only if we believe we have already seen it as an outcome, only if it was born in the past. This is why our "absolute" must be searched through a trip backward, some definitive nostalgia, and not by imagining various pathways forward. To go forward is to move into the unknown, but what can be remembered is known. What can be remembered, that is, what memories can be stimulated by fragments retrieved, by photographs, paintings, recordings, all traces still available outside the context of their world.

As to whether it is patently a mythology we search in our going back, a way of providing explanation, a method of organizing the disparate details of experience, or instead another taste of what was tasted before, a way of ensuring the reality of our memory of some pure involvement for its own sake—no logic will tell. But it is certain that moving backward, away and away from the conflagrations of our Now, we lose ourselves, if only for a breath. We lose the orientation of the bridge we were crossing, perhaps even the recognition that it was a bridge, so nervous were we in our passage, heading to know ourselves for the first time.

Figure 13.1. Benjamin (Dustin Hoffman) racing across San Francisco's Bay Bridge to find the love of his life in *The Graduate* (Mike Nichols, Lawrence Turman/Embassy, 1967). Digital frame enlargement.

Works Cited

Friedenberg, Edgar Z. "Calling Dr. Spock!" *New York Review of Books*, March 28, 1968. http://www.nybooks.com/articles/1968/03/28/calling-dr-spock/.

Goffman, Erving. *Frame Analysis: An Essay on the Organization of Experience*. Cambridge, MA: Harvard University Press, 1974.

Steiner, George. *Nostalgia for the Absolute*. Toronto: Anansi, 1974.

14

Nostalgia Ain't What It Used to Be

WILLIAM ROTHMAN

IN HIS ORIGINAL PROPOSAL FOR THIS volume, Matthew Leggatt posited, lucidly and provocatively, that our current media environment manifests a "turn toward both nostalgia and 'nostalgia,' both a genuine penchant to return and a willing responsiveness to commodified (finally hopeless) masquerades of a faded, but appealing, yesterday." Listing movies including *American Hustle* (2013), *La La Land* (2016), a succession of Disney reboots, and *TRON: Legacy* (2010), he asserted that "we have spent more time over the last decade living in the past, indeed in various 'pasts.'"

I believe, to the contrary, that over the past decade we—that is, Americans; our British friends across the pond have wallowed as much as ever in reliving Britain's "finest hour"—have spent as little time as possible "living in the past," certainly far less than Americans did in the 1940s and early 1950s, when nostalgia was a dominant element in innumerable movies. To name just a small handful: *How Green Was My Valley* (1941), *The Strawberry Blonde* (1941) (itself a remake) and its musical remake *One Sunday Afternoon* (1948); *Yankee Doodle Dandy* (1942); *Our Vines Have Tender Grapes* (1945); *Life with Father* (1947); *I Remember Mama* (1948); *Singin' in the Rain* (1952); and so on. Furthermore, a number of films of that period—*The Magnificent Ambersons* (1942), *Casablanca* (1942), *Shadow of a Doubt* (1943), *Meet Me in St. Louis* (1944); *It's a Wonderful Life* (1946), and *Sunset Blvd.* (1950) immediately come to mind—both invoke nostalgia and are about nostalgia, its pleasures, and its dangers.

Such films of the 1940s as *How Green Was My Valley* and *I Remember Mama* are "overtly nostalgic""; *American Hustle* and *La La Land* are not, although the former, a film I enjoy, at least has a few moments with a nostalgic element. I'm thinking especially of the fateful encounter, which Jennifer Lawrence makes memorable, her character has with the microwave she calls "the science oven." (Lawrence, on screen, has a genuine star quality that makes me nostalgic for a time when movie stars were really stars.) *La La Land*, a film I do not enjoy, is too frenetic, too hopped-up, to elicit or display nostalgia or appeal to the tender emotions or feelings such a nostalgia should provoke. Like virtually all contemporary American movies, especially blockbusters, it altogether lacks nostalgia's requisite wistful yearning, its longing for a happier, freer time that has slipped into the past, like childhood, and is now accessible only in memory. Indeed, I don't think it's possible to experience nostalgia without knowing, in one's heart, that one's childhood is past, that one is no longer entitled to the privileges and responsibilities (or rather, irresponsibilities) we grant to children. I first knew that my own childhood was over one night in my junior year of high school when I watched a performance of *The Cherry Orchard* on WNET's *Play of the Week*, with my sister out on a date and my parents hosting a New Year's Eve party in the living room. Anya's recognition that she was no longer a child so moved me and, to be honest, I so lusted after the young Susan Strasberg, who played her with such passion, that it hit me like a ton of bricks that I was no longer a child. Remembering this makes me nostalgic, but at the time, the tears I wept then were bitter, not bittersweet.

When Roy Orbison sings "I'm going back someday, come what may, to Blue Bayou," we hear in his voice that he knows there's no going back, no way of bringing back those happy times. (When it's Linda Ronstadt singing, we hear this, too.) To know that our childhood is over is to know, really know, that we are mortal, fated to die, and that it is impossible to turn back the clock or stop time in its tracks. As humans, knowledge of our mortality can make us feel, in dark moods, as if we have been sentenced to life in prison, without hope of parole, behind an impassable barrier. But the barrier that is impossible to cross—the speed of light, for example, or the screen that separates our world from the projected world—is not a real barrier, not really a barrier, however natural it may be for us to imagine that it is.

In the opening voiceover of *How Green Was My Valley*, Huw, the film's protagonist (Roddy McDowall in the body of the film; Irving Pichel speaks the narration), now grown up, speaks a truth about the reality of being human:

> There is no fence nor hedge around time that is gone. You can go back and have what you like of it, if you can remember. So, I can close my eyes on my valley as it is today, and it is gone, and I see it as it was when I was a boy. Green it was, and possessed of the plenty of the Earth. In all Wales, there was none so beautiful.

Huw speaks another truth about human reality when he says, "Strange that the mind will forget so much of what only this moment has passed, and yet hold clear and bright the memory of what happened years ago—of men and women long since dead." But then he adds, "Yet who shall say what is real and what is not?" In saying this, he is expressing skeptical doubt about what we ordinarily assume are further truths about human reality: you cannot make the past the present again; the present is real in a way the past is not; the living are alive and the dead not, our allotted time on this mortal coil has, to use Huw's own metaphor, a fence or hedge around it. Then again, the world of *How Green Was My Valley*, like the world of any film, is not reality; it is reality transfigured by the medium of film. And the world on film, that transfigured reality, is "a moving image of skepticism," as Cavell puts it ("More" 188). In the world on film, the separateness of past and present, inviolable in the one existing world, is overcome or transcended. Once *How Green Was My Valley* puts its nostalgic prologue behind it, the past is indistinguishable from the present. Is it that the past has become the present? Or has the present become the past, as Cavell more or less suggests when he observes that as we experience movies, our powerlessness to affect the events unfolding in the projected world makes those events akin, temporally (he adds, "mythically"), to the past, not the present?

When we're feeling nostalgic, the past reveals itself as possessing a precious beauty that we feel is missing from our lives in the present. But what makes the past appear so precious cannot be separated from the warm glow with which our nostalgia infuses it, nor from our knowledge that it *is* the past, that it is unreachable except by memory. We are powerless to alter the past, just as we are powerless to intervene to alter the events of a film. When we are in a nostalgic mood, what we most cherish about our memories is the sense they fleetingly allow us—is it illusory?—to be transported back to a time when a world of possibilities for the future that have since become closed off were still open to us, as if we had regained the lost freedom of childhood. But this glimpse of freedom comes at a price. When the nostalgic mood slips into the past, it brings home to us that the past cannot become the present again. The freedom of childhood is gone forever. Nostalgia cannot bring it back. We cannot become free by living in the past, if only because the past is fixed; unalterable. It allows us no freedom. The only way to be free of the past is to acknowledge that it *is* past.

Knowledge of the irrecoverable loss of something precious to us is what makes nostalgia possible. Then how can nostalgia be pleasurable? That there's nothing we can do to make the past the present, nor anything we can do to keep the present from slipping into the past, is key to the fact that nostalgia gives us pleasure—a bittersweet pleasure akin to what the Japanese call *mono no aware*, the exquisite sense of the fleetingness of all beauty. What separates the past from the present is only time itself, the inevitability of change, the condition of our finitude as human beings—a condition for which no one is to blame. Shame, guilt, and rancor haunt so much of our lives that we are often fearful of remembering the past, but when we feel nostalgic, we look back at our past without fear.

Most recent American movies are addressed rhetorically to viewers who assume—as do nearly all of my students these days, and I don't doubt they are more or less representative of the film industry's target audience—that there is no past that is "relatable"; that being "relatable," like being "engaging" (another word my students favor), is an attribute or quality some films simply have and others do not—as if establishing a meaningful relationship with a film were entirely up to the film and in no way up to the viewer. Viewers assume that only movies called "modern," not ones they call "old," can be "relatable" and that "modern" movies are more *advanced* ideologically and technologically, than "old" movies. "Modern" viewers, which so many moviegoers now assume they are, are likewise more advanced in their way of thinking than viewers could possibly have been in the era of "old" movies. What gives young people today such an idea that they are justified in making these assumptions? How has it come about that they think this way? I will return to these questions.

"Modern" movies assert their *presentness*, as I like to call it, denying any connection or indebtedness to the past. This is what distinguishes them from "old" movies, in my students' estimation—what makes them "modern," what locates them in the present, not the past. Because the Bradley Cooper/Lady Gaga film *A Star Is Born* (2018), for example, is a "modern" movie—if in doubt, experience it in buttocks-battering Dolby—my students assume that it is "relatable" and that the 1937, 1954, and 1976 versions—"old" movies all—are not. I also find the 2018 version, elevated by a performance by Lady Gaga that is beyond praise (as was Judy Garland's performance in the 1954 version) to be the best of the pack. But in my experience its "modern-ness," its assertion of its own presentness, weakens as well as strengthens the film. This movie goes to excessive lengths to provide the Bradley Cooper character with a backstory that is supposed to make him "relatable" by providing a psychological explanation for his behavior, an explanation of how his troubled past caused him to become the way he is in the present, vulnerable to addiction (understood in present-day terms as a disease, not a character flaw or moral failing)—a backstory that serves to deny him any blame, any responsibility for his actions, any moral agency. (That's what makes him "relatable," I suppose.)

A Disney film like *Frozen* (2013) asserts its presentness with its CGI technology, which deprives the film of the visual beauty that cel animation enabled "old" Disney films, like *Bambi* (1942), to achieve—a beauty that appeals to tender emotions and feelings. It also asserts its presentness by declaring its political correctness. I am thinking, above all, of the moment Kristoff, handsome but a lowly ice seller, kisses Princess Anna and his kiss fails to save her, although in the film's world true love has the power to melt her frozen heart. As it turns out, the love of Elsa, Anna's sister, possesses that power. Evidently, her love is stronger, truer, than Kristoff's, even though we are given no reason to believe that there is anything lacking in Kristoff's love or that his love is in some way untrue. He's not a fairy tale Prince Charming, which is what villainous Hans appears to be. Kristoff is a regular guy whose actions, not his looks or class, prove him a worthy suitor. Only the film's need to assert its presentness anoints the sisterly Elsa, not the sincere suitor Kristoff, with the power to save Anna. Perhaps it takes the wisdom of King Solomon—rarer than ever these days, it seems—to know that if two people's love is true, one's love can't be truer or stronger than the other's. The movie ends with Anna and Kristoff together. But if their love for each other is somehow lesser than the love between Anna and Elsa, their relationship must fall short of a real marriage, as judged by the standard of what Cavell, in *Pursuits of Happiness*, dubbed "comedies of remarriage"—or by my standard. Ideologically, *Frozen* is not more advanced than "old" movies. It's hogwash—politically correct, but hogwash nonetheless. And, while I'm feeling churlish—or am I just feeling nostalgic?—I will add that I would say the same about more than a few of the most critically acclaimed recent movies. (*Get Out* [2017], I'm thinking of you.)

In Terrence Malick's *The Tree of Life* (2011), a rare "modern" film that is steeped in nostalgia and utterly devoid of false "nostalgia," a number of the protagonist's memories reflect experiences common to any number of American boys of his (and Malick's) generation, such as doing unspeakable things to frogs or chasing DDT trucks. Yet even these collective memories, the film makes clear, are ultimately personal, particular to this one individual (and perhaps to Malick). I can feel nostalgia only for my own past—the only past that I can look back on, the past only I can look back on. Nostalgia is *always* personal, although in some incidents it makes me nostalgic to think I was with companions at the time. Reminiscing together can be a special pleasure. (These days, my sister Judy is the only person left with whom I can reminisce about childhood.)

As Cavell put it in the opening sentence of *The World Viewed*, memories of movies are strand over strand with memories of our lives. Or at least they were. It makes me nostalgic to remember the first time I watched *Casablanca* with my two best friends in high school, Jerry and Richie, on the TV in Jerry's basement. But when my students, sixty years from now, reminisce about the past—if the practice of reminiscing, one of the perks of being human, hasn't died out by then—will memories of *TRON: Legacy*, say, or of any of the metastasizing mass of Marvel films (the politically correct *Black Panther* [2018] is not really more advanced than the others), be strand over strand with memories of their lives? I don't see how they could. In asserting their presentness, such blockbusters may be "relatable" to impersonal media clichés, but not to the human reality of their viewers' lives. As I've said, most of my students assume that their experience of watching "modern" films has nothing to do with "living in the past." Too often, it also has nothing to do with living in the present.

Watching home movies my father shot a lifetime ago makes me feel nostalgic—even those taken before I was born, because it was my father who took them, enabling them to be a link to my memories of him. But Hollywood movies, past or present, are different. No matter how strongly I may identify with their characters—whatever exactly that means—their experiences are not my experiences. Hollywood movies do not address me personally. The events in the world projected on the screen, however analogous they may be to incidents in my own life, are not *my* past. Whose past are they? Our outsideness to the film's world, our powerlessness to intervene in the events unfolding before our eyes, makes those events, as I have said, akin to the past, not the present. But insofar as the events projected on the screen are unfolding before our eyes, they're not, in reality, anyone's past. They're our present. How can we be nostalgic when we're watching them? Strictly speaking, we can't be.

To be nostalgic is to look back at the past from a position in the present, with a bittersweet awareness of the barrier-that-is-no-real-barrier that keeps past and present apart, keeps the past from becoming the present again, makes the past unreachable except in memory. But the medium of film makes the impossible not only possible but necessary. The projected world fuses past and present, in effect, overcoming or transcending their separation. When I'm watching a movie, I can't feel nostalgia for the events in the film's world for two reasons. First, these events are unfolding before my eyes and are thus temporally like the present, not the past, to me. Second, my outsideness to the film's world, my powerlessness to alter them, makes these events temporally like the past to me—but it is not my past, and nostalgia is always personal. When I'm watching a movie of any period, it thus can't be nostalgia as such that I feel. But because we are outside the film's world (through no fault of our own), we are outside the world of the past, and we can watch movies as we can think of the past when we're feeling nostalgic, free of shame, guilt, and rancor. Movies can engender a pleasure analogous or comparable to nostalgia—a wistful longing, a bittersweet awareness that something we wish were possible—to be free of responsibility for our lives—is in reality impossible. We cannot escape from our lives in the world by seeking asylum in the world of a film, just as we cannot escape our responsibilities in the one existing world by living in the past.

It was in the 1940s that nostalgia became prominent in Hollywood movies. Not coincidentally, it was in the 1940s, too, that flashbacks became prevalent. Innumerable Hollywood movies of the 1940s and early 1950s begin with a voiceover spoken by the film's protagonist, who begins to tell the story—before a flashback takes over—of the events in his life that led him to the crossroads at which he now finds himself. In *Double Indemnity* (1944) and in the many postwar film noirs for which it served as a prototype, the mood cast by the protagonist's opening voiceover is anything but nostalgic. He is unburdening himself of memories that are painful, not pleasurable. In *How Green Was My Valley*, nostalgia enters the picture not through its setting in the past—*The Americans* (2013–2018), for example, is set in the 1980s but never permits a moment of nostalgia for the period—but by mediating our experience of the events of the film through Huw's nostalgic voiceover. Nostalgia isn't contagious. Huw's nostalgia doesn't make us long for the lost past he longs for. His valley isn't our valley. But his nostalgic mood casts a lingering spell over us, a spell sustained and deepened by Arthur C. Miller's luminous cinematography, which accords the film's world a precious visual beauty—as if it were bathed in nostalgia's warm glow.

Because the events in a film's world don't make us nostalgic in themselves, and because nostalgia is always personal, nostalgia only enters even "overtly nostalgic" movies by way of someone's nostalgia. Hence it was common for movies of the 1940s and early 1950s, even those that did not incorporate a nostalgic voiceover or embed the body of the narrative in a flashback, to dwell empathetically on the nostalgia of characters whose longing for the past, longing for the present to be like the past, colors our experience of the film as a whole. It is possible for the "someone" whose nostalgia bathes a film in a warm glow to be not a particular character but, rather, the film's director. Watching *The Quiet Man* (1952), for example, it is John Ford's wistful longing for Ireland, not that of John Wayne's character, that colors our mood as we watch the film.

Is Hollywood of the 1940s and early 1950s my once-green Welsh valley? No. For me, Hollywood's "Golden Age" was the period between 1934, the year of *It Happened One Night*, and the entrance of the United States into World War II—the period in which what Cavell later calls "Emersonian perfectionism" was ascendant in Hollywood, as it was in America in the New Deal era. In *The "I" of the Camera* (Rothman), I sketched a view of the history of the popular American cinema that envisions the shift from prewar to postwar Hollywood less as a liberation from constricting generic formulas than as an intensifying repression of the moral and philosophical perspective that granted American movies of the 1930s their combination of extreme popularity and extreme seriousness. What Emerson called "the wonderful way of *life*" is a matter of looking ahead, taking steps to create a better future, not looking back and longing to return to the past. The past is to be acknowledged, so that we can move on, walking in the direction of what Emerson calls "the unattained but attainable self" and moving America a step closer to becoming the "more perfect union" that was—is—its promise. Thus, it was no accident, I believe, that the repression of the Emersonian outlook of the prewar Hollywood years coincided with Hollywood's turn toward nostalgia. Increasingly, in the 1940s and early 1950s, nostalgia in Hollywood movies was a manifestation of Hollywood's willful forgetfulness, its self-imposed amnesia, about its own recent past.

More than today, remakes were a staple of Hollywood production in the 1940s and early 1950s. Almost without exception (Douglas Sirk's 1950s remakes of fine John Stahl melodramas of the 1930s are exceptions), these remakes are aesthetically and intellectually grossly inferior to the originals. *In the Good Old Summertime*, the 1949 musical remake of Ernst Lubitsch's great *The Shop Around the Corner* (1940), is a case in point. Judy Garland throws herself into her role, as always, and belts out her mediocre songs as if they were worthy of her, but the screenplay (by the husband-and-wife team of Albert Hackett and Frances Goodrich) censors out every bit of the seriousness, the dark undertones, in Samson Raphaelson's original screenplay. For example, the remake replaces the emotionally profound subplot in the original that climaxes in the suicide attempt by Mr. Matuschek (Frank Morgan) with an aggressively silly—no, *stupid*—storyline revolving around the boss's Stradivarius violin. And in shifting the setting from (what was then) present-day Budapest, at the historical moment Europe as we knew it was facing an existential threat from Nazi aggression, to a conventionally "nostalgic" turn-of-the-century, post-Exposition Chicago, the remake loses the original's conviction that something important is at stake in the fate of its characters; lost, in short, is the original film's moral and philosophical outlook. And the way *Good Old Summertime* trivializes *Shop Around the Corner* is all too typical of remakes of the 1940s and early 1950s. As befits a musical of the period, *In the Good Old Summertime* is in color, and in that way it declares its newness—but does not, in the fashion of *La La Land*, assert a presentness, a "modern-ness," that affirms a complete break with the past. Because all of the departures from *Shop Around the Corner* so obviously weaken *Good Old Summertime*, its commercial success was contingent on the public not remembering, not knowing, or not appreciating, the original's aesthetic and moral achievement.

The same can be said of such other musicals of the period as *One Sunday Afternoon* (1948), a vastly inferior remake of *The Strawberry Blonde* (1941), which, like *The Philadelphia Story* (1940), feels more like a 1930s film than a 1940s film. *The Strawberry Blonde* was itself a remake—a remake superior to the 1933 original, a fine film but a box-office flop, early 1930s audiences evidently not being receptive to its brand of nostalgia. Another example is *High Society* (1956), a disposable remake—even with Grace Kelly and a turn by Louis Armstrong—of *The Philadelphia Story*. None of these inferior remakes would have had a chance to be hits—indeed, they would not have been made—if it weren't for America's inability or unwillingness to acknowledge the value—or the values—of prewar Hollywood movies underwritten by what Cavell calls "Emersonian perfectionism." Such remakes not only exploited that amnesia, they actively reinforced it.

So did the genre Kathrina Glitre dubbed the "career woman comedies" that effectively shoved prewar-style comedies of remarriage off American screens during the wartime and postwar years. Films such as *Woman of the Year* (1942), *Take a Letter, Darling* (1942), *She Wouldn't Say Yes* (1945), and *Without Reservations* (1946), among numerous others, share many of the features of comedies of remarriage but with a glaring ideological difference. The "career woman," in learning to embrace her nature as a woman, embraces domesticity and motherhood as well. Even *Woman of the Year*, the best of these films, humiliates its "leading lady"—played by Katharine Hepburn, no less!—and does so not to open her eyes to her longing to become more fully human (as in *The Philadelphia Story*) but to shame her into conforming to an essentialist view as to which forms of life are and are not appropriate for women, as if for a woman to pursue a career is for her to deny her true nature, to deny what makes a woman a woman. A woman's nature is best expressed, these films assert, by marrying a man and embracing the life of domesticity and motherhood that "naturally" follows marriage. Comedies of remarriage revolve around a woman's quest for selfhood. Career woman comedies mock that quest. And they promoted a fake nostalgia for a prewar America that never existed—a place where women knew and happily embraced their God-given roles. To find these films funny, audiences had to forget that prewar America was not such a place, as Hollywood movies of the period make clear.

Postwar film noirs reinforced that collective amnesia in a different way—not by turning toward nostalgia, nor by turning away from it. The typical film noir protagonist has no past, or at least no past that is in any way relevant to his present identity—or to the film. When he begins to relate, in voiceover, the events that led him to his present dire situation, it is as if, apart from the particular events he is remembering, the past doesn't exist for him or for us. Remembering these events doesn't make him feel nostalgic; it causes him pain, not pleasure. Although *Double Indemnity* was in many ways a prototype for postwar film noirs, it is different in this regard, in that its protagonist Walter Neff (Fred MacMurray) has a past very much relevant to his present identity—and to the film. Walter has worked for so many years at the same insurance company, with Barton Keyes (Edward G. Robinson) his boss and mentor, that his past *is* his present, his present his past. He doesn't long nostalgically for a past when his life was better; he longs for a better future, the future he dreams of. His is a romantic dream, a dream of romance (or is it sex?) he has in common with all his fellow film noir protagonists—a dream of a future he tries to make real for himself by betraying his past, in the person of Keyes.

Keyes no more feels nostalgia for the past than Walter does. Rather than longing for a lost past, he is committed in his work to keeping alive, in the present, what he values about the past that he personifies, a time when insurance companies were run by men for whom insurance was not a business but a calling, as it still is for Keyes. And he believes that Walter feels the same way and will keep alive his dream for the future. But when Keyes reveals that he had overheard the confession Walter recorded—illustrated by the flashback that makes up the body of the film—Walter knows that his dream for the future is dead. And Keyes knows, from Walter's confession, that his own dream for the future is dead, too.

Meet Me in St. Louis is set in a turn-of-the-century St. Louis in the year leading up to the World's Fair that epitomized an America embracing the changes the new century was ringing in. But the film used its nostalgic setting to make a point about the (then) present—the moment in World War II when the outcome was no longer seriously in doubt. Esther (Judy Garland), fearful of the family's impending move to New York, wants her life to stay as it is. Like the daughter in Yazujirô Ozu's *Late Spring* (1949), another film about a society in the throes of change, Esther is, as we might put it, nostalgic for the present. She doesn't want her life to change. But life *is* change. In the end, the family stays in St. Louis but, as the film's ending at the World's Fair affirms, Esther now accepts the necessity of change and looks to the future in a spirit of adventure. So, too, must America, the film is saying, when the war is over, as it soon will be, and we are faced with the challenges of making America a more perfect union and helping create a better world.

Double Indemnity was made the same year as *Meet Me in St. Louis* and is also mindful of the time soon to come when the United States would no longer be at war. But unlike *Meet Me in St. Louis* and Vincente Minnelli's 1953 musical *The Band Wagon*, which find no real conflict between looking toward the future and acknowledging the past and tap into the hopeful spirit of prewar Hollywood movies, Billy Wilder's film is less hopeful. At the end of *Double Indemnity*, the future doesn't belong to either Walter or Keyes, who are both dreamers. The future belongs to young Lola and her boyfriend, neither one a dreamer, who have a shot at a future together, and to the "heartless so-and-so's" (to borrow a term from *Sunset Blvd*.) like Keyes's boss, representative of a new breed of insurance company executive, for whom the bottom line and his own ego are the only things that matter and who will run the new America, an America unfit for dreamers. *Meet Me in St. Louis* makes it clear where Minnelli stands, but in *Double Indemnity* Wilder is more ambivalent. He does not take a stand, as Minnelli does, against forgetting—repressing—the moral and philosophical outlook of prewar Hollywood, and to not take a stand is to participate in that repression, whether one likes it or not. In prophesying a postwar America in which dreamers have no place and heartless so-and-so's hold the power, Wilder is not casting his lot with the dreamers.

Double Indemnity focuses on the insurance business, in which men like Keyes who have actuarial tables running through their veins were giving way to corporate types for whom insurance was a commodity like any other. But Wilder's *Sunset Blvd.* is explicitly about Hollywood, as are a number of other Hollywood movies of the period, the most famous of which is *Singin' in the Rain* (1952). *Singin' in the Rain* is another film whose popularity depended on audiences not knowing, remembering, or appreciating, what prewar Hollywood movies, and the America to which they gave expression, were really like. Set in Hollywood during the transition from silent films to talkies, the film looks back at the period with affection, but not with nostalgia. We would rather live in the present than live in such a past, even if we could. *Singin' in the Rain* depicts American movies of that period, the men who made them, and their audiences as hopelessly naïve, childish at worst and childlike at best, granting license to the film's viewers to believe—indeed, take for granted—that they are superior to viewers of that period and entitled to look down on them.

In a direct way, then, *Singin' in the Rain* at once exploits, promotes, and furthers America's deepening repression of an Emersonian worldview that was ascendant in prewar Hollywood. In a more indirect and complex way, so does *Sunset Blvd.*, Wilder's most brilliant film, in which a clash between Hollywood's present and its past has tragic consequences. One might have expected Wilder to depict the film business the way *Double Indemnity* showed the insurance business, focusing on the parallels between them. After all, the moguls who built and ran the Hollywood studios lived and breathed movies, not number crunching, but they were a dying breed, like Keyes, inevitably to be replaced—as has really happened—by corporate types for whom movies are a commodity like any other. But *Sunset Blvd.* refrains from implying that present-day Hollywood is run by heartless so-and-so's, reserving that category for reporters and paparazzi, who are also the target of Wilder's scorn in *Ace in the Hole* (1951). When Norma (Gloria Swanson) has Max (Erich von Stroheim), her chauffeur and driver (and, as he later confides to Joe [William Holden], her first husband and the once-famous film director whose films made her the great star of the silent screen that she was) drive her to Paramount so she can have a face-to-face conversation with Cecil B. DeMille, many of the older studio hands warmly welcome her back. And DeMille himself, depicted as a bridge spanning the chasm between Norma's Hollywood and present-day Hollywood, treats her kindly and respectfully. To be sure, the film makes clear that there are people at Hollywood studios like Cole, who keeps phoning Norma not because the studio is interested in the script that Joe wrote with her but because the studio wants to rent her luxurious car, a rare antique. But as long as there are still dreamers like DeMille in Hollywood, *Sunset Blvd.* implies, the film business isn't heartless. It's the newspapers, magazines, radio, and the new medium, television, that have made America forget Norma. Hollywood hasn't forgotten her. But that doesn't mean that Hollywood would produce her comeback film.

Key to the film's depiction of present-day Hollywood is the character of Betty Schaefer (Nancy Olson), a young script reader for Paramount, whose harsh criticism of one of Joe's scripts dooms it at the studio. She is looking for scripts that have something to say, not a slick, derivative rehash of material that was never meaningful to begin with. Later, though, she finds "potential" in a scene in another of his scripts. Even as Joe is being "kept" by Norma and working with her on what he knows is a hopelessly bad, old-fashioned screenplay for what she deludes herself into believing will be her comeback as a star, he is secretly meeting with Betty, who helps him complete a screenplay that develops his potential as a writer—and who falls in love with him, even though she is engaged to another man. *Sunset Blvd.* gives us no reason to question Betty's acuity as a script reader, and hence no reason to doubt that, judged by Hollywood's criteria at the time, the screenplay Joe writes under her tutelage would make a successful film. But if that screenplay were to be produced, the resulting film wouldn't—couldn't—be a film like *Sunset Blvd.*, which has at its heart Joe's perverse, conflicted, tormented relationship with Norma, a relationship that ultimately dooms him—that is utterly beyond Betty's ken. Like young Lola in *Double Indemnity*, Betty is not a dreamer, but in the world of *Sunset Blvd.* she has a future in the film business. Joe does not. Joe is doomed. We cannot simply assume that Wilder's film is asserting its superiority to the kind of movie Betty believes in, the kind Hollywood believed in at the time, as *Sunset Blvd.* would have it, since Betty's boss evidently respects her judgment as a reader. Betty believes that films should have something to say, but she wouldn't know what to make of a film that says what *Sunset Blvd.* says.

In any case, there's a major discrepancy between 1950s Hollywood as it really was and Hollywood as *Sunset Blvd.* depicts it. In the real Hollywood, *Sunset Blvd.* was a smash hit that won three Academy Awards and was nominated for eight more. In the film's America, audiences of the time wouldn't have loved *Sunset Blvd.* And in the film's "Hollywood," Paramount wouldn't have made it. Betty would have nixed it. But there is an even more telling discrepancy between Hollywood's glorious past and Hollywood past as the film invokes it. Start with Erich von Stroheim, who was nominated for a Best Supporting Actor Oscar for playing Max. True, we learn that Max was the director whose movies made Norma a star, but that knowledge doesn't keep us from seeing him as almost as delusional, almost as pathetic as Norma. The film offers no sense of von Stroheim's stature in film history. For the vast majority of viewers in 1950, von Stroheim would be at most a famous name, but no more. *Sunset Blvd.* doesn't help this great artist to be remembered; it helps him and his art to be forgotten. The same is true of Gloria Swanson, also nominated for an Oscar. She certainly threw herself into her performance, mugging and grimacing and chewing up the scenery in ways that may have been appropriate for the histrionic character she was playing but that convey no sense of the down-to-earth quality and the comic touch that were Swanson's calling cards as a star in the silent cinema and beyond. Rather, the film turns the fifty-one-year-old actress, still possessing star quality, into a grotesque and demented old hag, anticipating the way *What Ever Happened to Baby Jane* (1962) treated Bette Davis and Joan Crawford, both actresses then only in their mid-fifties. There is only one passage in *Sunset Blvd.* that allows us a glimpse of what Swanson was really like at the height of her stardom. It occurs when Norma makes Joe watch one of her old movies and the sequence incorporates four brief shots—glorious but brief—from *Queen Kelly* (1932), the ill-fated, never completed von Stroheim film in which Swanson is cast—or miscast—against type as an innocent convent girl, which she definitely was not. These shots are followed by a close-up of Norma in the present, backlit by the projector beam and framed as if this, too, is a shot from the old silent film. The shot doesn't serve to reveal that she is as radiant as ever. Rather, it underscores how pathetic she has become—and how monstrous, an effect enhanced by the fact she is screaming hysterically, like an angry and bitter madwoman, a grotesque contrast with her silence in the old film. In what kind of world could such a woman ever have been a beloved movie star?

When in their initial awkward encounter Joe first recognizes Norma and says, "You used to be big," she replies, in one of the film's most famous lines, "I *am* big; it's the pictures that got small." To viewers who know the silent cinema at its glorious best, most movies of 1950—even those "with something to say" that Betty would have advocated—*are* small. But *Sunset Blvd.* is addressed primarily to viewers who—thanks to what I have been calling America's collective amnesia about Hollywood's past glories, an amnesia increasingly exploited and reinforced by Hollywood movies themselves—do not know, do not remember, or do not appreciate, regardless of how "big," in Norma's sense, "old pictures" once were. And Wilder's film forgoes the opportunity to help awaken America from this amnesia. Rather, like *Singin' in the Rain*, it reinforces most viewers' assumption, endorsed in innumerable ways by the culture as a whole, that they are superior to viewers of the past and entitled to look down on them. How "big," then, is *Sunset Blvd.*? "Bigger" than most movies of the period, I would say. But not as "big" as the most glorious silent films, or the best films of the prewar years. At the climactic moment of the film, it fails a crucial test. To quote the fine synopsis of the film on the Internet Movie Data Base:

> The scene returns to the opening. Still narrating, Joe expresses fear over how Norma will be unable to cope with the disgrace, and the discovery of how forgotten she truly is. By the time the police arrive, however, she has completely broken with reality and slipped into a delusional state of mind, thinking the news cameras are set up for a film shoot. To help the police coax her down the stairs, Max plays along with her hallucination

that she is on the set of her new film. He verbally sets up the scene for her, and cries "Action!" Norma dramatically descends her grand staircase. Joe, in voice-over, remarks that life has decided to spare her the pain of that discovery, and that "The dream she had clung to so desperately had enfolded her." Norma makes a short speech declaring how happy she is to be back making a film, and delivers the film's most famous line: "All right, Mr. DeMille, I'm ready for my close-up."

As if taking pity on Norma, Wilder withholds the pathetic close-up we imagine the newsreel camera to be "really" capturing, thus distancing itself from the heartless so-and-so shooting footage for the sensational news story about the once great movie star's emotional breakdown. But Wilder also withholds the glorious close-up that Norma, in her madness, imagines DeMille's camera to be capturing—a transcendent close-up with the power to reclaim her stardom and ensure her immortality. In so doing, Wilder is renouncing or forgoing his own camera's capacity for revelation. Unwilling or unable to reveal Norma Desmond—to reveal Gloria Swanson, the great star who incarnates Norma, as older but still radiant—to be "positively the same dame" the camera revealed her to be in her silent movies, Wilder's camera symbolically obliterates her image.

I began this chapter by suggesting that Americans today spend far less time "living in the past" than they did in the 1940s and early 1950s, when nostalgia was a dominant element in innumerable movies. Paradoxically, however, in American movies of that period, nostalgia was a manifestation of a willful forgetfulness, a self-imposed amnesia, about Hollywood's and America's own recent past. Indeed, the 1940s and early 1950s was the period in which the assumption that is almost universal among my students these days—the assumption that what they think of as "modern" movies, and their audiences, are incomparably more advanced than in the past—first emerged in American popular culture and began to be cultivated by Hollywood movies. It may be a long way from *Singin' in the Rain* to *La La Land*, but it was down a slippery slope.

Works Cited

Cavell, Stanley. "More of *The World Viewed*." *The World Viewed: Reflection on the Ontology of Film*, enlarged ed. Cambridge, MA: Harvard University Press, 1979. 162–230.

Cavell, Stanley. *Pursuits of Happiness: The Hollywood Comedy of Remarriage*. Cambridge, MA: Harvard University Press, 1981.
Glitre, Kathrina. *Hollywood Romantic Comedy: States of the Union, 1934–1965*. Manchester: Manchester University Press, 2006.
Rothman, William. *The "I" of the Camera*, 2nd ed. New York: Cambridge University Press, 2004.

Contributors

Matthew Leggatt is Senior Lecturer at the University of Winchester. He is the author of the monograph *Cultural and Political Nostalgia in the Age of Terror: The Melancholic Sublime* (2017). Other recent publications include the journal articles "Deflecting Absence: 9/11 Fiction and the Memorialization of Change" (*Interdisciplinary Literary Studies*, 2016), "You've Gotta Keep the Faith: Making Sense of Disaster in Post-9/11 Apocalyptic Cinema" (*Journal of Religion and Film*, 2015), and "Another World Just Out of Sight: Remembering or Imagining Utopia in Emily St. John Mandel's Station Eleven" (*Open Library of Humanities*, 2018).

Vera Dika holds a PhD in cinema studies from New York University and has taught at University of California, Los Angeles, University of Southern California, and New York University. She is currently Associate Professor of cinema studies at New Jersey City University and is the author of three books, *The (Moving) Pictures Generation: New York Downtown Film and Art* (2012), *Recycled Culture in Contemporary Art and Film: The Uses of Nostalgia* (2003), and *Games of Terror: Halloween and the Films of the Stalker Cycle 1978–1983* (1991). Dika has recently guest curated film shows at the Centre Pompidou, the Walker Arts Center, and the Museum of the Moving Image. She is a founding editor of *Millennium Film Journal*.

Ross P. Garner is Lecturer in television studies in the School of Journalism, Media and Cultural Studies at Cardiff University. He has published articles in peer-reviewed journals, including "'It is Happening Again': Paratextuality 'Quality' and Nostalgia in Twin Peaks's Dispersed Anniversary" in *Series: International Journal of TV Narratives* (2017), along with articles in *Popular Communication* and *Critical Studies in Television*.

He is currently preparing the monograph *Nostalgia, Digital Television and Transmediality*.

Fran Mason is Senior Lecturer at the University of Winchester, where he teaches film studies and American literature, within which areas he teaches a range of courses including those relating to postmodernism, crime fiction and film, science fiction, cyberculture, and contemporary writing. He wrote his doctoral thesis on American postmodernist fiction of the 1960s and 1970s with a particular interest on more politically or socially engaged fiction by Thomas Pynchon, Ishmael Reed, William S. Burroughs, Robert Coover, Ronald Sukenick, and Joseph McElroy. He has published widely on film, literature, and contemporary culture, including *American Gangster Cinema: From "Little Caesar" to "Pulp Fiction," Hollywood's Detectives*, two editions of *The Historical Dictionary of Postmodernist Literature and Theater*, plus articles on gangster movies, assassin films, heist films, contemporary fiction, and more.

Tracey Mollet is Lecturer in media and communication at the University of Leeds. Her research interests include Disney animation, contemporary American television, and American popular culture. She has published in various volumes on the relationship between popular culture and American cultural identity and is the author of *Cartoons in Hard Times: The Animated Shorts of Disney and Warner Brothers in Depression and War* (2017). She has presented and published widely on *Stranger Things* and is currently coediting a collection on the series.

Ian Peters is Assistant Professor of mass communication at Brenau University. He earned his PhD from Georgia State University in 2015, and his dissertation explored themed space exhibitions and museum pedagogy in Britain, Canada, and Japan. Previous publications include chapters in *Transformative Works and Cultures* and *Battlestar Galactica and Philosophy* and *Anime and Philosophy*. His present research interests focus on cultural hybridity in media texts, Japanese popular culture, and contemporary Cold War narratives.

Murray Pomerance is an independent scholar living in Toronto and Adjunct Professor in the School of Media and Communication at RMIT University, Melbourne He is author of *Virtuoso: Film Performance and the Actor's Magic*; *A Dream of Hitchcock*; *Cinema, If You Please: The Memory of Taste, the Taste of Memory*; *The Man Who Knew Too Much*; *Moment of Action: Riddles of Cinematic Performance*, and more.

William Rothman is Professor of cinema at the University of Miami. His books include the landmark study *Hitchcock—The Murderous Gaze* (1982; expanded edition 2012), *The "I" of the Camera* (1988; expanded edition 2004); *Documentary Film Classics* (1997); *A Philosophical Perspective on Film* (2000); *Cavell on Film* (2005); *Jean Rouch: A Celebration of Life and Film* (2007); *Three Documentary Filmmakers* (2009); *Must We Kill the Thing We Love? Emersonian Perfectionism and the Films of Alfred Hitchcock* (2014); *Looking with Robert Gardner* (2016); and *Tuitions and Intuitions: Essays at the Intersection of Film Criticism and Philosophy* (2019).

Steven Rybin is Associate Professor of film studies and director of the Film Studies program at Minnesota State University, Mankato. He is the author of *Geraldine Chaplin: The Gift of Film Performance* (forthcoming) and *Gestures of Love: Romancing Performance in Classical Hollywood Cinema* (also from SUNY Press), among other books. He is editor of *The Cinema of Hal Hartley: Flirting with Formalism* and coeditor with Will Scheibel of *Lonely Places, Dangerous Ground: Nicholas Ray in American Cinema* (SUNY Press).

Jason Sperb is Visiting Assistant Professor at Oklahoma State University. He is the author of *Flickers of Film: Nostalgia in the Time of Digital Cinema* (2015), *Blossoms and Blood: Postmodern Media Culture and the Films of Paul Thomas Anderson* (2013), and *Disney's Most Notorious Film: Race, Convergence, and the Hidden Histories of* Song of the South (2012). He recently completed a book manuscript on representations of Hawai'i in twentieth-century US mainland film and television.

Christine Sprengler is Associate Professor of art history and an Affiliate Member of film studies at Western University, Ontario. She is the author of two books, *Screening Nostalgia* (2009) and *Hitchcock and Contemporary Art* (2014) as well as articles on British and American film and television, contemporary art, and the relationship between cinema and the visual arts. Her current book project, *Fractured Fifties: The Cinematic Periodization and Evolution of a Decade*, is under contract.

Daniel Varndell is Senior Lecturer in the English literature department at the University of Winchester. He is the author of *Hollywood Remakes, Deleuze and the Grandfather Paradox* (2014), and has published on Hal Hartley, Michael Haneke, John Barrymore, Peter Sellers, and John Frankenheimer. His forthcoming monograph will examine etiquette and torture in film performance.

Christina Wilkins is a researcher in the area of contemporary television and literature. Her work examines popular cultural narratives and their uses from working through trauma to embodying political turmoil. Her book *God Is (Un)Dead: Religion and Identity in Post-9/11 Vampire Narratives* (2018), focuses on the working-through of post-9/11 trauma in the cultural trope of the vampire. She is currently teaching at the University of Winchester.

Justin Wyatt is Associate Professor of communication studies and film/media at the University of Rhode Island. He is also the Associate Director of the Harrington School of Communication and Media. Wyatt is the author of *High Concept: Movies and Marketing in Hollywood* and *The Virgin Suicides: Reverie, Sorrow and Young Love* and the coeditor of *Contemporary American Independent Film: From the Margins to the Mainstream*.

Index

12 Years a Slave, 3
16mm film, 92, 97, 99
1920s, 56
1930s, 58, 94, 105, 117, 254–256
1940s, 9, 200, 243, 247–248, 253–256, 262
1950s, 5, 7, 9, 24, 26, 36, 39, 40, 41, 46–47, 92–102, 105, 110, 133, 218, 242–244, 247, 253–255, 260, 262
1960s, 3, 24, 39, 41–43, 93, 94, 96, 98, 110, 113, 191, 211, 218, 222, 244
1970s, 4–5, 7–8, 18, 20, 94, 96, 98, 105–118, 125, 156, 159, 160, 161, 191, 211, 222
1973 Energy Crisis, 106, 182
1980s, 1–2, 4–6, 8, 26, 105, 110, 111, 113, 121, 126, 138–147, 181–186, 188, 192–193, 211–212, 215, 217, 218, 220, 254
1990s, 3, 5–6, 19, 28, 39, 42, 54, 79, 96, 140, 184
2001: A Space Odyssey, 175
35mm film, 17
9/11; *see* September 11

The A-Team, 218
Abramson, Leslie H., 62
Academy Awards, 2–3, 8, 190, 260
accuracy; *see* nostalgia, accuracy

Ace in the Hole, 259
Across 110th Street, 114
action figures, 79
Adam's Rib, 165
adaptation, 124, 179, 182, 189–192, 199, 207–208; *see also* remakes
aesthetic; *see* nostalgia, aesthetic
affective; *see* nostalgia, affective
aging, 52, 54–56, 58, 60, 61–62, 65, 67, 69, 92, 130, 233–234
Airwolf, 218
Akira, 191
Akker, Robin van den, 37, 38, 48
Aladdin, 3–4
Alien, 78
All That Heaven Allows, 39
Altman, Rick, 18, 31
Altman, Robert, 116
AMC, 138, 212
America's Got Talent, 127
American Gangster, 105
American Graffiti, 24, 26, 105, 107, 112
American Hustle, 7, 105, 106, 108, 113–116, 118, 247, 248
American Idol, 126, 127
The Americans, 1–2, 8, 181, 186, 212, 214–222, 225, 254
amnesia, 203, 255–257, 261–262; *see also* nostalgia, memory
Anderson, Wes, 29, 38

269

Andrews, Julie, 55, 62–68
antinostalgia, 212–213, 221, 224, 225
Antonioni, Michelangelo, 244
Appadurai, Arjun, 76
Argo, 3, 21
Aristotle, 52
Armstrong, Louis, 256
Army of Darkness, 183
artifice; *see* nostalgia, authenticity
Arthur, 121
The Artist, 3, 40
Ashby, Hal, 97
Atomic Blonde, 181
Auerbach, Erich, 74
authenticity; *see* nostalgia, authenticity
autobiography, 16, 92–93, 96
Avengers: Infinity War, 71–72
The Aviator, 39, 95

Bacall, Lauren, 54
Back to the Future, 24, 26, 73, 184, 189, 191, 193–194
Bambi, 251
The Band Wagon, 258
Barthes, Roland, 16
Basinger, Jeanine, 55
Battlestar Galactica, 211
Baudrillard, Jean, 21, 75
Bauman, Zygmunt, 4–5, 107
Beatty, Warren, 91–102
Beauty and the Beast, 3
Beloved, 38
Ben-Hur, 243
Benjamin, Walter, 209
  Angel of History, 4, 10
  reproduction, 72, 74–75
The Big Bang Theory, 83
The Birdcage, 163
Birdman, 3
Birth, 54
Biskind, Peter, 96, 182
black and white film, 17, 39, 111; *see also* color; sepia; Technicolor
Black Mass, 105

Black Panther, 252
Blade Runner, 185, 205, 208
The Blair Witch Project, 167
Blanchett, Cate, 46, 243
Blast from the Past, 39, 40–42
blockbuster, 96, 122, 189, 191, 193, 248, 252
Blow-Up, 244
Boardwalk Empire, 138
Body Heat, 105
Bourdieu, Pierre, 76
box office, 2–3, 127, 129, 190, 256
Boym, Svetlana, 15, 18, 27, 36, 107, 118, 139, 148, 198
Brexit, 141
Bridge of Spies, 212
Browning, Elizabeth Barrett, 67
Bubley, Esther, 47
Bulworth, 94, 96
Bush, George H. W., 143

California, 236–238
Cameron, James, 58–60
Captain America: The First Avenger, 95
Carol, 7, 37, 46–47, 243
Carroll, Noel, 156, 159–160
Carter, Jimmy, 113
Casablanca, 247, 252
casting, 39, 56, 58, 129–130, 158, 243; *see also* stars
Caught, 95
Cavell, Stanley, 68, 249, 252, 254, 256
cel animation, 251
celluloid film, 18, 139
CGI, 251
Cherry, Brigid, 71
The Cherry Orchard, 248
Chicago, 128, 137, 255
childhood; *see* nostalgia, childhood
Chinatown, 105, 107, 112, 117
Christmas, 22, 46
CinemaScope, 38, 39
cinematography, 17, 38, 39, 46, 48, 254

civil rights, 26–27, 38, 43–45
class; *see* identity, class
classical cinema, 17, 38, 51–55, 58, 61, 92, 164–165, 176, 247–262
close-up, 53, 60, 128, 173, 175, 176, 200, 233, 261, 262
Cline, Ernest, 179, 182, 185, 189, 190–192
clinical; *see* nostalgia, homesickness
clothing; *see* fashion
Coen Brothers, 111, 112
cognitive estrangement, 187
Cold War; *see* war
Collins, Lily, 91, 93, 100
color, 38–40, 43, 48, 94, 114, 200, 239, 241–243, 255; *see also* black and white; sepia; Technicolor
coming-of-age, 24, 25, 139; *see also* aging; nostalgia, childhood
commercial; *see* nostalgia, commodified
commodification; *see* nostalgia, commodified
The Conformist, 105, 107
Cook, Pam, 6, 19, 27, 30, 36, 186, 200, 203
Cooper, Bradley, 114, 251
cosplay, 74, 79–85
counterculture, 24, 96, 106, 110, 220
Crawford, Joan, 260
crime, 105–118
The Crown, 243–244
cultural studies, 74, 76
The Curtain, 61

Dancing with the Stars, 127
Daughters of the Dust, 27–29
Davis, Bette, 260
Davis, Fred, 16–17, 18, 19, 25, 138
Death in Venice, 101
defamiliarization, 187–188
déjà-vu, 234
DeLorean, 73, 189, 191
dementia, 233; *see also* amnesia; nostalgia, memory

DeMille, Cecil B., 259, 262
Demme, Jonathan, 94
Deutschland 83, 8, 186, 212, 214, 215, 219–225
Deutschland 86, 8, 212, 214, 215, 219–225
Deutschland 89, 219
Diamonds are Forever, 95
DiCaprio, Leonardo, 60, 95
Dick Tracy, 96
Dika, Vera, 8, 36, 107
Disney, 3–4, 20, 29–30, 56, 63, 247, 251
Dittmar, Claudia, 222
Doctor Who, 77, 243
Dogville, 54
Dolby, 251
domesticity, 40–42, 44, 80–81, 84, 98, 115, 143, 217, 256; *see also* identity, gender
Double Indemnity, 254, 257–260
Down with Love, 39, 41
Draaisma, Douwe, 199, 209
Dracula, 162
Drake, Philip, 125
drama, 44, 46, 127, 128, 132, 161, 162, 171, 186, 191, 217, 221
dress; *see* fashion
Duffer Brothers, 139
Duffett, Mark, 82
DVD, 5, 237, 241; *see also* VHS
Dwyer, Michael, 5, 26, 36
Dyer, Richard, 19, 20, 30, 36
dystopia, 113–115, 192; *see also* utopia

editing, 98–99, 132, 164; *see also* cinematography
Edwards, Blake, 63
Egoyan, Atom, 233
Ehrenreich, Alden, 92
Eisenhower, Dwight D., 24, 243
Emerson, Ralph Waldo, 67–68, 254–255, 256, 258–259
Endless Love, 121

escapism, 3–5, 21–22, 115, 117, 118, 138, 180, 189, 233, 253; *see also* romance
E.T. The Extra-Terrestrial, 145, 146, 181, 183
Etsy, 71–72
Ex-Machina, 208
Eyes Without a Face, 161, 166, 168–170, 176

Facebook, 133, 193; *see also* social media
Fame, 8, 126–127, 130, 133
family, 16, 27, 43–44, 46, 65, 81, 98, 102, 122, 128, 137, 140, 142–144, 163, 207, 217, 221
fandom, 4, 71–85
Fantastic Voyage, 187–188
Fantin, Emmanuelle, 212
Far from Heaven, 39, 40–41, 46–47
Fargo, 111
Fargo season 1, 113
Fargo season 2, 7, 105, 108, 111–113, 118
fashion, 79–83, 105, 106, 109, 110, 112, 114, 115, 123, 128, 133, 212, 224
Father of the Bride, 165
feminist movements, 26, 145; *see also* identity, gender
Firebox, 71
Fisher, Mark, 4–5, 193
Fiske, John, 72, 76, 79
flashback, 20, 23, 202, 253–254, 257
Footloose, 8, 126, 128–130, 133
Forbidden Planet, 71
Ford, John, 154
The Fortune, 96
Fox, 130
Frampton, Hollis, 16
Frankenstein, 171
Freaks and Geeks, 19, 24
Free Fire, 7, 105, 106, 108–111, 118
The French Connection, 114

Freud, Sigmund, 161, 162
Friday the 13th, 139, 157
Friedenberg, Edgar Z., 236–240, 242
Fright Night, 121
Frozen, 251–252

G.I. Joe: A Real American Hero, 218
Game of Thrones, 76, 78
Garland, Judy, 251, 255, 257
gender; *see* identity, gender
genre, 17–19, 20, 30, 35, 37, 107, 112, 116, 138, 155, 157, 160–162, 197, 199–200, 207, 218, 254; *see also* crime; drama; horror; melodrama; musical; noir; road trip; romance; science fiction; the western
Geraghty, Lincoln, 73, 75, 82, 83
Gerry Anderson's New Captain Scarlet, 211
Get Out, 8, 155–176, 252
Ghostbusters, 78, 145
Gibbons, Alison, 47
Gigi, 231–232, 234–235, 240
The Girl with the Dragon Tattoo, 124
Glee, 127
Glitre, Kathrina, 256
The Go-Between, 234
Goffman, Erving, 243
Gold Diggers of 1935, 58
Goldman, Bo, 92, 94
The Good German, 39
Good Night, and Good Luck, 39
The Goonies, 145
Gorton, Assheton, 244
Gosling, Ryan, 38, 116
The Graduate, 8, 235–239, 242, 245
Grainge, Paul, 6, 36, 139, 198, 203, 205, 208
The Grand Budapest Hotel, 20, 24, 25, 29
Gray, Jonathan, 74
Grease, 129
Grease Live!, 8, 126, 129–133

Grease Sing-a-Long, 129
Greeks, 15, 52, 180
Green Book, 3
Guardians of the Galaxy, 138, 181
Guess Who's Coming to Dinner, 158, 161, 162–166, 176
Guffey, Elizabeth, 36

Halloween, 139, 157, 166–167
Halt and Catch Fire, 186
Harry Potter, 76
Hartley, L.P., 234
Hathaway, Anne, 63
To Have and Have Not, 54
Haynes, Todd, 39, 46–47, 243
HBO, 8, 138, 197
Heaven Can Wait, 96
Hell's Angels, 92, 94, 95, 97, 99, 100, 101
The Help, 26
Henry, Buck, 236
Hepburn, Katherine, 164–165, 256
Hi Diddle Diddle, 56
Hidden Figures, 7, 37, 43–46, 47
High School Musical, 127, 130
High Society, 256
Hills, Matt, 72, 75, 77, 82
Hitchcock, Alfred, 48, 161, 173
Hobbes, Thomas, 52
Hoffman, Dustin, 236, 240
Hollows, Joanne, 81
homage, 15, 48, 144, 184, 185, 188; *see also* intertextuality
home; *see* nostalgia, home
home movies, 16, 184, 252–253
homesickness; *see* nostalgia, homesickness
horror film, 8, 138, 139, 155–176
How Green Was My Valley, 247–249, 254
Howards End, 233
Hughes, Howard, 91–102
Hugo, 40
The Hunger Games, 192

Hutcheon, Linda, 36, 206
Huyssen, Andreas, 206, 207

I, Robot, 208
I Remember Mama, 247, 248
identity, 5–6, 26–29, 42, 46, 74, 79, 81, 114, 115, 125, 141, 148, 180, 198, 199–201, 205–206, 208–209, 219, 224
  class, 43–44, 46, 76, 80, 110, 127, 157, 163, 222
  gender, 7, 26, 27, 39, 40–46, 47, 55, 61, 68, 80, 92, 96, 143, 146–147, 200, 216, 232, 256
  masculinity, 29, 47, 75, 107, 117, 142, 143, 145, 147, 148, 200
  race, 3, 26–29, 38, 39, 42–46, 80, 127, 141, 145, 155–176, 182, 213
  sexuality, 3, 6, 27, 39, 42–43, 46–47, 96–97, 127
In the Good Old Summertime, 255
In the Mood for Love, 27
Industrial; *see* nostalgia, industrial
Inglorious Basterds, 111
The In-Laws, 163
Inside Man, 54–55
intellectual property, 72, 125, 182, 185, 187, 191; *see also* intertextuality
intertextuality, 7, 8, 48, 54, 61, 83, 96, 112, 115, 139, 142, 147, 157, 159–160, 166, 182–183, 185, 197; *see also* adaptation; intellectual property
The Invisible Man, 58
The Irishman, 105
The Iron Giant, 183
It, 139
It Happened One Night, 254
It's a Wonderful Life, 247

Jackie Brown, 125
James Bond, 20, 216

Jameson, Fredric, 6, 17, 18, 36, 37, 39, 52, 105–108, 112, 138, 139, 156, 159–161, 197–198, 203, 205–206; *see also* postmodernism
Jenkins, Henry, 123, 124, 125
Jet Pilot, 95
Johnson, Catherine, 72, 77
July, Miranda, 38
Jurassic Park, 79, 184, 191

Kackman, Michael, 213, 216–217
Kant, Immanuel, 48
Kaplan, E. Ann, 61
Kay, Jilly Boyce, 36
Kelly, Grace, 256
Kennedy, Robert, 94, 101–102
Kill the Irishman, 105
King, Martin Luther, 44
King, Stephen, 138
The King's Speech, 3
Kirkpatrick, Ellen, 80–81
Kundera, Milan, 54, 61–62

La La Land, 7, 37, 38, 47–48, 247, 248, 255, 262
Lady Gaga, 251
Lamerichs, Nicolle, 74, 80, 82–83
Landsberg, Alison, 185–186
Late Spring, 257
Lawrence, Jennifer, 115, 248
Le Sueur, Marc, 18, 21, 39, 198
Lee, Christina, 193
Leggatt, Matthew, 220, 223–224, 247
Let There Be Light, 15
Leviathan, 52
Levitt, Helen, 47
Life with Father, 247
Lili, 241
The Lion King, 3–4
Lister, Linda, 65
literature, 37–38, 74, 223; *see also* adaptation; intertextuality
Lizardi, Ryan, 5, 145, 187

Locke, John, 55
The Long Goodbye, 116
Los Angeles, 92, 107, 116, 237
Losey, Joseph, 234
Lowenstein, Adam, 169
Lubitsch, Ernst, 255

M.A.S.H., 218
Mad Men, 25, 122, 134, 138, 242–243
The Magnificent Ambersons, 247
Mahoney, Cat, 36
Malick, Terrence, 252
The Man from U.N.C.L.E., 218
The Man Who Loved Women, 63
The Man Who Wasn't There, 113
Mandingo, 167
Manhattan, 114
Mantel, Hilary, 51, 54
Mara, Rooney, 46, 243
Marshall, Gary, 63, 65
Marvel Universe, 71–72, 252
Marx, Karl, 76
Mary Poppins, 63, 65, 68
masculinity; *see* identity, masculinity
The Master, 15
matte painting, 38, 39, 41
McDowell, James, 38
McGovern, George, 102
Meet the Fockers, 163
Meet Me in St. Louis, 247, 257–258
melancholy, 15, 19, 20, 23, 28, 41, 67, 69, 198
melodrama, 39, 217, 255
Melvin and Howard, 94, 95
memory; *see* nostalgia, memory
merchandise, 7, 71–85, 139
metamodernism, 7, 36–39, 42, 46–47, 48
Metropolis, 187
Middleton, Peter, 106–107
Mighty Morphin Power Rangers, 73
Miller, Arthur C., 254

Miller's Crossing, 112
mimesis, 74–75, 77, 79, 187; *see also* mimetic; simulation
mimetic, 71–85; *see also* mimesis; simulation
Minnelli, Vincente, 231, 258
mise-en-scène, 19, 21, 23, 164, 173
Mission Impossible, 218
mode; *see* nostalgia, mode
modernism, 36–37, 44, 48, 75; *see also* postmodernism; metamodernism
Monroe, Marilyn, 99, 212
montage, 112, 115; *see also* editing
mood; *see* nostalgia, mood
The Moon Is Blue, 92
Moonlight, 3
The Moon-Spinners, 56–57, 60
Morimoto, Lori, 82
Morrison, Tony, 38
Murder My Sweet, 175
music, 23–24, 38, 65, 99, 101, 109, 125, 126, 128, 145, 167, 182, 200, 211, 217, 220–221, 224, 231–232, 234, 236, 238–239, 241
musical, 8, 38, 55, 65, 91, 100, 121–134, 247, 255, 256, 258

Nadel, Alan, 218–219
narrative; *see* nostalgia, narrative
national; *see* nostalgia, national
NBC, 126, 130
Nebraska, 16, 17, 20, 23
Negri, Pola, 55–57, 58, 60, 61, 67, 68
Netflix, 5, 139, 140, 190, 243
New Hollywood, 62, 96
New York, 41, 47, 113–114, 126–127, 158, 235, 257
The Nice Guys, 7, 105, 106, 108, 116–118
Nichols, Mike, 235–238
Niemeyer, Katharina, 36, 138, 140, 198, 204, 206

Night of the Living Dead, 176
Nightmare: Return to Elm Street, 139
Nixon, Richard, 102
No Country for Old Men, 112
noir, 116–117, 254, 256–257
Nosferatu, 124–125
nostalgia
  accuracy, 3, 8–10, 35, 45, 82, 109, 113, 232–234, 237, 239, 243, 260
  aesthetic, 3, 31, 35, 38, 39, 43, 45, 47, 71, 73, 139, 161, 212, 242–244
  affective, 3, 7, 19–20, 24, 32, 75, 107, 122–123
  artifice; *see* nostalgia, authenticity
  authenticity, 3, 35, 37–38, 44–48, 82, 92, 106, 109, 116, 132, 133, 184–187, 197, 201–202, 209, 232, 238–239, 243–244, 247, 252–253
  childhood, 17, 21, 24, 39, 51, 78, 139, 142, 144–147, 183, 187, 188, 192, 199, 240, 248, 250, 252; *see also* coming-of-age; nostalgia, generational
  clinical; *see* nostalgia, homesickness
  commercial; *see* nostalgia, commodified
  commodified, 3–7, 18, 19–20, 23, 24, 25, 30–32, 41, 71–85, 121–134, 139, 186, 198, 201–202, 209, 242, 247
  fidelity; *see* nostalgia, accuracy
  generational, 3–4, 19, 24, 94, 106, 122, 123, 127, 129, 140, 148, 242; *see also* aging; nostalgia, childhood
  home, 8, 17, 21, 39, 40–49, 68, 137–148, 162, 188, 204–205, 207
  homesickness, 15, 23, 28, 35, 42, 138, 139
  industrial, 3–7, 19, 23, 24, 31, 71–85, 121–134, 139

nostalgia *(continued)*
  memory, 2, 8, 51–52, 62, 67, 92, 107, 123, 198, 202–209, 232–235, 237, 244–245, 248–250, 252–253; *see also* amnesia; prosthetic
  mode, 43, 139, 198, 203–204
  mood, 42–43, 198, 203–204, 206
  narrative, 3, 7, 17, 20–21, 24, 31, 32, 108–110, 123, 168–171
  national, 211–225, 247
  period; *see* 1920s; 1930s; 1940s; 1950s; 1960s; 1970s; 1980s; 1990s
  peripheral, 7, 19–20, 32
  reflective, 27, 28, 31, 94–95, 101, 118, 198, 235, 243
  representational, 7, 20–21, 24, 31, 32, 36, 186, 244
  restorative, 27, 198, 235
  revisionist, 107, 108, 110, 111, 114, 116, 117, 198
Nostalgia, 16
nuclear weaponry, 41, 219–221, 223; *see also* war, Cold War

The Old Dark House, 58–60, 162
One Sunday Afternoon, 247, 256
Orbison, Roy, 248
Orkin, Ruth, 47
Oscars; *see* Academy Awards
Our Vines Have Tender Grapes, 247
Ozu, Yazujirô, 257

Paramount Pictures, 52, 259, 260
pastiche, 17–20, 29, 30, 31, 32, 35–36, 38, 116, 160, 161; *see also* intertextuality; postmodernism
Peele, Jordan, 8, 155, 156, 160, 161, 166, 169, 171, 172, 174, 176
performance, 52–55, 60, 62, 68, 74, 94, 98–99, 234, 243, 260; *see also* stars
period; *see* 1920s; 1930s; 1940s; 1950s; 1960s; 1970s; 1980s; 1990s
periodization, 36

peripheral; *see* nostalgia, peripheral
The Philadelphia Story, 256
photography, 15–16, 25, 28, 46–47, 241, 244–245
Pixar, 20, 21
Pleasantville, 39, 40–41, 43
Plummer, Christopher, 64, 233
Poitier, Sidney, 164–165
Pokémon, 78
Pomerance, Murray, 62
Pop! Vinyl, 71
popular culture, 16, 18, 29, 31, 32, 76, 77, 116, 130, 138, 142, 145, 146, 181, 182, 186, 206, 211, 212, 215, 217, 220–221, 262; *see also* music
postmodernism, 4, 18, 35–37, 38, 39, 41–43, 45, 47, 48, 74, 105–107, 111, 116, 138, 139, 159, 160, 161, 203, 208; *see also* Jameson; pastiche
The Princess Diaries, 55, 63, 67
The Princess Diaries 2, 63, 65–67
propaganda, 218, 222–223
prosthetic memory, 185–187, 193; *see also* nostalgia, memory
Psycho, 157, 158, 161, 162, 172–173

Queen Kelly, 52–54, 261
The Quiet Man, 254

race; *see* identity, race
Rahman, Osmand, 74, 80, 82
Raiders of the Lost Ark, 105, 181, 183
Ready Player One, 8, 139, 179–194
Reagan, Ronald, 2, 6, 24, 26, 110, 111, 140, 141–143, 146, 147–148, 181–182, 216, 218
rear projection, 39
reboots; *see* remakes
Reds, 96
reflective; *see* nostalgia, reflective
remakes, 3–4, 6, 8, 17, 20, 23, 121–134, 139, 157, 247, 255–256; *see also* adaptation; intertextuality

Remember, 233
representational; *see* nostalgia, representational
restorative; *see* nostalgia, restorative
revisionist; *see* nostalgia, revisionist
Rick and Morty, 77
Ricoeur, Paul, 60, 108–109
Ringu, 161, 172, 173–174
RKO Studios, 91, 97
road trip, 3, 17, 21–23
Robocop, 121, 128
The Rocketeer, 95
Rocky Horror Picture Show, 158, 162
romance, 3, 10, 26–28, 58, 60, 62, 96, 114, 144, 147, 187, 216, 241, 251, 257;
  as genre, 35, 46, 96, 161–162, 193
  Romantic period, 75
Romeo and Juliet, 163
Ronstadt, Linda, 248
Rosemary's Baby, 160, 167
Rules Don't Apply, 7, 91–102
The Running Man, 192

San Francisco, 163, 164, 237–238, 245
Santo, Avi, 72, 73, 79
Saturday Night Fever, 114, 115
Saturday Night Live, 130
Saved by the Bell, 19, 130
science fiction, 2, 8, 111, 138, 139, 180, 187, 189, 193, 197, 200, 202, 205, 211
Scorsese, Martin, 95
Se7en, 112
sepia, 39, 43; *see also* black and white film; color; Technicolor
September 11, 8, 23, 138, 180, 211, 219, 223; *see also* terrorism; War on Terror
Serres, Michel, 36
sexuality; *see* identity, sexuality
Shadow of a Doubt, 248
Shampoo, 97, 98, 102
The Shape of Water, 3

Shaw, Caitlin, 36
She Wouldn't Say Yes, 256
The Shining, 160, 188
The Shop Around the Corner, 255
Shumway, David, 122–123, 125
silent film, 52–53, 56, 258–261
The Silver Chalice, 243
Simon and Garfunkel, 236, 240
The Simpsons, 78, 83
simulation, 5, 17, 20–21, 23, 42, 80, 106, 179, 205–206, 241;
  see also Baudrillard; pastiche; postmodernism; prosthetic memory
Singin' in the Rain, 247, 258–259, 261, 262
Sirk, Douglas, 39, 40, 47, 255
The Skin I Live In, 171
slow motion, 19, 200
Smith, Matt, 243
Snow White, 58
social media, 133, 160, 193
Somewhere in Time, 234
Sorkin, Aaron, 243
The Sound of Music, 55, 63–68, 130
Sperb, Jason, 36, 94
Spielberg, Steven, 138, 142, 145, 180, 181–184, 189–190
Spotlight, 3
Sprengler, Christine, 5–6, 18, 36
Stahl, John, 255
Stand by Me, 145
Star!, 62–63, 65
A Star Is Born, 251
stars, 20, 52–57, 60–62, 65, 68–69, 91–102, 129–130, 164–165, 248, 259, 260–261; *see also* casting; performance
Star Trek, 76, 81, 218
Star Wars, 4, 78, 79, 105
State of the Union, 165
Steiner, George, 231, 244
Stenport, Anna Westerstahl and Garrett Traylor, 124–125, 126, 129, 133

step motion, 19
The Stepford Wives, 160
Stewart, Kathleen, 18
Stewart, Susan, 73, 74, 76–77, 78, 83
Stories We Tell, 16, 20, 23, 30
Stranger Things, 8, 137–148, 181, 186, 190
Strasberg, Susan, 248
The Strawberry Blonde, 247, 256
Stroheim, Erich von, 54, 259, 260, 261
Stuart, Gloria, 55, 58–60, 61, 67, 68
suburbia, 24, 26, 40–42, 46, 93, 110, 138, 157, 166
Suburbicon, 243
Sunset Blvd., 52–54, 63, 248, 258–262
Super 8, 16
Super 8, 138
Super 16, 47
Suvin, Darko, 187
Swanson, Gloria, 52–54, 56, 61, 67, 68, 259–262
Szwarc, Jeannot, 234

Take a Letter, Darling, 256
Taussig, Michael, 75
Taxi Driver, 55, 114
Technicolor, 39, 43, 48; see also black and white film; color; sepia
Teenage Mutant Ninja Turtles, 183
terrorism, 8, 23, 106, 109–110, 138, 211, 213, 219, 221, 223; see also September 11; War on Terror
Texas Chainsaw Massacre, 157, 158, 162
theater;
  cinema, 129, 130, 160, 185, 192, 235–237, 241
  stage, 130, 133, 232
Things to Come, 192
The Three Musketeers, 58
time travel, 2, 21, 22, 23, 25, 107, 122, 189, 193, 242
Titanic, 58–61

Tomorrowland, 29, 31
Total Recall, 128
Town & Country, 94
Toy Story 4, 3
Tracy, Spencer, 165
Transformers, 123
transmedia, 122–126, 129, 132–134, 139; see also intertextuality
trauma, 15, 22, 23, 39, 161, 168, 169, 172, 175, 176, 233; see also war
The Tree of Life, 252
TRON: Legacy, 247, 252
Trump, Donald, 2, 141, 145, 147–148, 181–182, 213, 215
Tucker: The Man and His Dream, 95
Twilight Zone, 25

utopia, 42, 107, 180, 183, 187, 189, 191–193, 240; see also dystopia

Vacation, 22
Vendetta, 95
Verhoeven, Paul, 128
Vermeulen, Timotheus, 37, 38, 48
Vertigo, 48
VHS, 174, 237; see also DVD
Victor Victoria, 63
video games, 18, 147, 180, 183, 185, 186, 189, 190, 192, 202
Visconti, Luchino, 101

The Walking Dead, 75
WALL-E, 21
Walters, Charles, 241
war, 15, 22, 23, 26, 186;
  Afghanistan, 217
  Cold War, 8, 41, 43, 44, 110, 137, 211–225
  Vietnam, 26
  War on Terror, 211, 213, 216, 219
  World War II, 15, 29, 254, 257
Warner Bros., 130, 182
The Warriors, 114
Watergate, 106

Wayne, John, 95, 254
Weisberg, Joe, 214–216
Wentz, Daniella, 138, 140, 204
the western, 22, 111, 197–209
Westworld, 8, 197–209
Wetmore, Kevin, 138, 181, 190
Whale, James, 58, 67, 158, 162, 171
What Ever Happened to Baby Jane, 260
Wilder, Billy, 258–259, 260, 261, 262
Williams, Raymond, 37
Wilson, Janelle, 46, 140, 141, 148
Winslet, Kate, 58–60

Wise, Robert, 62
Without Reservations, 256
The Wolf of Wall Street, 21, 108
A Woman of the World, 56–57
Woman of the Year, 256
Woo, Benjamin, 73, 74, 81, 83
Wood, Robin, 160–161, 162, 163
Woods, Tim, 106–107
Wordsworth, William, 54, 55–56, 69, 235

Yankee Doodle Dandy, 247
YouTube, 132, 160, 192, 193

Also in the series

William Rothman, editor, *Cavell on Film*

J. David Slocum, editor, *Rebel Without a Cause*

Joe McElhaney, *The Death of Classical Cinema*

Kirsten Moana Thompson, *Apocalyptic Dread*

Frances Gateward, editor, *Seoul Searching*

Michael Atkinson, editor, *Exile Cinema*

Paul S. Moore, *Now Playing*

Robin L. Murray and Joseph K. Heumann, *Ecology and Popular Film*

William Rothman, editor, *Three Documentary Filmmakers*

Sean Griffin, editor, *Hetero*

Jean-Michel Frodon, editor, *Cinema and the Shoah*

Carolyn Jess-Cooke and Constantine Verevis, editors, *Second Takes*

Matthew Solomon, editor, *Fantastic Voyages of the Cinematic Imagination*

R. Barton Palmer and David Boyd, editors, *Hitchcock at the Source*

William Rothman, *Hitchcock: The Murderous Gaze, Second Edition*

Joanna Hearne, *Native Recognition*

Marc Raymond, *Hollywood's New Yorker*

Steven Rybin and Will Scheibel, editors, *Lonely Places, Dangerous Ground*

Claire Perkins and Constantine Verevis, editors, *B Is for Bad Cinema*

Dominic Lennard, *Bad Seeds and Holy Terrors*

Rosie Thomas, *Bombay before Bollywood*

Scott M. MacDonald, *Binghamton Babylon*

Sudhir Mahadevan, *A Very Old Machine*

David Greven, *Ghost Faces*

James S. Williams, *Encounters with Godard*

William H. Epstein and R. Barton Palmer, editors, *Invented Lives, Imagined Communities*

Lee Carruthers, *Doing Time*

Rebecca Meyers, William Rothman, and Charles Warren, editors, *Looking with Robert Gardner*

Belinda Smaill, *Regarding Life*

Douglas McFarland and Wesley King, editors, *John Huston as Adaptor*
R. Barton Palmer, Homer B. Pettey, and Steven M. Sanders, editors, *Hitchcock's Moral Gaze*
Nenad Jovanovic, *Brechtian Cinemas*
Will Scheibel, *American Stranger*
Amy Rust, *Passionate Detachments*
Steven Rybin, *Gestures of Love*
Seth Friedman, *Are You Watching Closely?*
Roger Rawlings, *Ripping England!*
Michael DeAngelis, *Rx Hollywood*
Ricardo E. Zulueta, *Queer Art Camp Superstar*
John Caruana and Mark Cauchi, editors, *Immanent Frames*
Nathan Holmes, *Welcome to Fear City*
Homer B. Pettey and R. Barton Palmer, editors, *Rule, Britannia!*
Milo Sweedler, *Rumble and Crash*
Ken Windrum, *From El Dorado to Lost Horizons*
Matthew Lau, *Sounds Like Helicopters*
Dominic Lennard, *Brute Force*
William Rothman, *Tuitions and Intuitions*
Michael Hammond, *The Great War in Hollywood Memory, 1918–1939*
Burke Hilsabeck, *The Slapstick Camera*
Niels Niessen, *Miraculous Realism*
Alex Clayton, *Funny How?*
Bill Krohn, *Letters from Hollywood*
Alexia Kannas, *Giallo!*
Homer B. Pettey, *Mind Reeling*

www.ingramcontent.com/pod-product-compliance
Lightning Source LLC
Chambersburg PA
CBHW030527230426
43665CB00010B/799